T0026302

BLOCKCHAIN RADICALS

BLOCKCHAIN RADICALS

HOW CAPITALISM RUINED CRYPTO AND HOW TO FIX IT

JOSHUA DÁVILA

Published by Repeater Books

An imprint of Watkins Media Ltd

Unit 11 Shepperton House

89-93 Shepperton Road

London

N1 3DF

United Kingdom

www.repeaterbooks.com

A Repeater Books paperback original 2023

1

Distributed in the United States by Random House, Inc., New York.

Copyright Joshua Dávila © 2023

Joshua Dávila asserts the moral right to be identified as the author of this work.

ISBN: 9781914420856

Ebook ISBN: 9781914420702

Printed and bound in the United Kingdom by TJ Books Limited

*TO ALL THOSE WHO HAVE SUPPORTED
ME THROUGHOUT THE YEARS AND WHO
CONTRIBUTED AT BLOCKCHAINRADICALS.ETH*

CONTENTS

DISCLAIMER

The purpose of this book is to provide educational information and encourage thought and discussion on the political applications of blockchain technology and cryptocurrency. It is not intended as a guide for financial gain or investment advice. The projects mentioned in the book serve as a mix of examples, highlighting both the challenges and potential benefits of crypto through a radical political lens.

It is important to note that the information contained in this book is based on the best available data at the time of writing, and the crypto industry is rapidly evolving. As such, some of the projects mentioned in the book may no longer exist or may have changed significantly by the time the book is read.

Readers should approach this book with an open mind and critically evaluate the information contained within. It is not intended as financial advice and readers are encouraged to seek professional guidance before making any investment decisions.

INTRODUCTION
FORGING A NEW MAP OF THE CRYPTO TERRITORY

Writing has nothing to do with meaning. It has to do with land surveying and cartography, including the mapping of countries yet to come.

— Gilles Deleuze

In early 2022, truckers protested against vaccine mandates for crossing the US border in Ottawa, the capital of Canada. This "Freedom Convoy" campaign later became a protest against general COVID-19 restrictions. In response to several crowdfunding campaigns that raised millions of dollars from Canadians and, problematically, Americans associated with far-right political groups, Canada's Prime Minister Justin Trudeau invoked the 1988 Emergencies Act for ten days. This declared that the government could freeze the bank and payment service provider accounts of individuals suspected of being part of the convoy without needing to go through the court system. This also included platforms that used cryptocurrencies and led to a decree by the Canadian government that specific **cryptocurrency** firms had to give information about any assets being used in the campaign.

A month or so later, a week into the Russian invasion of Ukraine, long-term Putin foe Pussy Riot singer Nadya Tolokonnikova started a **blockchain**-enabled DAO (**decentralised autonomous organisation**) and used the much-derided medium of NFTs to raise money for the

Ukrainian resistance, announcing on Twitter that blockchain was an important part of the fight against dictators.[1] In Kyiv meanwhile, the besieged government also made public several cryptocurrency **wallets** that supporters could donate to. By the end of February 2022, they had raised over $60 million in **bitcoin**, **ether** and other cryptocurrencies, spending the funds on fuel, food and other supplies like bulletproof vests and night-vision goggles for soldiers. Alex Bornyakov, the deputy minister of the Ministry of Digital Transformation, which facilitated the spending of the cryptocurrency, stated that cryptocurrency "is easier, not complicated, transparent, and faster in comparison to a SWIFT transaction, which could take more than a day."

Suddenly **crypto**, once a shorthand for **cryptography** and now also for cryptocurrencies, was, for the first time since Occupy Wall Street and the financial blockade of WikiLeaks, occupying centre-stage in a political and economic crisis. However, while these developments are headline-grabbing and not unambiguously politically progressive, it is also important not to overlook the myriad ways in which cryptocurrency is also being used by others experiencing state repression, for example in Palestine and elsewhere in countries with economic sanctions, or by sex workers who are constantly in a fight against financial service providers due to the legal grey area in which they work. For many who don't have the privilege of proper financial services, turning to cryptocurrency has been one of their lifelines.

Why then has blockchain been greeted with such hostility and scepticism by much of the left? One of the earliest critiques of Bitcoin, the first and most famous of the cryptocurrencies, was David Golumbia's *The Politics of Bitcoin: Software as Right-Wing Extremism*. His argument was largely that Bitcoin's right-libertarian origins meant it was predisposed to having utility and application only for a right-wing agenda (if any at all). This has continued with left-wing publications like *Jacobin*, which in 2022 published several articles related to crypto, with nearly all of them concluding that cryptocurrency is a scam, a Ponzi scheme and something that the left should stay away from. A look through many of the claims made and the sources cited in these articles shows that few of the writers properly understood many of the basic technical principles and workings of the technology, making their claims weak for people who are actually working on the infrastructure they are critiquing. It seems that their audience is not those who are closest to being able to answer their critiques (i.e., people working in the industry), but instead others who are jockeying for position within what might be termed the "Critique Economy", a largely discursive and academic mini-industry that seems to have consumed too much of the left's energy of late, as its actual institutional power has declined.

Blockchain is not a simple technology, so while technical inaccuracies can be forgiven, what is disturbing about the many articles written by incorrect but otherwise intelligent journalists and academics is how their claims inadvertently serve the crypto industry. By taking the socio-political descriptions of what cryptocurrencies or blockchains are at face value, these critics are inadvertently doing the job of the crypto-marketers and hypemen they so despise. At the same time, they also try to enshrine themselves as gatekeepers of what constitutes appropriate left-wing endeavours and resources. The truth is that crypto-marketers use right-wing libertarian rhetoric in order to attract a particular audience (whether or not either would describe themselves as libertarian is beside the point) because it is also one that is willing to part with their government-backed money. This is not meant to disparage that audience — the marketing is designed to tap into the disillusion and sense of disenfranchisement that many people feel, and especially the idea that there is something wrong with the monetary system. This is twisted into the adoption of a right-wing politics that has gained in popularity and become very profitable for some. In the past decade or two, there has been a process of implicit and explicit association that has led many to believe that anything crypto-related is right-wing and libertarian, an attitude adopted and promoted by many of its figureheads.

What the left-wing Critique Economy has failed to grasp, however, is that this has all been intentional as a way to keep the left out of the sphere of influence, limiting its capacity to decide on the direction that this new technological space should take. It was a poisoning of the well that the gatekeepers, writing scathing pieces as part of the Critique Economy, have continued to add yet more poison to. They have inadvertently re-enforced the legitimacy of an incorrect framework created by the crypto industry, and thus provided a poor map for helping others on the left navigate this space. Responses to crypto tend to be either excessively boosterish or completely sceptical, but this book instead argues that blockchains can both support existing political strategies on the left and open up new ones — novel strategies that blockchains made visible, legible or possible.

A typical writer of the Critique Economy attacks "techno-determinism", the idea that progress in "technology" is the key to society's development as well as its cultural values, making it the main agent of societal change. Optimistic techno-determinism is usually what is called upon by Silicon Valley elites to justify pushing more and more technological solutions, with the presumptions that "improving" technology helps progress society and therefore leads to more progressive outcomes. Sometimes this is referred to as "techno-utopianism" or "the Californian Ideology", a term coined in an essay by Richard Barbrook and Andy Cameron that claims its origins can be traced to the philosophy of the right-libertarian author Ayn Rand. Pessimistic techno-determinism as a counter-claim has emerged largely on the left after promises about technology leading us to more fulfilled and prosperous lives have repeatedly failed. This can more broadly be characterised as the feeling that most, if not all, new technology that has come about can only be used in ways that are exploitative or against your goals if you're on the left of the political spectrum.

This book is not techno-deterministic in either direction, and is instead meant to recognise the positives and the negatives of this emerging technology, an approach needed in order to make important assessments as to what this technology will feasibly allow us to do that will be beneficial to society as a whole and not just those that control the means of technological "innovation". Instead of viewing technology as deterministic, we can see it as probabilistic, recognizing that the current situation we're in significantly favours the haves over the have-nots, but also understanding that it doesn't have to be this way — the left has an opportunity to alter the status quo, perhaps with the very technology supporting it. The advancement of new technology is not the only agent for political change, but we cannot separate it away neatly from our social relations, especially in a world where so many of these social relations are mediated by the advanced and complex infrastructure that makes up the Internet. Ultimately, social movements are what lead to political change, but technology has always been important for movements — without the printing press, many important ideas would never have been spread. The advance of technology creates the material conditions for what is possible, but it's important for people seeking social justice to recognise their own agency in influencing what is done with it. How much agency is recognised and how it is used is what tips the scales for or against the public benefit. I would name this position and framework as "techno-probabilism".

Techno-probabilism is a framework for thinking critically about the potential futures enabled by a particular technology given certain conditions and uncertainties. It avoids both optimistic and pessimistic techno-determinism by attempting to recognise the full spectrum of practical possibility. It is a way of thinking about technology that is more open-ended and exploratory. It allows for space to think about the potential conditions that would need to be had in order to steer us towards particular futures. It understands that the same technology built with the intention to be used in one application or one political ideology is often not loyal to its creators and can be used for multiple other situations. This is especially the case for cryptocurrency and blockchains as will be covered throughout the book.

By applying a progressive political view to this framework on the technological space inhabited by blockchain and cryptocurrencies, we can begin to develop a strategy that recognises the potential of technology to enable collective action, while also taking into account the political conditions and risks that accompany technological development. It is a strategic framework that gives us permission to reappropriate technology developed with **capital** in mind to sustain collective liberation, while also being aware of the need for strategic duplicity in order to navigate the contradictions of a globalised, technologised political economy.

New technology has always been a political consideration, from new smithing techniques for creating stronger metals for swords, to companies implementing systems that make half their workforce redundant, to state-issued identity cards. There is a growing likelihood that cryptocurrencies and blockchains will creep into the mainstream, whether or not the values of cryptocurrencies ever reach the unrealistically high levels their hypemen predict on social media. If that's the case, it's important to have an appropriate map of the territory in order to create strategies and tactics that heighten the probability for desired outcomes.

This book will demonstrate that crypto and blockchain have played a much more complex role in attacking and circumventing traditional power structures in ways which are amenable to a number of ostensibly contradictory political projects. While much of the focus on it since then has been from either boosters or sceptics, its emergent qualities and the ways in which people have been actively engaging with it in ways that would be interesting for the left is largely the focus of this book. The left sceptics around crypto and blockchain have been by far the most vocal and strident voices, often drowning out more tentative and exploratory practitioners, artists, activists and programmers. I am not claiming that blockchain is a panacea, but the insistence that you need not investigate it yourself because the relevant academics have already done that for you and have decided it is fruitless is another part of the set of presumptions this book hopes to work against. Based on my experience of working in this space in various capacities and talking to precisely those artists, activists and programmers working within the blockchain space who are committed to an egalitarian politics, we need to have a fuller and clearer understanding of the strengths and limitations of blockchain.

I would argue it is precisely blockchain's emergent properties, its newness and plasticity, and the ways it might be imaginatively developed, that is what makes it both exciting and troubling to many. Of course nothing that develops out of and under **capitalism** is going to avoid hucksterism, scams, volatility, exploitation and straight criminality. Unfortunately, there is no pure space in which the revolution can be organised, only a set of conditions of no one's choosing that have to be grappled with. While there were constructive reactions to the rise of the Internet, like 1990s cyberfeminism and the left blogosphere around Mark Fisher's *k-punk*, the larger left does not have the time to make the same mistakes it made with the Internet and again with social media, by ignoring it until a crisis like the 2008 recession occurs. When just a couple of decades ago left-wing institutions and groups were deriding the Internet as just another bourgeois distraction, today social media is undoubtedly essential for organising and collective action, yet relies on centralised platforms owned by some of the most powerful tech companies in the world. While there were groups on the left fighting over the political terrain of early cyberspace, their successes were limited. The left needs to be engaged in building its own technological infrastructure if it wants to stay resilient in the future.

The blockchain space is fraught with all kinds of questionable practices — a messy, complicated and developing territory pulling in numerous directions. The questionable or even outright illegality that is associated with cryptocurrency can be particularly deeply offputting to many, especially left-liberal commentators, who have trust in dominant institutions and want a measured and measurable progress within well-defined and narrow parameters. But it is from the potentially disturbing foment of the blockchain space, I would argue, that the new is likely to emerge, partly because now that the more conventional electoral and parliamentary models of the attempt to push toward socialism have been thwarted (Sanders in the US and Corbyn in the UK, to give the two most pertinent examples for Anglophone readers), so the energy that animated those concerns will flow elsewhere. Into other more militant forms of worker organising no doubt, but also, given the centrality of online life in the twenty-first century, into digital networks that are attempting to create more equitable and open forms of mutualism, sociality and interrelation. What's certain is that the impulses toward socialism, communism, economic democracy (call it what you will) develop in lockstep with capital, wrestling it all the way. At the moment blockchain is a new frontier and it's there that we must also contest territory, rather than merely cede it as always-already belonging to the right.

The Map Is Not the Territory

In the 1930s, the Polish-American scientist and philosopher Alfred Korzybski made the remark, "the map is not the territory", or that abstraction derived from a thing is different from the thing itself. His view was that many people confuse conceptual models of reality with reality. For example, the map of Peru's geography is still very different from the actual geography of Peru. The symbols used on the map to denote where the Andes mountains are are helpful in limited ways, unless the map zooms in closer and contains more details, but even then, it will differ from actually being in the Andes. This is not to say that conceptual models are useless, but that they need to be paired with critical thinking because, as another aphorism goes, "all models are wrong, but some are useful". While these observations are more common to academic circles for semantics, linguistics or statistics, among other fields, they are also important for understanding politics, including the politics of technology.

Gilles Deleuze was a French post-Marxist philosopher born in 1925, who witnessed the civil unrest throughout France in May 1968 that saw the largest general strike ever attempted in the country's history, as decentralised wildcat strikes popped up in support of ongoing protests against capitalism, consumerism and imperialism. While there were significant gains made by workers once the Gaullist government realised that increased police violence was making the situation worse, the call for revolution made by socialists and communists didn't succeed. No Western country had come so close to a political revolution in the past several decades. In the midst of this event, Deleuze published his magnum opus, *Difference and Repetition*, a critique of representational thinking which would then heavily influence his two most popular books, co-written with Félix Guattari: *Anti-Oedipus* and *A Thousand Plateaus*

Deleuze's work is notoriously difficult to understand, but has been a significant influence on me in trying to better understand crypto while writing this book. The most fundamental part of his critique of representational thinking, or what is also commonly referred to as "skeuomorphic thinking" by others, is the framework I use for the structure of this book. To understand Deleuze's critique of representational thinking, we can turn to a video made by the popular YouTube video essayist Jonas Čeika.[2]

To explain Deleuze's critique of representational thinking, Čeika uses the example of the drum machine. The drum machine was originally created as a tool for musicians to use in a situation where they may not have a drummer for their musical ensemble. From the viewpoint of representational thinking, the drum machine is simply a lesser version of a drummer with a real drum set, a representation that does not match the ideal. Representational thinking is thus arborescent, or similar to a tree, with branches (representations) stemming from the base (the ideal drummer and drum set). This type of thinking, however, is extremely limiting for understanding the drum machine and does not map well onto the ways in which drum machines have actually been deployed.

Instead of limiting the drum machine to this representation, musicians ended up pushing the drum machine to do things that a drummer with a drum set could never do, thus starting the creation of new genres of music. This new box of repeated synthetic sounds became the basis of not just the Cambrian explosion of electronic music genres, but is now used to complement already existing genres of music. These first experimental musicians were thus not limiting themselves because they were not asking what the drum machine represents, but instead asking "What can the drum machine do?" Deleuze calls this a form of "rhizomatic thinking". You can think of a rhizome as a network that lacks a clear centre, and it is by thinking rhizomatically that we are able to understand the possibilities in present that allow for the creation of the new, uninhibited by representations.

For Deleuze, many people are trapped in representational ways of thinking that are limiting their understanding of the world. These representations can also be seen as tracings, or stickers that we try to put on top of the world to make it easier to understand, even if they are ultimately incorrect. My argument in this book is that representational thinking is also rampant in the crypto industry as a way to market crypto to a large audience quickly, as well in the minds of the critics of crypto. Discussions and debates between hypemen and gatekeepers of crypto tend to happen over a map which is covered in tracings derived from representational thinking, creating unresolvable tensions because neither are talking about the actual territory.

This is obviously problematic if the left wants to be able to respond to the changes being brought on by the introduction of crypto and blockchains. The left cannot be using an incorrect map, or a conceptual model, to derive a response. The left must also be cognizant that whatever model or mapping is created will be wrong or limited to some extent. The point is to try to make one which is at least useful. The book therefore asks readers to not ask what crypto represents, but instead ask, "What can crypto do?", without too much concern for the current map of the territory they may have in their head.

The purpose of this book is to provide a more useful map of the crypto territory to help you and the social movement you may be a part of to navigate it safely. By understanding the way past social movements from the right and the left have influenced the trajectory of crypto, and by making new connections that are not made in mainstream discourse as it exists at the time of writing, a new map can be drawn to lead us into new futures. One that is neither overly optimistic and utopian about a future with crypto, nor deterministically pessimistic. Another important consideration to keep in mind is that the map drawn in this book is just a snapshot of a particular moment in time in a space that is rapidly evolving. The projects mentioned in this book should not be considered an endorsement or financial advice (I am not a good person to listen to for that) and are all likely to be different (or bankrupt) to varying degrees by the time you read this book. They should only be seen as examples for helping us draw a more useful and rhizomatic map.

Collective Emergence

Using Deleuze's framework for his critique of representational thinking, I go through various different common representational models used by crypto hypemen and describe why they are wrong, but also why just because they are wrong does not mean that crypto is useless for the left, as many of its critics would have you believe. This book is separated into three sections that move from the worst to least bad form of representational thinking common in the crypto world. In the first section we will explore the idea of crypto as money, which was the original idea that propelled Bitcoin into existence. Taking a critical analysis of these claims, it is not hard to see that bitcoin, and cryptocurrency generally, is not money. However, the fact that it is not money can be a good thing, especially for its radical political potential. It is this very fact, along with the many properties that cryptocurrencies share with money, that allows cryptocurrency to be used for circumventing financial blockades by states or banks in various contexts through counter trade, as has been the case for WikiLeaks and Sci-Hub among others. The flexibility of the system also allows us to explore alternative democratic monetary systems that would otherwise not be possible and that defy the "digital metal" narratives expounded by right-wing libertarian hypemen.

In the second section we explore the next most common representation, which is crypto as finance. Starting with a dive into **Ethereum**, and its innovative creation of smart contracts, we see how this attempt at cryptographically enforced contracts written in computer code do not actually prove the common dictum from the crypto hypemen that "code is law". The affordances of smart contracts are however important for the functioning of the very quickly growing **Decentralised Finance (DeFi)** space in which many financial products that would normally only be available to those on Wall Street are available to anyone through a blockchain. While much of this space is a reformulation of many of the most capitalistic financial products, representational thinking can limit our abilities to look into the details of these mechanisms and discover the potentials of smart contracts and crypto **tokens**. The differences between the traditional financial system and

DeFi are important to understand for developing strategies that subvert financial systems for different ends than profit. We will also cover the phenomena of **non-fungible tokens (NFTs)** and how, similar to many DeFi mechanisms, they are commonly misunderstood and can be repurposed for more collective ends.

The third section will take a critical look at the least worst representational model used to understand this space, which is crypto as coordination. While many of the most well-meaning people in the crypto space like to use the metaphor of the monetary system and economy as a coordination system, this type of thinking ends up overlooking the importance of power relationships. In this section we will map out the similarities and differences between decentralised autonomous organisations (DAOs) and cooperatives; the burgeoning Regenerative Finance (ReFi) movement looking to combat the climate crisis and claims about energy usage in blockchain systems; and how blockchains can be used to not only enhance democratic systems, but also for new forms of political resistance and new collaborative cultural practices. While this book largely focuses on Bitcoin and Ethereum, the penultimate chapter goes through a few of the different existing technical infrastructures, including but not limited to blockchains, and how the technical decisions behind these create different social outcomes and possibilities. I conclude with an argument for taking a techno-probabilist approach to crypto. Techno-probabilism is a concept I'm using to help us understand our relationship with the potential futures for the left created by new technologies, moving beyond a toxic relationship with the Critique Economy and the false dichotomy between structure and agency.

Given our history living under capitalism, it should be a surprise to no one that extractive capital and deceptive business practices have been present in a space where very innovative technologies are being created and tested. This is surely a problem, but it is not a new one. Due to the free market fundamentalist, libertarian-inspired representational models used by crypto marketers, many get the impression that crypto is therefore only useful for this extremely restricted and dystopic world view. By moving past these models and instead trying to understand what these tools do and how they work, we can recognise and begin to create new tools and models that foster a new collective and collaborative imagination of the future. By doing this we can see the crypto space as one for collective emergence that questions older models of currencies, markets, information, politics and their limitations. We can begin moving past the question of why the future has seemed to be standing still for so long and start pre-figuring and designing the non-alienating systems of relations we would prefer to live under instead, by collectively wielding the technological tools we have at our disposal for pro-social ends, creating a new generation of **Blockchain Radicals**.

SECTION 1
CRYPTO AS MONEY

Derived from the original intention behind Bitcoin as a "peer-to-peer electronic cash system" that emulated certain properties of an idealised version of a gold standard — "It's a better form of money" is the most common framing for explaining what cryptocurrency is to newcomers. It is clear however that most if not all cryptocurrencies have not achieved the status of money. Critics will say that this means all cryptocurrencies are not fit for purpose. While cryptocurrencies do have some of the same properties as money, the fact that cryptocurrencies are not money can in fact be a positive for subverting the constraints of the dominant monetary system, especially for those interested in challenging currently-existing capitalist institutions. The ability of cryptocurrency to circumvent financial blockades by states or banks through counter trade should be taken seriously as a tactic for any group with enemies among the financial elite. Additionally, the flexibility of the system allows us to explore alternative democratic monetary experiments that would otherwise be impossible.

CHAPTER 1

BITCOIN: THE UNFORTUNATE GENESIS

The Times 03/Jan/2009 Chancellor on brink of second bailout for banks.

— Bitcoin Genesis Block

One of the difficulties of writing a book about a technical subject like blockchain or cryptocurrencies for a general audience is answering the question, "What in the world is this stuff?" in a way that is not drowned in unapproachable jargon. While I will do my best to avoid it as much as possible, I will need to introduce some technical concepts and definitions throughout my explanations of how crypto and blockchains work and how they are used. The truth is that many areas like digital technology and finance sometimes intentionally use complicated language as a way to keep people outside of their circle confused. This makes it difficult for the general public to understand and assess for themselves the merits of what is being sold to them.

Information asymmetry is a common weapon for venture capitalists and scammers alike. Therefore, equipping yourself with an understanding of how it all works can act as a good defence against what "decentralisation"-boosting profit maxi misers are trying to sell you as cryptocurrencies continue to enter the mainstream. This makes it essential that we cover the fundamentals of what makes the technology work so that we can assess its political implications and co-opt it for more radical and democratic means.[1]

While digital technologies have improved people's lives in certain respects, we have also been oversold on technological solutions and platforms owned by multinational but largely American corporations who have centralised large parts of the once more decentralised Internet. Although Silicon Valley elites may continue to push for the adoption of cryptocurrency with some amount of radical messaging about re-decentralising the web, it is largely with the intention of increasing their own wealth and power. However, this does not negate the more radical potentials of these technologies. We are facing a critical moment in time where several futures are laid out in front of us in terms of what is prioritised for the development of this emergent technology.

While the majority of the most well-known cryptocurrencies use a blockchain as their underlying architecture, not all of them do. Blockchains are just one type of **distributed ledger technology (DLT)** although it is the most well-known. DLTs have many different uses today and many non-blockchain DLT architectures are used for other cryptocurrencies, but for this book we're going to mainly stay focused on blockchains.

Before we get too deep into technology, whenever I speak to crypto-curious people, I like first to give a bit of the history and context that bitcoin, the most widely known cryptocurency, was birthed from, because I think it helps to explain why someone would create it. This then improves people's understanding of how it works and what it means for those of us more interested in the collective good than just personal financial gain.

Where Did Bitcoin Come From?

If you were around in 2008, you will probably remember the historical event now called the "Great Recession" — the collapse of the subprime real estate mortgage market in the United States, which triggered many more collapses around the world. It was the most severe economic and financial meltdown since the Great Depression in the 1930s, and yet little was done by the political class to ameliorate the situation for the working class. Governments pumped money into the very same banks that designed and speculated on the complex financial products that created the crash, on the grounds that they were "too big to fail". Even after receiving bailout money from the government, companies like AIG still paid out $218 million in bonuses to their financial services division, despite the company posting a loss of $61.7 billion in the first quarter of 2008.[2]

Millions of people lost their jobs and homes due to the poor incentive structures inherent to a financial system enforced by the government but ultimately designed in the interests of financial elites. It was a period defined by a marked increase in the distrust of state and financial institutions and distress caused by economic uncertainty, something which manifested in the Occupy Wall Street protests. Still, even with all the anger from the masses, only one banker in the United States ever went to jail. The crisis spilled over into other countries too, leading to the European debt crisis with Greece as the worst example and the failure of all three major Icelandic banks. Of the forty-seven bankers who were jailed in all, about half of them were from Iceland.

The same financial institutions that for decades had been pushing for neoliberal reform to "free up" markets by decreasing the power of government agencies to regulate them were now dependent on central banks and government regulatory bodies to stay afloat, and at taxpayers' expense. Their already existing influence over the state was used to ensure policy accommodated their interests, even though newly elected politicians had ridden a populist wave promising "hope and change". Politicians simply did not have the courage to fulfil the promises they made in the face of pushback by some of the most wealthy and powerful people in society.

The effects of the Great Recession and the reactions to it can still be seen today. Many millennials in the United States who graduated during its peak have significantly less wealth and more debt compared to previous generation at the same age. In Europe, Greece still has the highest ratio of debt to GDP in the EU after more than a decade,[3] and yet Iceland, a small island country which saw a similarly large economic collapse but put many more bankers into jail, has seen one of the best economic recoveries since then.[4]

It was into this socio-economic context in 2008 that the Bitcoin white paper was introduced, in a "cypherpunk" mailing by a pseudonymous account list named Satoshi Nakamoto (Nakamoto's true identity at the moment of writing has still not been discovered) who called on other cypherpunks and cryptographers to help them build it.[5] Cypherpunks will be explained in more detail shortly, but often they advocate for the use of cryptography, the study and practice of secure and private communications under the threat of attackers in which only the intended receiver can know the contents of a message, largely through the use of encryption and many advanced mathematical theories. Cryptopgraphy has become extremely important under late capitalism, for example in modern warfare, where it is used to protect secrets from opposing militaries and for creating secured networks over the Internet.

The paper, titled *Bitcoin: A Peer-to-Peer Electronic Cash System*, described a value transfer system that was not reliant on a third party or central authority like a central bank, Wells Fargo, Western Union, Visa or any other financial institution. If it worked, we wouldn't need to trust the same banks that had screwed people over to make money from gambling on subprime mortgages, at least in theory.

The idea of using the Internet for facilitating a system of transferring money between people without the need for banks or governments was not new. One of the first attempts at digital cash over the Internet was DigiCash, founded by David Chaum in 1990 and based on his own 1983 research paper. The paper detailed a protocol with every proposed element of the Bitcoin blockchain except for **Proof of Work** (more on that later) but did not experience the same success as bitcoin. Part of the reason that DigiCash didn't achieve the same success is that it still required banks to adopt it, and few were inclined to do so at the time. Based on the technical specifications of DigiCash, a user had to trust that the company and the banks would follow through on their transaction. This is unlike how cash works. When I give you cash, we don't need a third party to make the transaction happen. This makes cash **peer-to-peer**, whereas DigiCash was still an electronic form of money reliant on the company's servers and banks to send the currency, even if there were solid cryptographic protocols that directed the system.

Chaum's research is said to be a direct inspiration for "cypherpunks". The term was coined by Jude Milhon (or St Jude, as she was sometimes referred to),[6] a civil rights activist and cyber-feminist in the 1960s and 1970s, to mean computer users who were dedicated to online privacy through encryption. In 1992, a small group of cryptographers and early Internet advocates, including St Jude, started the *Cypherpunks* mailing list, which was used like a forum to discuss a plethora of different topics that revolved around privacy over the Internet, both from a political and a technical standpoint. Many of the subscribers to the mailing list went on to become notable open source developers, privacy researchers, entrepreneurs and activists. While it's difficult to say where exactly the cypherpunks lay on the political spectrum, the people involved could be largely described as civil libertarians, with the desire to use technology to get around, or make obsolete, any form of censorship that could be imposed by states and governments.

DigiCash also inspired other early attempts at cryptographic digital currencies from other cypherpunks like Hashcash, Bit Gold and B-Money. Unsurprisingly, then, the release of the Bitcoin source code and start of the network in January 2009 was an exciting moment for many cypherpunks. It was a moment of truth. Could this grand experiment work? Would it be secure without centralised control? Would there be enough **nodes** willing to participate in the network, or would it crumble under its own weight before adoption could become mainstream? While it may not look exactly how the original cypherpunks thought it would, at this point, we can safely say that bitcoin and cryptocurrencies in general have reached the mainstream.

In the past decade and a half the institutions that people were told had their best intentions at heart have failed them, and the cypherpunk ethos of distrust of institutions and prioritisation of personal liberty has become a compelling story. The appeal of cryptocurrencies is the promise of the creation of new institutions that are resilient and pose a better alternative to the status quo. While you may already have opinions on whether cryptocurrencies like bitcoin achieve both of these objectives, in order to get a full grasp of the current situation, let's start to peek under the hood technologically but still in a way that laymen can understand. Don't worry if you don't feel that you're technologically inclined, take your time and remember to refer to the glossary if you need a reminder or another explanation of a word. Now, let's see how Bitcoin solved "the double spending problem", something which makes it unique compared to previous attempts at digital currency.

How Bitcoin and Blockchains Work

Sometimes the words "bitcoin" and "blockchain" are used interchangeably, so what is the difference between them? You can think of bitcoin as a concerted attempt to create a resilient digital cash system without the need for a centralised authority. After its creation it was realised that the technological structure underpinning it could be abstracted in a way that allowed for its modifiable parts to be changed to create any number of designs. While the word "blockchain" is never mentioned in the Bitcoin white paper, Bitcoin was the first blockchain. Within the code were particular assumptions about economics and money which created the impression that all blockchains make the same assumptions. However, the modifiability and default open source nature of blockchain code makes it just as possible to apply different assumptions.

But first, in order to understand how Bitcoin and blockchains works, we need a top-down view of how most Internet architecture is configured today. In the vast majority of applications users are likely to interact with (most of which are developed or owned by a Big Tech corporation), the data that they see and manipulate comes from servers owned by the company. When we post on Facebook or Twitter, or interact with any other big tech company online, we are sending a request to those servers. Once that post finishes going through an automated system of approvals to make sure the post doesn't contain anything blocked on the platform, it appears on other users' clients (or apps). All of this takes a couple of seconds at most usually. This is commonly referred to as a "client-server model".

The implications of this architecture is that these big tech corporations have significant control over what information gets displayed. While those on the right decry tech corporations for censoring conservative voices in the United States, it has also been shown that companies like Google and Meta have censored left-wing activists as well. Indeed, prominent figures across the political spectrum have been denied access to their accounts for various reasons revolving around adherence to the company's terms and conditions.

While some argue that these companies have a right to censor who they want on their platforms because it is their private domain of business, it is undeniable that this has very serious political implications when the Internet is also seen as public infrastructure for communication. The client-server model of network architecture gives excessive power to the owners of the server (Big Tech). An additional issue is that there are single points of failure that, if compromised, can lead to complete outages of communication infrastructure that people are dependent on.

An alternative to the client-server model of architecture is the peer-to-peer (P2P) model, where the network infrastructure is not held or owned by a single entity but is instead spread out across a network of connected computers or servers. Computers on the network have equal permissions and responsibilities for processing the data and peers can be both suppliers and consumers of resources as needed. This is done largely through the use of open protocols as opposed to creating walled gardens as in the case of Big Tech platforms. While this may sound like a foreign concept for some, there's a chance you have benefited from P2P networks before if you've ever used services like Napster, LimeWire, BitTorrent or any other file sharing service to download movies, music or other media. P2P networks have been very influential in the media industry and have led to rapid changes in how media is consumed. As consumers we're able to gain access to an almost limitless library of media for free. This led to a drastic decrease in total profits in the music industry from 1999 to 2010 as people bought fewer CDs, and led to the rise of streaming giants like Spotify and Netflix. This is a situation which has its own problems, but the point is that by using a different underlying network architecture, the relationship people had with institutions changed drastically.

Bitcoin uses a P2P network to try to create a digital monetary system that does not rely on current financial institutions or state actors that have control over monetary data. However, there are problems with using this type of architecture to do this. When you share something over the Internet, you're not giving others the same thing you're seeing on your screen. For example, if you send an email to Karen in HR explaining how Todd in Finance keeps eating noisily at his desk, Karen's email application receives a *copy* of the email you sent. Now both you and Karen have a copy of the same email. Compare this to a letter, where you physically write on a piece of paper about how Todd's mess is stinking up your floor of the office and that same piece of paper is sent to Karen so that she can then refer you to section 4.2 in the employee handbook on "conflict resolution in the workplace".

What previous P2P networks like Napster showed was that computers and the Internet are amazing copying machines, and this power was leveraged to provide you with a free digital copy of that U2 album you didn't want to buy. However, this power creates particular difficulties in using P2P networks for a global monetary system without a central authority. If I try to send a dollar through email, all I've done is created another dollar; now there are two dollars, when I wanted to just send one. One way to solve this problem is by adding a central authority who decides that only the second digital dollar has worth and the first one doesn't. The problem here is that this authority would now have the power to censor specific parties by deciding which digital dollars count or not, taking us back to the initial problem. This is essentially how banks use computers to share information very quickly and manage your money. In fact, about 92% of the world's money is digital, held on digital ledgers owned by various financial institutions. This issue with making a digital monetary system free of states and financial institutions while also ensuring the integrity of the ledger is called the "double spending problem". So how does Bitcoin solve this?

As alluded to, bitcoin uses a P2P network of computers, also referred to as nodes, to share a digital ledger that tracks how much bitcoin everyone on the network has. Similar to how nodes on P2P networks like Napster shared information about music or movies, nodes on the Bitcoin network share the information about bitcoin, a type of economic information. Another difference between a P2P network like Napster and Bitcoin is that a node on Napster sharing a U2 album can disconnect from the network without much issue and repercussion for the person sharing the album. This dynamic is not possible for something trying to create a monetary system in which people need to be confident that it won't be hacked or destroyed by a bad actor. The way Bitcoin solves this is through economic incentivisation using a cryptographic competition utilising *hashes* that helps keep the network secure from direct manipulation.

A hash is a cryptographic function that can take any sized input and create a corresponding fixed sized output. What's different about a hash compared to other types of functions though, is that it only goes in one direction, meaning that if you have the input, you can easily produce the output, but by knowing the output, you cannot say what the input was. It is one way in which messages or data can be hidden inside another piece of data without others knowing unless they know about what is being hidden. In the table below you'll see that for each input for the SHA256 hashing algorithm, we get a radically different output with no relation to one another.

Input	Hash Output
Blockchain Radicals	1c402875f66d1284ca0fa601a534d30b3110df7f6c2dd903f66383c-d42a87991
Blockchain Radicals!	f5a53722dfbdc322b48b3ba70c98ab-23f78e688dc71a72257fbbcb8cd-b6146a0
blockchain radicals	df981e7faec6a3a62e783dc-c274e35140268f33038cdfe-3830a67bcdc720249a
(Combination of the three hashes above)	ca11a8c0a3480358a421551e6f-e7358891c9d88bca1e228b4cec-50f3ae5f2051
Blockchain Radicals by Joshua Dávila	a4aa88a0677e1c1e0a8c89bbb-5f252e9d72d5a4f46884154e51d-efb52d50dd0d

The properties of a good hash include:

1. It only operates in one direction
2. It is highly unlikely to generate the same hash twice[7]
3. Slight changes in the input data significantly change the output

What you'll notice in the table is that by making a very small change in the input, we can produce a very different output in which there is no way to tell that actually both inputs are almost identical. This is because knowing the output tells us nothing about the properties of the input. Someone looking at just the first three hash outputs would have not way of telling that all three of them say essentially the same thing in slightly different ways.

Additionally, we could combine the hashes above to create one hash that holds all of these hashes, therefore using half of the space needed to store both. What's also neat is that I could even use a hash to prove I am the writer of this book. To keep it simple, let's say that the entirety of my book is just the title like what is shown in the last row of the table. I can now append "by Joshua Dávila" to the end of that text and create the hash of my book. If this hash is provably stored somewhere and I were to notice somebody plagiarising my work, I could recreate the above hash which includes the text I wrote along with my name. Since my name and the text recreate the hash that existed before the plagiarised version of the book, this could serve as evidence against the plagiariser that they are stealing my work.

As you may be able to tell, there are many different ways this kind of hashing function could be used. For the Bitcoin network, hashes are used for a "Proof of Work" (PoW), a method of cryptographic proof by which the prover proves to the verifiers that a certain computational effort was expended. It was first proposed as a way to prevent denial-of-service attacks by slowing down the speed that bad actors can flood online sites or services as well as send spam email. However, here it's used as a way to ensure the security and validity of the P2P network of nodes and the digital ledger of bitcoin they track.

The name for the nodes on the Bitcoin network that help upkeep the network's security are commonly referred to as miners. Bitcoin miners however are not mining for gold, but for hashes in a cryptographic competition that earn them the right to add a block of bitcoin transactions to the Bitcoin blockchain, as well as some newly minted bitcoin cryptocurrency and the transaction fees included in all of the transactions in the block as a reward. The reward serves as an incentivisation for miners to continue the job of securing the network.

As bitcoin transactions are sent to the network (Alice sends 1 bitcoin to Bob), they are used as inputs for a hash function. The "block" in blockchain refers to a group of transactions that are organised by a miner to be added to the ledger. Miners compete by inputting as many bitcoin transactions as possible (up to two to four megabytes), along with the hash of the previous block of transactions added, and a random number added called a "nonce", into a hashing function to create an output with enough preceding zeros. Since a property of the hashing function is that the output of the function is impossible to predict until you process the inputs, the more preceding zeros that are required in the output to win, the more difficult the competition becomes. The difficulty of the problem is adjusted regularly to ensure that each block is added at approximately every ten minutes. Since the competition is purely based on probability and a miner's ability to exert computational work (or commonly referred to as hashing power), the more energy a miner is able to exert, the higher chances they have at winning the competition at each block interval up until the point they are not profitable many times due to the increasing energy costs incurred.[8] So the creation of a winning hash with appropriate inputs acts as a proof of work

Problem: Can you make a hash that includes recent bitcoin transactions, a hash of the previous block, a nonce, and begins with at least 4 zeros?

Reward: Newly minted bitcoin

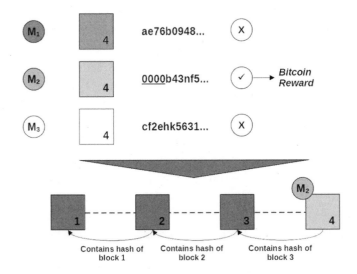

that bitcoin miners need to show to win the cryptographic competition. Proof of work is also commonly referred to as the **consensus mechanism** of the network since it is how nodes that are part of the Bitcoin protocol come to consensus about the current state of the Bitcoin ledger.

The "chain" part of the blockchain is the pattern of including the winning hash of the previous block in newly added blocks to the ledger. By repeating this pattern, the protocol creates a publicly verifiable record of the ledger that shows the relative chronological order of transactions made. You can think of a blockchain as a shared database like a Google Sheet (but without Google) that is hosted redundantly by each node in the network, however, since we're using a P2P architecture as opposed to a centralised client-server architecture, Bitcoin uses this proof of work competition as a way to solve the double spending problem inherent to attempting digital cash without a centralised authority. Attempting to do something like

Bitcoin using Google's infrastructure would effectively make Google the centralised authority over the ledger, defeating the purpose in the first place.

When we interact with centralised services on the Internet, like ones owned by Google and other Big Tech companies, most times we first need to create profiles that include some personally identifiable information which is then used to link our identity to the actions that we take using their services, which is also stored as part of our personal profile in their servers. This collection of data at a scale of millions or even billions of users allows Big Tech platforms to create more and more focused "user profiles" to sell as advertising products to their real customers — businesses that buy advertisements on their platforms. Want to advertise to college-educated men aged twenty-five to forty-five who are tech savvy, earn over $100k per year, are located in one of the New York City boroughs, vegan and recently searched for meal replacement powders? There's likely an advertising product for that user profile. This is all legal within certain limits and is what users agree to when clicking on the terms and conditions of Big Tech's walled gardens.

Instead of creating a profile with your personal information, accounts are made on a blockchain through public key cryptography to create a key pair. A private key is a series of numbers and letters that you keep as a secret and do not share with anyone, which if you run through the appropriate one-way cryptographic hashing functions will give you your public address which you can then share with anyone so that they can send bitcoin to your account. You can think of it as how you would access your online bank account. Your private key acts as the username and password to access the account online which you never share with anyone, and your IBAN (similar to an account and routing number if you're in the United States) can be shared with anyone so that they can send you money without needing to know anything about your username and password. This also means that people's identities on the network are a random string of numbers and letters, making them pseudo-anonymous and giving some layer of theoretical privacy protection. Because of the properties of hashes noted previously, it is effectively impossible to be able to know someone's private key to access their bitcoin just by knowing their public address, making it a very secure mechanism for storing accounts.

On the Bitcoin network, and most other blockchains, in order to make a transaction, you "sign" it with your private key. This means that you prove you are the owner of the public address (sometimes also referred to as a wallet) that holds the bitcoin or cryptocurrency by proving you are the owner of the associated private key. As long as you are able to prove you know the private key, you are able to access the funds held in the wallet. There are important differences with this type of system compared to normal online banking, however. For one, if you forget your username or password for your online banks, it's not difficult to go through the process of requesting a new password. The reason they're able to do this of course is because you have provided them with personal information about yourself that only you should be able to answer to prove that you are you. Using public key cryptography in the case of blockchains like Bitcoin, if you lose your private key, you lose access to any of the cryptocurrency that may be held in your wallet. There is no customer service phone number to call for the Bitcoin network. This inherently puts quite a bit more onus on the individual to store the private key in a safe spot where it can be retrieved. Since it's just a string of numbers and letters, it can be stored written on a piece of paper, as an encrypted file or on a hardware device (usually the most secure option).

So let's walk through the entire process of the creation of one block on the Bitcoin blockchain. Users who are connected to the Bitcoin network sign transactions with their private key to send to the receiver's public address along with a market determined transaction fee. These transactions are then

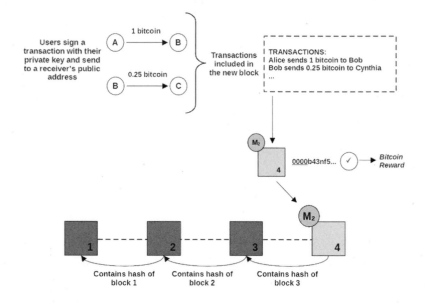

requested to the P2P network of miners who are competing to create hashes with a predetermined amount of zeroes in the front using the requested transactions, the hash of the previous block and a "nonce". When a miner is able to create a block meeting the criteria, this serves as a proof of work to other miners that they won the competition for that block, and the winning miner receives newly minted bitcoin as well as the transaction fees paid by users whose transactions are included in the block, and the process repeats itself.

This entire process makes it extremely difficult to change the balances of users on the Bitcoin network by bad actors. Let's say miners on the bitcoin network are working on block #400 and you made a very large transaction back on block #100 that you want to reverse. In order to accomplish this, you would need to re-mine block #100 as well as all of the blocks between it and the most current block being mined by all the other miners on the networks and then beat the other miners on mining the most current block to broadcast to the rest of the network. This is because nodes on the Bitcoin network default towards the largest chain of blocks that is shared with them. However, in order to achieve this practically, you would need to have more than half of the total hashing power of the rest of the network, which would not only be extremely expensive but require a significant amount of energy that few have access to. This is called a 51% attack, which becomes much more difficult to pull off as the transaction desired to be changed falls further behind the current block of transactions being mined.

Bad actors are also disincentivised to cheat the Bitcoin network because even if they were to pull off such an attack, the price of bitcoin would very likely fall since it would be proven that the network is not as safe as believed. Therefore any bitcoins stolen would lose their value significantly, making their heist less valuable. Of course this may not be as much of a concern if the bad actor did not care for the price of bitcoin and instead just had the intention of throwing off the network.

Another important thing to note about how Bitcoin works is that in the design of the protocol, new bitcoin is minted at a fixed rate that decreases over time until there is a total of 21 million, at which point no new bitcoin will ever be created. This means that over time, bitcoin has a deflationary effect (theoretically becomes more valuable) and has similar properties to gold in that there is a limited supply that can exist. In the context of the 2008 financial crisis, where "too big to fail" banks were receiving bailout packages from governments, this was seen as a better alternative. This has consequently attracted many "gold bugs", those who think that the gold standard was a better basis for the global monetary system, to the bitcoin community. Whether intended or not, this was an assumption baked into the very technology itself. However, it's important to keep in mind that not only can different assumptions be made and baked into cryptocurrencies, but already existing ones can be "disloyal children" to support political endeavours that go against their creators' politics, and in the next section we'll look at such undertakings.

CHAPTER 2

THE COMMUNISM OF SCIENCE AND CENSORSHIP RESISTANCE: A DOUBLE-EDGED SWORD

The communism of the scientific ethos is incompatible with the definition of technology as "private property" in a capitalistic economy.
— Robert K. Merton, *The Normative Structure of Science*

WikiLeaks is a giant library of the world's most persecuted documents. We give asylum to these documents, we analyze them, we promote them and we obtain more.
— Julian Assange, *Der Spiegel Interview*[1]

In April 2022 Virgil Griffith, a former developer for Ethereum, the second largest cryptocurrency by market capitalisation behind Bitcoin, was sentenced to five years in prison for allegedly giving presentations to the North Korean state on how to use cryptocurrencies to evade sanctions imposed by the United States.[2] Griffith pleaded guilty in September 2021 to conspiring to violate the International Emergency Economic Powers Act, a law prohibiting US citizens from exporting goods, services and technologies to North Korea without obtaining authorisation from the Treasury's Office of Foreign

Assets Control (OFAC). This showed the seriousness with which the US took sanctioned countries using cryptocurrency to evade their sanctions.

This was reinforced in August 2022 when OFAC sanctioned Tornado Cash,[3] an anonymisation tool that protects the privacy of users in the otherwise public Ethereum network by decoupling sender and recipient. It was alleged that sanctioned countries like North Korea were using it to launder cryptocurrency that state-sponsored hackers were stealing. The decision was controversial as Tornado Cash was not a company, it was instead a set of **smart contracts** (more on what these are in the next section) on a blockchain, a piece of autonomously running code. Because OFAC's statutory authority limits it to sanctioning "persons" or "entities" — and a smart contract is neither — crypto advocates argued that the government overstepped its authority. After the sanctioning, however, many of the self-described censorship-resistant applications and organisations in the crypto world started adhering to the lists of sanctioned wallets published by OFAC to stay in their good graces.

While these shows of force can be intimidating, it deflects from the reality that sanctions don't really work.[4] Sanctions are imposed by governments to punish dictatorships or "bad guys" in other countries. The idea in the liberal or conservative mindset on geopolitics is that by intentionally harming the general population in those countries, by denying them food, medicine and other goods they need or value, they will create disorder and rebellion which will change the government's policies. Almost always, however, sanctions have limited effects: they harm innocent people in the targeted country and not those in charge, who will always find ways to get food and medicine. Instead of an uprising, the internal propaganda machine turns on, convincing the people that those implementing the sanctions are the enemy, heightening nationalist fervour. Sanctions also run up against the problem of being a tool used against autocratic regimes, as an autocratic regime does not have the democratic infrastructure needed for people to make changes even if they wanted to. The real autocratic regime for these countries is the US, which tries and fails to be the world police.

One of the more radical selling points for cryptocurrencies has been their censorship resistance, playing an important although complicated role in regards to sanctions. While the examples above show that cryptocurrencies are not as censorship-resistant as crypto hypemen claim, there is clear evidence that sanctioned countries like Venezuela have used bitcoin to purchase imports from Iran and Turkey.[5] It's also been proven that Iran uses bitcoin mining as a way to get around economic sanctions as well as to purchase imports.[6] In 2021 Cuba announced they would be regulating and authorising the use of cryptocurrencies, likely also in a bid to circumvent sanctions from the US.[7]

With the recent Russian invasion of Ukraine, it's unsurprising that many were worried Russia would also use cryptocurrencies as a way to evade sanctions. However, the ensuing moral panic and assertion that cryptocurrencies should be banned in order to stop Russia from evading sanctions was short-sighted. This was not only due to the complex geopolitical circumstances around the situation, with sanctions failing to do what was expected in tanking the Russian economy, but also because Ukraine itself was benefiting from cryptocurrencies. The Ukrainian government was able to raise $10.2 million in cryptocurrency just four days after the start of the invasion, and since March 2022 $100m worth of crypto has been raised via the "Crypto Fund for Ukraine". The benefits of using cryptocurrency were that it was less influenced by geopolitical or macroeconomic factors like the depreciation in the value of the Ukrainian hryvnia and the speed with which the funds could be received — traditional money wires can take twenty-four hours, but cryptocurrency is much faster.

As with so much about crypto, the truth is that censorship resistance is a double-edged sword, and in a world where decentralised technologies are being used to subvert authoritarian control, they've increasingly become important factors in geopolitical competition. At the same time, crypto is not only important at the geopolitical level, but also at the individual level for marginalised people.

Sex Workers' Struggles for the Right to Be Paid

One of the earliest memes to come out of the crypto world was the phrase, "Not your keys, not your coins", which meant to remind newcomers especially that if you did not yourself own your private key to access your cryptocurrency funds, then you did not actually own your cryptocurrency. The hacks of exchanges like Mt. Gox in the early days saw people lose all of their bitcoins in an instant when the exchange was allegedly hacked, as well as the Bitcoin wallets that held its customers funds. This was because the Mt. Gox, like all crypto exchanges at the time, was ultimately the custodian of their customers' bitcoins. Critics may argue that forcing individuals to keep their keys safe is overly burdensome, but in many situations, this self-custody imposition also makes cryptocurrencies resistant to censorship.[8]

For many in the sex industry, cryptocurrency can be a lifeline, as due to pressure from conservative groups traditional payment service providers and financial institutions continually oscillate between tolerating and banning those suspected of working in it. In August 2021 one of the most popular platforms for sex workers, OnlyFans, stated they would no longer allow "sexually explicit" content, in order to comply with requests from its banking and payment providers. The CEO of OnlyFans even stated that, "The change in policy, we had no choice — the short answer is banks".[9]

While OnlyFans users also include non-sex workers, the vast majority are, and many had joined the platform in order to get away from more predatory forms of sex work, as the platform facilitated direct relationships between clients and performers. While the decision was reversed less than a week later after gaining more assurances from banking partners, actions like this from financial institutions are not new. In 2018, Pornhub announced it would accept cryptocurrency payments. It then switched to only accepting cryptocurrency for its premium service after being axed by Visa and Mastercard in 2020.

Some of the acceleration towards the acceptance of cryptocurrency in the sex industry has been caused by the passing of the Fight Online Sex Trafficking Act (FOSTA) and Stop Enabling Sex Traffickers Act (SESTA) in the United States in April 2018. While the legislation was meant to counter sex trafficking through online platforms, advocacy groups have pointed out that it has disproportionately affected sex workers and is essentially an Internet censorship bill. The legislation has made it more difficult for online platforms to stay in business since they require teams of lawyers to evaluate multiple scenarios of risk at the state and federal level. This has meant that some have gone out of business, forcing many sex workers back into more dangerous forms of work like street prostitution, which includes a much higher risk of human trafficking. What conservative activist groups fail to realise is that no matter the moral position you take, like the war on drugs, prohibition of sex work has rarely if ever succeeded in eradicating it.

With these short-sighted attempts at censorship by powerful institutions, it is the self-custodial aspects of cryptocurrency and its lack of direct control by these same institutions which make it a necessary option for those working in the sex industry. Paying for services with cryptocurrencies means that you are not going through financial service providers who can censor your transaction due to pressures from well-funded political groups that would rather you not exist. By facilitating more direct relationships between clients and service providers (whether or not those services are sexual in nature) through the Internet, cryptocurrencies can protect some of the most vulnerable or prosecuted in society.

WikiLeaks: Whistleblowing and State Retaliation

Founded in 2006 by Internet activist and cypherpunk Julian Assange, WikiLeaks is an organisation dedicated to the publication of censored or otherwise restricted documents involving war, spying and corruption that has published more than ten million documents and associated analyses. This includes classified documents related to the mistreatment of civilians through torture and solicitation of child prostitution, among other international war crimes committed in the Afghan and Iraqi wars under President George W. Bush. This includes the WikiLeaks-released "Collateral Murder" video in April 2010, showing United States soldiers shooting eighteen civilians, including two *Reuters* journalists, from a helicopter in Iraq. These two mega leaks are referred to as the "Afghan and Iraq War Logs" and were first published through three media partners: the *New York Times*, the *Guardian* and *Der Spiegel*.

More recently, in March 2016, WikiLeaks was also responsible for publishing over twenty thousand pages of emails from John Podesta, a former White House chief of staff and chair of Hillary Clinton's 2016 US presidential campaign, which included transcripts of Clinton's speeches to Wall Street and the revelation that Donna Brazile had given Clinton some questions in advance of her debate with Bernie Sanders on CNN. It's been speculated that the release played a part in Clinton's drop in the polls right before the election of Donald Trump. WikiLeaks is certainly a controversial organisation, but whatever else may be said about them, they stick to their principles of being against censorship of restricted documents.

Events in 2010 and 2011 were a major turning point for the organisation. Besides the release of the Afghan and Iraq

War Logs, 2010 saw the start of the "Cablegate" leaks which revealed the internal discussions and intelligence-gathering tactics of US diplomats, including collecting the credit card numbers, frequent flyer miles and biometric information of foreign officials. It also first revealed then-President Obama's administration's war in Yemen against suspected terrorists, Saudi Arabia's urging to bomb Iran, and that in the weeks before the US-led invasion of Iraq in 2003, UK and US diplomats spied on UN Secretary General Kofi Annan in apparent violation of international treaties prohibiting spying at the UN. According to WikiLeaks, it was the largest set of confidential documents ever to be released into the public domain. The leaks during these two years are considered to be of the same scope as the Pentagon Papers, which had demonstrated, among other things, that the Lyndon B. Johnson Administration had systematically lied, not only to the public but also to Congress, regarding the US military's actions in the Vietnam War, boosting the anti-war effort.

US politicians, including many Republicans and Democrats, called for immediate action against WikiLeaks and anyone related to the leaks, including Assange. It was soon revealed that it was Chelsea Manning, an intelligence analyst in the US army, who had leaked most of the documents published by WikiLeaks in 2010, which led to her arrest under the Espionage Act. An investigation in the US began to prosecute Assange under the same law and at the same time charges were levelled against him in Sweden for sexual assault, charges he claimed were false and were being used to extradite him to the US. The charges in Sweden have since been dropped but led to his claim for political asylum in the Ecuadorian embassy in London, where he stayed from August 2012 to April 2019 in an office-turned-studio apartment. London's Metropolitan Police stood guard outside to arrest him if he stepped outside.

The "Cablegate" leaks in 2010 soon kickstarted a financial blockade against WikiLeaks. PayPal, Amazon, Visa and

Mastercard, among others, all stopped processing donations to WikiLeaks as a result of US government pressure, causing a 95% decrease in revenue for an organisation largely dependent on donations through these financial intermediaries.[10] Additionally, the Swiss bank PostFinance froze Assange's personal account. Kristinn Hrafnsson, spokesman for WikiLeaks, described the situation as:

> the privatisation of censorship, because this is being done because of extreme pressure by the US Government... It's extremely important to fight back and stop this process right here and now so that we won't see in the future... where we have the financial giants deciding who lives and who dies in this field.[11]

Many allied organisations did what they could to help WikiLeaks raise funds for sustaining its infrastructure and paying salaries by accepting donations on their behalf. For example, the French non-profit FDNN (Fund for the Defense of Net Neutrality/ Fonds de Défense de la Net Neutralité) set up a Carte Bleue fund for WikiLeaks. Carte Bleue, the French national credit card system, had a contractual agreement with Visa and Mastercard that barred them from cutting off merchants through their system. Other efforts included auctioning off eight seats to a lunch with Assange and the Slovenian Marxist philosopher Slavoj Žižek,[12] as well as auctioning the server that hosted the Cablegate documents on eBay.[13] This was one of the first opportunities for the recently created bitcoin to prove its worth in being able to facilitate transfers of value across the Internet, circumventing these very financial intermediaries it was theoretically made to fight against.

Soon after these companies stopped working with WikiLeaks, in December 2010, a debate erupted on the official Bitcoin web forum regarding the potential risk that bitcoin donations to WikiLeaks would spur unwanted attention from governments. Satoshi Nakamoto, the pseudonymous inventor of Bitcoin, weighed in:

> The project needs to grow gradually so the software can be strengthened along the way. I make this appeal to WikiLeaks not to try to use Bitcoin. Bitcoin is a small beta community in its infancy. You would not stand to get more than pocket change, and the heat you would bring would likely destroy us at this stage.[14]

They continued, "It would have been nice to get this attention in any other context. WikiLeaks has kicked the hornet's nest, and the swarm is headed towards us."

At that moment, WikiLeaks agreed with the assessment made by Satoshi and decided to wait until Bitcoin was more established before accepting donations. Infamously, just six days after posting the message warning WikiLeaks about kicking the hornet's nest, Satoshi disappeared from the bitcoin community and has still yet to be heard from or identified. At the time of the comments made by Satoshi, the price of bitcoin stood at around $0.25, and about six months later on 9 June 2011, it jumped up to an all-time high of $29.60.[15] It seemed that people had begun to see the advantages of censorship-resistant transactions. On 14 June 2011, it was decided that Bitcoin had become a viable alternative for raising money and WikiLeaks tweeted that they would begin accepting bitcoin donations.[16] Despite it being incorrectly reported by *Forbes* (and by WikiLeaks itself) that bitcoin was an anonymous and untraceable currency,[17] perhaps due to its association with the Silk Road, an anonymous marketplace that used bitcoins to sell contraband, including a wide range of illegal drugs, donations flew in to the WikiLeaks Bitcoin address. Earlier that month, Senators Chuck Schumer and Joe Manchin had called for the shutdown of Silk Road and referred to Bitcoin as "an online form of money laundering used to disguise the source of money, and to disguise who's both selling and buying the drug". Years later, Ross Ulbricht, the pseudo-anonymous founder of Silk Road, would be caught and arrested due to forensics software made for the Bitcoin blockchain, other tactics from law enforcement and the very public nature of bitcoin transactions. It's likely that the WikiLeaks financial blockade combined with the popularisation of the Silk Road during this time helped propel bitcoin's price for its first bull run.

While it's unclear how many bitcoins WikiLeaks earned in the first campaign due to the possibility of WikiLeaks owning several Bitcoin addresses, in February 2020 it was reported that the original WikiLeaks Bitcoin address received 4,043 BTC.[18] The exact dollar amount that would equal varies based on the price of bitcoin at a particular moment and when WikiLeaks chose to spend it. At the time of writing, the price of one bitcoin is hovering around $20,000, making the 4,043 BTC worth about $80,860,000. Since the spending of the bitcoin collected can be tracked on the bitcoin blockchain, there is evidence that at least 3,500 BTC has been spent, having gone to the known address of BitPay, a bitcoin payment processing service, likely to convert it into fiat currency like US Dollars or Euros.[19]

While the original financial blockade eventually ended, WikiLeaks never removed the option to donate via bitcoin, something which came in handy when a new financial blockade was enforced in 2017. In fact, they have since expanded to accept other popular and privacy-oriented cryptocurrencies. The choice of continuing to accept bitcoin donations ended up being not only a smart move for circumventing the blockades, but also as an investment. According to Assange in 2017,[20] WikiLeaks' donated bitcoin generated a 50,000% return. He thanked the US government for pressuring them to make the move, as each time action was taken against WikiLeaks it gave the organisation a boost in bitcoin donations.[21]

On 11 April 2019, the Ecuadorian embassy stopped offering Assange political asylum without due process and invited the London police to arrest him on charges of a breach of bail, considered a minor violation in UK law, for the dropped charges in Sweden. He was quickly found guilty and the same day charged with conspiracy to commit computer intrusion (i.e., hacking into a government computer), which carries a maximum five-year sentence, in relation to allegations related to helping Chelsea Manning.

Since his arrest Assange has undergone multiple trials to decide whether the UK will extradite him to the United States to face likely much more significant punishment and worse treatment. So far, while the assigned judge has agreed to most of the charges, extradition seems to have been prevented largely because of Assange's deteriorating physical and mental health. Throughout his time in the Ecuadorian embassy, it had been revealed that Assange underwent multiple forms of psychological torture, being refused contact with his lawyers, family and friends, in addition to being spied on by multiple governments including the US, Ecuador, the UK and Spain. In February 2020, an organisation called Doctors for Assange published an open letter in a medical journal in which they said Assange was in a "dire state of health due to the effects of prolonged psychological torture in both the Ecuadorian embassy and prison", which could lead to his death, and that his "politically motivated medical neglect sets a dangerous precedent".

Documents revealed by WikiLeaks showed that this was an explicit effort by state security agencies to wear down Assange and his defenders. It was additionally revealed that organisations like the CIA and others had made plans to assassinate Assange if needed. Extradition has been strongly opposed by multiple news, journalism and reporter organisations as there could be very serious implications for a free media when it has always been clear that the leaks released by the organisation were important for public interest in exposing the multiple war crimes and human rights violations being committed by governments in the name of peace and justice.

At the time of writing, Assange is still being kept in a UK jail and WikiLeaks is again unable to process donations in fiat money without the help of European partners like the Wau Holland Foundation. If you would like to help support the organisation continue its mission, you can donate through cryptocurrency or fiat money at *https://shop.wikileaks.org/donate*. The fact remains that, for those who believe in the fundamental tenet of true net neutrality and non-violent content free from censorship by business interests or through government force, WikiLeaks is an important counter-institution to challenge the neoliberal capitalist order. It's important for those wanting to see radical political change away from the status quo to support their efforts, even if it means donating cryptocurrency to get around financial blockades.

Sci-Hub: Making Science Like Communism

In 1942 Robert K. Merton, considered to be the founding father of modern sociology, published *The Normative Structure of Science*,[22] in which he laid out a set of four principles that need to be adhered to for society to benefit from the fullest measures of scientific achievement. For Merton these principles are imperative for scientific institutions to follow since together they describe the ethos of modern science. The principles are: universalism, disinterestedness, organised scepticism and communism. That's right, communism.

Merton explains that science requires full and open communication as opposed to secrecy. Scientific goods and discoveries should not be held back by turning them into intellectual property, since all findings in science benefit from the social collaboration of scientists that came before them as well as their peers. He cites the court's decision in the case of US v. American Bell Telephone Co., which states that "The inventor is one who has discovered something of value. It is his absolute property. He may withhold the knowledge of it from the public", as being detrimental to science, while praising scientists like Albert Einstein who used patents as a way to make sure their work was available to the public. Collective collaboration is required for science to reach its fullest capacity. Therefore, having communism in terms of communication is part of the essence of science. However, unfortunately, in line with the trend of general institutional failure in modern capitalist society, this principle is not adhered to by many large scientific institutions, especially scientific journals.

Unsurprising to those who have published in academic journals, but surprising to those outside of them, many articles published in academic journals, some filled with work funded by public grants, are behind a paywall. Academic journals can charge somewhere from $30 to upwards of $70 per PDF download. Not only that, but it is also common practice for scientists who want to have their papers published after rigorous peer review to need to pay the journal for it, something which can cost upwards of $5,000 in addition to the non-refundable application fee to have your article even considered for peer-review and publication. On top of that, journals earn revenue from organisations, including universities, companies, non-profits and others that need access to academic articles, by selling them subscriptions. In 2012, Harvard's Faculty Advisory Council revealed that the school spent $3.75 million annually on academic journal subscriptions with some costing up to $40,000 every year.[23] On top of all this, the authors of the articles being purchased do not receive a cut of the sales of their publication. It's easy to see how these pricing and revenue practices can be detrimental for institutions that don't have the same deep pockets as universities with large endowments.

Even though much of the research being published comes from public money, the most prestigious journals for scientists to publish in, that are of most to help their careers, are private companies whose purpose is to maximise their profits. The top for-profit scientific publishers report profit margins of nearly 40% higher than that of companies like Apple and Google.[24] This privatised model has caused the centralisation of wealth, influence and market share for the top journals. In the natural and medical sciences, the top five largest for-profit academic publishers now publish 53% of all scientific papers.

If you are a part of an organisation without the deep pockets needed to have access to all of the top scientific journals, what do you do? One answer is to go to Sci-Hub to download for free nearly any paywalled academic journal article or any that are open-access already. Over eighty million articles are available in their databases. In order to access the site, you may potentially need to use a VPN or try many different top level domains like .ru,.st,.se or others (for me, www.sci-hub.ru has worked the best) because, as you can imagine, Sci-Hub is blocked and illegal in many countries. In fact, some large journals have put forward lawsuits in several countries to censor the site for copyright violations, demanding millions in damages.

If the user provides either the URL of the paywalled journal article they want to read or the DOI number (an identifier that nearly all journal articles possess) into the search bar and clicks the big red button with a key in it that says "open", and assuming Sci-Hub has the article, a PDF that you can save directly to your computer pops up. Many times you can even just copy the title of the article or something close enough into the search bar and get the exact article you were looking for. It offers an extremely fast service not only because of the fact that people don't need to go through the usual paywall on an academic journal sites, but the page usually loads very quickly as well, making it a much better experience than many journal websites.

If you manage to be able to access the Sci-Hub site or any of its mirror sites, on the About page you'll be greeted with an image of Vladimir Lenin with his hand out, on the left, rendered in a socialist realist art style once common in the Soviet Union, accompanied with this text: "Sci-Hub is the most controversial project in modern science. The goal of Sci-Hub is to provide free and unrestricted access to all scientific knowledge." [25] Scrolling down, you will also find statistics about the number of articles and books available to download from the site as well as more information about the goal of providing open access to science, a link to a list of lawsuits currently against Sci-Hub around the world, and a contact email to the founder of the site.

Originally from Kazakhstan, Alexandra Elbakyan was born in 1988 when the country was still a part of the Soviet Union and is the one-woman team behind Sci-Hub. For someone working on something so illegal, you would think that she would be a shadowy figure shrouded in secrecy with little information about them available. However when you click "Elbakyan" on the menu of the site,[26] you're greeted with a GIF of a woman with pale skin and brown hair, wearing a t-shirt with the text "Send" on it and waving at you with a slight smile. On the page, Elbakyan gives a detailed biography. She started programming at twelve and had an interest in neuroscience, going to university to study brain-computer interfaces (well before Elon Musk's Neuralink company), but failed to find a PhD program in the US that covered her research interests: "to connect networks of conscious experiences".

Further down there is a timeline of her life with her political views, "communism", and her religion, "new age hermeticism" listed, while just below that a collection of fifty-six photos from when she was a baby, through her childhood and into adulthood, working in labs, travelling, group photos with friends and colleagues, and other things ostensibly normal people do. Under that is a section titled "Works and Ideas". Under "communism", she writes:

I enjoy the idea of communism and consider it to be the true essence of science, information and knowledge. Communism and communication are the same-root words. So communism is the hidden idea behind any text and message — information by its essence is common.

While she may use the word communism to describe her beliefs on openly accessible information, it is perhaps less a political manifesto and more of a practical scientific conclusion.

The next idea she lists is "Information God":

> For ancient people information was sacred, language and writing and communication were manifestations of the god. That god was known by various names: Thoth in ancient Egypt or Hermes in Greece or Tir in Armenia; and this god is known in modern astrology as Mercury. These gods were also associated with knowledge and intellect, supporting the idea that knowledge is essentially common.

There is a collection of her writings on the topic, including an article and presentation in Russian and blog posts, including one titled "Why Stalin is a God", that can be read in either Russian or English.

Her final idea, "Global Brain", revolves around collective intelligence, framing a group of people as a collective brain with more knowledge than a single brain could ever possess. For Elbakyan, with technologies like the Internet and brain-machine interfaces, we can literally connect the brains of different people, creating the "global brain". It's clear that she not only preaches open access and transparency, but also practices and desires it to a radical degree

I was lucky enough to be able to speak with Elbakyan through a video call once. Using the contact email that was listed on the Sci-Hub website, I reached out to her to ask if she would be interested in an interview for my podcast. After several months of back and forth email and finding a Russian translator (Elbakyan can understand and read English but prefers to speak in Russian) we made the arrangements. When she came up on screen on the day of our interview, I was for some reason amazed that she looked exactly like the GIF of her waving at you on the Sci-Hub site. Speaking through the translator, she was remarkably normal, pragmatic and open for someone who was constantly facing lawsuits raised around the world. When I asked her what inspired her to start Sci-Hub, this is what she had to say:

Alexandra: So, there wasn't a specific single thing that inspired me to start the project. Well, first of all, I was a student myself and I was writing on and working on the topic of new computer interfaces. And then I faced a problem that most of the scientific articles that I needed for work were with paid access. And I thought I would need to come up with some sort of a program to deal with it and the logic was as follows. If we can access and download free movies or free music online, then why isn't there a thing for scientific papers? And second, I then noticed that a lot of people were faced with the same problem and would need a solution for it.

Me: It seems to come from a very practical reason for why you needed something like that... you had a problem and you needed to fix it.

Alexandra: Yes, that's about it. It's not like there was some new global idea and ideology behind it.[27]

Similarly to WikiLeaks, along with the legal troubles and constant site takedowns, Sci-Hub has also suffered from a financial blockade at the behest of the institutions that are challenged by its existence. While in the beginning she had an option for international supporters to donate through PayPal, through which she received about $2,000-3,000, after the large publisher Elsevier (which owns around 2,500 science journals) complained to PayPal about copyright infringement in 2015, PayPal refused access to any of the funds and the account. She was still able to receive donations through Yandex.Money,[28] a payment processor available largely in ex-Soviet countries, which covered many of the costs, but there was no way for her to receive donations from international supporters who wanted to help pay for the costs associated with running all of the servers and the site. This was when she first came across bitcoin.

After being recommended by several users, in 2015 she shared a Bitcoin wallet address so that international supporters could donate to her cause. University of Pennsylvania postdoctoral fellow Daniel Himmelstein and a group of other scholars found that Sci-Hub raised over 94 bitcoins with about 85 bitcoins seemingly withdrawn, leaving 9 bitcoin left by the start of 2018.[29] Assuming a price of $15,000 (the approximate price bitcoin was hovering around on 1 January 2018), that would be $135,000 left, presuming that the rest of the bitcoin was spent. This is also assuming that the bitcoin addresses publicly known to be owned by Sci-Hub are the only ones, when there is a possibility that Elbakyan could have reserved certain addresses for certain big donators.

By this point looking back, just like in the case of WikiLeaks, this bet to start accepting bitcoin donations was an incredible fruitful one. But this is not really the most important point to take home. What these examples show is the importance of having some form of censorship-resistant payment channel to assist efforts which have legitimacy but not legality.

Having the option to accept or use cryptocurrencies comes in handy when you may have legitimacy for your cause (people want to support it) but are considered illegal at the behest of capitalist institutions. In the case of Sci-Hub, it has legitimacy in challenging the current structure of how science publishing is done today as well as the entire existence of intellectual property in general, but this challenge comes at the cost of financial blockade, especially in countries that have the most to gain from intellectual property enforcement.

The reverse could also be said about the very journals that are trying to make Sci-Hub completely inaccessible on the Internet through claims of intellectual property and copyright infringement. They can be seen as illegitimate (many scientists do not agree with the way journal publishing is handled and financed) yet it is completely legal and uses that status of legality, as well as the legal frameworks around copyright, to profit. Elbakyan has countered that what these journals are doing is akin to violation of Article 27 of the Universal Declaration of Human Rights adopted by the United Nations General Assembly.[30] However, until countries like the United States, which have lawsuits against Elbakyan, have significantly less influence over the UN, it's unlikely that human right would be enforced universally. One of the likely reasons why Elbakyan hasn't faced the same dangerous threats as others who have similarly leaked information that the public deserves to have access to is because, unlike Julian Assange, Chelsea Manning or Edward Snowden, she does not reside in the US realm of influence. Additionally she does not have a team, instead doing most of the work on her own. As long as she stays outside of that realm of influence, she would likely stay safe from having to pay for any of the lawsuits against her or the prospect of jail time.

When you go to the English donation page of the Sci-Hub site, you will find that you now have the option to donate in bitcoin as well as ten other cryptocurrencies as a way to "diversify" risk in case one wallet or cryptocurrency is compromised. Further down the page, just as on the others, she gives a transparent and honest recount of the history of donations to Sci-Hub and how some academic publishers have made claims that her site was funded by and working for the Russian government in order to de-legitimise her work. Switching to the Russian language page you will find a Sberbank card number that people in Russia can donate to instead. Although some may argue that cryptocurrency donations are not necessary, it would be strange if Sci-Hub only relied on donations from Russian financial service companies, especially given the current geopolitical and economic situation in Russia as a result of the Ukrainian invasion.

If there's anything to take away from these examples it is the importance of having a contingency plan in place if you intend to fight capitalist institutions. There are various factors that make it difficult to directly compare the plight of Julian Assange and Alexandra Elbakyan, but what we have seen in the cases of both WikiLeaks and Sci-Hub is that one of the first attacks from capitalist institutions who are being challenged is financial blockade, and in the absence of any other alternative, as well as in terms of preparation for a future we cannot predict with absolute certainty, cryptocurrency is an important tool. For any radical group with legitimacy that still relies on some form of quasi-money to support its infrastructure, this must be taken seriously.

CHAPTER 3

"IS BITCOIN MONEY?" IS THE WRONG QUESTION TO BE ASKING

Money, it's a crime
Share it fairly but don't take a slice of my pie
Money, so they say
Is the root of all evil today
But if you ask for a rise it's no surprise that they're giving none
away
— Pink Floyd, "Money"

Despite the previous chapter's focus on the hype around cryptocurrencies and the use of Bitcoin to give money to entities under financial blockades, *this book is not really about money.* Although much of the marketing around cryptocurrencies has revolved around a particular critique of monetary systems with the conclusion that cryptocurrencies like bitcoin are "better forms of money", it's clear that this does not hold up under scrutiny. To dig into this, let's try to understand at a high level what money is and how it functions.

First of all, money is pervasive in modern capitalist society. Unless we live off-grid on self-subsistence farms or have the ability to live very alternative lifestyles, we need money to be able to buy food, pay for housing, pay taxes, bills and get access to the other things that make life enjoyable. Without money or a social safety net that can provide for us, either through welfare from the state or from our local community, we risk hunger, homelessness and violence.

Because of this, money has enormous power and influence over how people in society behave. How do we prepare when it looks like inflation is coming, decreasing the purchasing power of wages? Do we choose to do work that is good for society but poorly paid, or net-negative for society but very well paid? Do we buy the more expensive organic and fair-trade brand or the cheaper store brand? And what if there's nothing on the packaging to tell us the difference between two products and all we have is the difference in price? Would we even want to know that the cheaper brand was made with slave labour on a different continent after we chose it over the more expensive one? Would that change if the exploitation or pollution the company was creating was happening in our own community?

Friedrich Hayek, the libertarian Austrian School economist who inspired many of the men who had a hand in the creation of Bitcoin,[1] argued that money and prices were efficient signalling systems to facilitate the free market by aggregating vast amounts of information in a way that planned economies could never do. While prices certainly do coordinate markets as they exist currently, it's difficult to believe that prices "efficiently" reflect all of the information behind a product when, as shown above, just knowing the price of something does not tell us what went on in its creation. It seems more accurate to say that prices give something to agree on between consumers and producers, but it doesn't aggregate so much as collapse the information to facilitate trade at the expense of "externalities" which usually show up as pollution of our water and air, exploitation of our community or others in foreign countries, or any of the other unethical practices that large multinational companies participate in on a regular basis with few repercussions to their balance sheet. If using money and prices is an instrument for signalling preferences in an economy, it is an extremely blunt one that loses all of the finer details and qualities of what we as humans actually care about should we be given the opportunity to stop and think about it. What our dependence on money shows is that we have a monoculture of value expression that we rely on for our economy to function. Rather than having systems of value expression that can take into account the effects on the environment or the social fabric of communities, our economy almost exclusively revolves around financial value. What's worse is that this system is almost impossible to opt out of.

It's not just that we need money to survive, it's that money in a particular form has taken hold of many aspects of our lives; money that is recognised by the state. You may hear this referred to as "fiat money" from those who advocate for cryptocurrencies like bitcoin. It's not uncommon to hear bitcoin supporters speak of the fiat money system as being the root of all evil because governments can make the "money printer go brrr". In fact, this is an incorrect understanding of how money is created and exists in the first place. They will blame money printing by the US government for the Great Recession in 2008 and warn of it being a ticking time bomb for hyperinflation even though most, if not all, credible academics who study these areas will say that is not the case as drops in economic productivity are a much larger factor in creating inflation. They will likely claim that things were better when the world was ruled by the gold standard, or when money was backed by gold reserves (another assertion with little evidence to back it), and that Bitcoin emulates a similar monetary system except digitally.

While central banks are overseen by directors chosen by those elected to government, and central banks can increase the money supply through open market operations (where central banks provide liquidity directly to private banks in their currency like during the 2008 recession and more recently with COVID-19), the vast majority of money is created through the private banking system.

Similarly to the way that you may have a bank account with your bank, your bank likely has its own bank account with the central bank from which it can take out loans at a fixed interest rate which they then loan out to their customers at a higher interest rate in order to pay for the original loan. This is handled through digital ledgers between the involved entities and regulators. In this way, it is actually private banks that "print" most money, not governments. In fact, in most "first-world" countries, it is private banks who also facilitate digital payments, through private infrastructure, not government infrastructure.

Central banks also are generally in charge of the distribution of physical money (bank notes and coins) in order to help private banks give this form of money to their customers, though this makes up a very small percentage of the total money supply.[2] Essentially, we have two money systems that we as normal citizens take part in. The *state physical* (cash) and the *bank digital* (numbers on a digital ledger) money systems.

The writer Brett Scott, in his book *Cloudmoney*, has presented extensive evidence of how private banks have been influencing consumers and businesses to be more "cashless", hurting the state physical money system so that private banks can have more influence over the money supply and reduce their costs related to dealing with cash. Electricity and computers can move faster than a bank teller counting cash. This amounts to the privatisation of what was once the largely nationalised form of money system, since physical cash gives people real ownership over their money, compared to a number in a computer controlled by a bank. The COVID-19 pandemic in particular helped speed up this process, as some companies began to not accept physical cash in stores due to unfounded lies that the spread of the disease was happening through cash exchange, which has never been proven in studies. Whenever we use a digital or private bank-related infrastructure to make a purchase, we are using a payments system that exists on top of the monetary system, making these banks (and now many fintech companies) effectively middlemen. It is safe to say, according to Scott, that banks, with fintech companies as their partners, have declared a war on cash.

There is also a state digital money system, but the only actors who get access to it at the moment are private banks, through their accounts with the central bank which facilitates account clearing between banks. As it stands, they are the only ones who get access to the central bank, giving them the first rights on how to introduce money into the economy as private entities. This is problematic as private banks are also for-profit. Would private banks allocate money in a way that was good for the public if it also hurt their bottom line? Similarly to a company that may exploit workers or pollute the environment to lower costs, this causes externalities that are simply not accounted for in our common mental models for thinking about money. This means that monetary policy and the money supply are not democratic, and are instead largely handled through market-based adjustments to induce banks to borrow more or less with the hopes of certain outcomes in financial markets that cascade into the larger economy. We as citizens have essentially no influence over how money is created or introduced into society, as that power is reserved for those who have influence over central banks — the private banks.

Another important consideration is that since all money that is loaned out by central banks to private banks is done so at interest, as are the loans those private banks then make to their clients, there is always more debt owed by the economy than actual money in existence, making money a scarce resource. So how can these debts be paid off? This creates what has been termed a "Money Growth Imperative", or the systemic requirement for more money to be created in order to resolve the contradictions that arise in the competition between savers and debtors.[3] This results in the need for continuous extraction of the Earth's natural resources to sell on the market in the hope that money trickles down to you eventually. In a time when the natural disasters caused by climate change are ever increasing, this seems like a money system with a death wish. It has been designed by and for the elites of a capitalist system to ensure their wealth and power keeps growing, no matter the cost. Pink Floyd had the right idea here: "money, it's a crime". But it's also completely legal, even though if most were to look at it with a critical eye, it would be seen as an illegitimate system for a democratic society.

These are all issues however that you won't hear about from most of the hardcore cryptocurrency enthusiasts, as this is a more complicated story to tell potential future buyers. While they will agree with me in saying that the monetary system is legal but illegitimate, their narrative stems from an Austrian School-inspired belief that simplifies many more complex socio-economic issues. This simplified narrative is a seductive one for many due to its adherence to the ideologies promoted by many capitalist institutions: it does not prioritise the interest of a democratic society, as we'll see soon.

Is Bitcoin Money?

So, does Bitcoin achieve its goal as digital money? The answer will of course depend on who you ask. The more hard-line supporters of Bitcoin (commonly referred to as "bitcoin maxis") will say unequivocally, "Yes, it has achieved that and should perhaps even be used as an accepted global payment system". There are, however, some practical reasons to think this is not a desirable outcome, in part because Bitcoin does not fulfil every property of what money should have. The three functions of money are to be a:

1. Store of value: Money that you hold onto should have the same or close to the same value from one day to the next or even to the next year, the value should stay relatively stable.
2. Unit of account: Money is what we use to measure value in economic transactions and is therefore a good unit for setting prices of goods and services.
3. Medium of exchange: Money is something that is widely accepted for payment.

As it stands today, governments are fundamental to ensuring these three functions are still true of the money they issue. This is partially done through monetary policy and taxation. The US dollar is useful because people need it to survive in American society. You may need to pay taxes in it, most things are priced in US dollars and people generally believe that it will be useful for the foreseeable future. While many bitcoin maxis argue that this system is illegitimate for reasons revolving around distrust of governments and the state, a suspicion many people are sympathetic to, it is not correct that bitcoin achieves these functions in the way that the US dollar does. This is not to say that state backing is required for anything to be considered "money" (although this is the view of Chartalism), but it does require a significant and coherent system of social organisation to enforce itself.

Bitcoin does store value in that it can likely be liquidated into actual money in the future, but it does not have the same stability of value that money has. It is not uncommon for the price of bitcoin to fluctuate by upwards of 5% in price relative to the US dollar in a single day, which makes it more akin to speculative investment products like stocks. There may be some amount of inflation that changes purchasing power, but it does not come close to the fluctuations in an average week of a cryptocurrency. So bitcoin doesn't really fulfil the first function of money in the way the US dollar does.

The most attention-grabbing aspect of bitcoin and other cryptocurrencies, especially in the media, has been the price valuations and fluctuations. While bitcoin maxis may celebrate the increases in price, or take advantage of its volatility for trading opportunities (i.e., speculation), there is a contradiction between wanting the price of bitcoin to go up as fast as possible with the aim of it also being a system for digital money. Let's say you want to purchase some organic apples and are thinking about what they might cost. You probably wouldn't estimate their price in bitcoin, and even if you did estimate they might cost 0.000123 BTC, that could very well change almost immediately due to bitcoin's price fluctuations. Instead, however, you'd be much more likely to estimate the cost in your local state money because it is a unit of account.

An additional irony, when considering price, is that bitcoin is being priced in actual money, like US dollars. This is how we are able to make sense of bitcoin and its worth. We imagine cryptocurrencies as tokens which are priced in money. Where money is used for its stability, bitcoin and most other cryptocurrencies are largely bought with real money as an investment opportunity with the hope of returns in real money in practice.

While people can certainly choose to offer or accept bitcoin as payment for goods and services, and there are entire businesses that do this, it is clearly not widely accepted on global markets (although recently Russia has started accepting bitcoin to purchase its oil due to economic sanctions imposed after its invasion of Ukraine). Due to the power of the state, and its monopoly on legal violence, it has some ability in dictating the rules of payment and ensuring its own currency is the de facto money of its nation.[4] The borderless nature of the infrastructure bitcoin uses makes it difficult to be utilised by the state and declared as legal tender without significant amounts of centralisation (something like this is happening in El Salvador, with President Bukele declaring bitcoin as legal tender in the country).

There is a major contradiction and tension in cryptocurrency narratives. One is that cryptocurrency is a better form of money to spend and the other is that it is attractive to hold on to in the hopes of making a profit. What is clear about what makes money "money", is that it cannot be simultaneously an investment and something you spend for your everyday needs. This tension largely comes from already-existing ideas around what the "optimal" money system should look like, which is inspired by the theories of the Austrian School of economics. Due to this school of thought's belief in free markets above all else, they espouse a commodity theory of money. This is the belief that money comes from and ought to be something that is backed by some commodity, most commonly gold. Gold-backed money represents a type of money with some form of absolute value backing it, where the free market decides what that absolute value is. This approach typically ignores that judging value is a relative phenomenon and that markets under capitalism are essentially undemocratic, with the rich having more say than the poor.

Reverence for the gold standard stems from an incorrect understanding of where money comes from in human history, usually referred to as the "Myth of the Barter Economy", or the idea espoused by many early economists that, before money, humans relied on a barter economy which was slow because it relied on a "coincidence of wants". It was then decided to use gold as money to facilitate trade, then later paper money and now digital money. However, according to anthropological studies by Caroline Humphrey, "No example of a barter economy, pure and simple, has ever been described, let alone the emergence from it of money; all available ethnography suggests that there never has been such a thing."[5] By continuing with this commonly believed but incorrect story about money, conservative libertarians are able to idealise this past system of commodity-backed money returning with added digital flair. It is also easy to imply that states are not necessary for a monetary system to function since gold has "intrinsic value" that lies outside of state authority, a position that is also compatible with libertarian beliefs.

This idealised, non-existent past is contrasted with the current fiat money system we use, which views money as a form of credit and does not need to be "backed" by anything in order to function (except for maybe the state), even though the way we speak about money often implies it to be a commodity. However, in a credit theory of money, money is seen as just a type of paper promise which you can spend on goods and services where it's accepted, like an IOU. This acceptance is largely driven by the fact that businesses and citizens need to use it in order to pay taxes to the state. This gets to the actual story of the origins of money based on the anthropological evidence from Humphrey and the late David Graeber's book, *Debt: The First 5,000 Years.* Money was never a physical thing created to facilitate easier trades, but was instead created as a tool for comparing things in proportions, making exchanges and tracking debts — essentially it is a tool for accounting which is easier to accomplish through record-keeping than sending small pieces of metal to each other. According to Graeber's anthropological work, the oldest monetary systems viewed money as debt, and for every debt, there must be a credit.

In the mind of the conservative Austrian School economists, the lack of a material object (i.e., gold) that backs money makes it manipulable by the evil state in order to impose tyranny through money printing. In their view, having money backed by a commodity would make it a purer and fairer form of money. This belief however ignores the history of the gold standard when countries kept reserves of gold and other rare metals in order to back their money, ignoring how states manipulated the price of gold in order to achieve their political goals through spending. For those who adhere to this Austrian School view, however, bitcoin represents a type of "digital gold" that can facilitate a digital form of the gold standard, but with theoretically increased transparency, giving it "digital materiality" — in effect it can be the best of both worlds. The opaqueness of actually-existing cryptocurrency exchanges and many schemes using cryptocurrency, however, makes such a claim difficult to believe.

The argument runs that Bitcoin simulates gold due to its planned inflation schedule. In the same way that there is a limited supply of gold on Earth, it is estimated that bitcoin will run out in 2140 when 21 million have been mined. Due to this scarcity, it is considered a fairer form of money than allowing governments to print money into the economy (even though, as shown before, this is not the case), something which causes inflation (also a short-sighted misunderstanding). This over-indexed fear of inflation also makes bitcoin attractive, since the theory goes that once bitcoin reaches its 21 million cap, it would become a deflationary money system, meaning that each bitcoin would rise in value because supply would stop increasing, while demand for it would increase. This is an extremely flawed proposed solution to the broken monetary system we have today.

In a deflationary economy, lenders (people who make loans) have more power over debtors (people who take out loans, usually working-class people). If you're a working person who only makes money through their labour and took out a loan to make ends meet, over time, as deflation occurs, it becomes more and more difficult to pay off the loan because money is more difficult to find, while the loan stays the same. Only those who have a lot of money when deflation occurs are those who really win out in the end. While inflation also generally hurts working people, this is a consequence of the undemocratic nature of the current monetary system. When banks get first rights on new money creation, they also get the upper hand in acquiring financial assets with that new money. New money very rarely goes directly to the population, who will make the most positive impact on the economy. Turning money into a deflationary digital commodity is still an undemocratic solution to this problem. In order to make their ideal digital commodity-based monetary system a reality with Bitcoin in the current conditions, it is only possible through speculative markets and re-enforcing the flawed but simplistic narrative about money, inflation and governments. This is why there is a need to attempt to resolve the contradiction of "better to spend" versus "attractive to hold".

This is not to say that bitcoin is completely useless other than for speculating on price. Some of the things that make it not viable as money make it advantageous for other things that radicals are interested in. Bitcoin may not be money as such, but it certainly can do some of the same things that money can, which makes it, alongside other cryptocurrencies, a useful tool, something which will be detailed throughout the rest of the book. First, let's take a closer look into how bitcoin does simulate particular properties of money.

If bitcoin isn't money, then how are organisations like WikiLeaks and Sci-Hub, and countries like Venezuela and Iran under economic sanctions, and citizens of a country like El Salvador, using cryptocurrency, if not as money? According to Brett Scott, when people are spending their cryptocurrency on something, they are engaging in what is known as countertrade.[6] If you go to an online store of a company that allows their products to be purchased in cryptocurrency, they will still show their prices in US dollars, euros, pounds, etc. When you checkout to purchase the product, the e-commerce store will use a service to convert the money amount into the equivalent amount of cryptocurrency and ask you to send it through their service. In effect, you have spent an amount of cryptocurrency that is equal to the agreed upon money price. This conversion will change based on the market prices at the moment of purchase, so in a world of volatile cryptocurrency prices, the price could be different as soon as an hour later, or even sooner.

This is exactly how all the other examples of organisations or countries that accept cryptocurrency spend it. They use cryptocurrency as a *stand-in* for money. The cryptocurrency they receive can then be traded into money through exchanges. It's important to note that the only reason countertrade works is because there is already a money price associated with cryptocurrency through speculative markets. But it is exactly through this countertrade capability that they can get around the payment rails that enforce financial blockades. This essentially means that bitcoin does fulfil the third function of money as a medium of exchange, but it still does not make it money.

But if bitcoin and other cryptocurrencies aren't money, then what's the point in their existence? It's important to understand cryptocurrency and the affordances it creates in order to realise its potential and not restrict ourselves to thinking of cryptocurrency as a better or worse representation of money. But what if you do want to use a blockchain to facilitate some kind of monetary system that fulfils the functions of money?

Mutual Credit on the Blockchain

One of the main issues with the current fiat system is that the ability to create money is only reserved for the elite. Central banks can directly inject money into the economy through open market operations like quantitative easing, but most money is created through private banks giving out loans to their clients. In addition, these private banks prioritise their largest clients, who are usually multinational corporations that themselves prioritise their own profits over the well-being of the environment or society. But what if instead of keeping the power to create money centralised in just a few hands, we had a money system that decentralised this power so that anyone could create money if they needed it?

Mutual credit is an alternative form of money where the power to create money can be given to individuals or institutions who are a part of the system. Anybody who's part of the system can create a line of credit with anybody else. It's actually very similar to how banks hold accounts with each other. Mutual credit systems however can be designed to not only give that power to banks. They can be made so that the power to create money is distributed across many or even all actors in the system. The "credit" in a mutual credit system can also be measured in any currency desired, such as US dollars, euros, beer or even time (these systems are sometimes referred to as "time banks").

Mutual credit systems are most commonly used at a business-to-business level. For example, SardexPay is a mutual credit system that started in 2009 on the Italian island of Sardinia during the peak of the recession when businesses were desperate to find alternatives to traditional banking. Businesses that are a part of the SardexPay network all start with a balance of 0 and can offer goods or services to other businesses in the network to earn Sardex credits, denominated in euros, in order to purchase goods and services from other businesses in the network. Additionally, businesses are allowed to go into debt up to a certain limit without needing to pay any interest, with the expectation that they will make up for their debt by selling their services to the network of over ten thousand businesses which have exchanged over 220 million credits denominated in Euros since 2019.[7] This allows for businesses to exchanges goods and services with each other without the need of "real" euros by facilitating mutual exchange and trust.

Mutual credit systems disincentivise hoarding and do away with the paradigm of fear of inflation vs deflation that digital gold proponents put forth with Bitcoin, because they see money as a tool for measurement that anybody can have the power to wield. This makes those who engage in these systems more interested in building trust and community rather than seeing themselves as isolated consumers in competition. Part of the reason why recessions happen is because private banks lose trust in both one another and consumers, and so they slow down or stop giving loans or credit.

While mutual credit systems have clear rules on how much wealth can be hoarded based on credit limits (you can usually only have an account balance below or above a fixed number of credits), the fiat money system has no ceiling. This creates an endless competition over who can become the wealthiest person in the world. Trying to do the same in a mutual credit system would just clearly demonstrate to your community that you are not giving others the chance to earn credits. And as mutual credit systems don't include interest, there is no drive towards endless economic growth which inherently demands more extraction of natural resources.

For those who adhere to a commodity theory of money, a mutual credit system might not look like a monetary system, but that's because it is a type of money system that we are not regularly exposed to, if at all. Mutual credit systems have been around for a long time and actually predate the current fiat monetary system, but are always quite difficult to keep going once they reach a certain size.[8] You may even have a small-scale, unacknowledged mutual credit system happening among your friends if you have a habit of getting rounds of beer at the bar for each other but making sure that everyone takes their turn to buy. SardexPay uses digital technologies to help make the clearing of credit between businesses faster and more streamlined than through more manual means in order to accommodate many more parties, and while it has been incredibly successful and beneficial to the businesses that are a part of its network, it is still a centralised system for mutual credit that relies on the SardexPay company to function. As long as the businesses trust Sardex, everything should theoretically go well — but what if you wanted a mutual credit system on a more decentralised infrastructure?

One such project is Trustlines, which has created a decentralised network of mutual credit systems built on top of Gnosis Chain, a side chain on Ethereum using **proof of stake** (more on all this in the next chapters).[9] With Trustlines, users can choose to be a part of any currency network that already exists, including not just hundreds of different national currencies, but also hours, beers and favours, or they can create a completely new currency network that fits their needs. Once a currency network is chosen, a user needs to begin creating bilateral credit lines (called "trustlines") with the people they trust who are also a part of that network. For example, Simon and Bob are friends who want to track who owes beers to whom, and so they create a trustline between each other using the beer currency network on the Trustlines application, with a credit limit of 10 beers. After Simon buys the first two rounds of beer, Simon's account balance is +2 while Bob's balance is -2, showing Bob owes Simon for the two rounds. Simon can purchase up to 8 more rounds of beer before reaching the credit limit, after which he will no longer be able to buy more rounds of beer and Bob will need to start buying rounds to make up for the deficit.

What if we start to add more people to our beer currency network? Let's say that Bob has a friend named Alice and they create a trustline with a 10 beer credit limit when Alice joins Bob and Simon for a drink. Wanting to be friendly, Alice buys two rounds of beer for both Bob and Simon. Even though Alice and Simon don't have a trustline, they can still transact with each other through their mutual friend Bob, whom they both trust. After the two rounds the account balances are updated. Alice has +4, Bob has -4 and Simon has 0. Essentially what happened is Bob received 2 beer credits from Simon and then Bob gave 4 beer credits to Alice in order to facilitate the exchange. You should notice that if you add up all of the debits and credits across everyone in the network, it will always equal out to zero.

This example was used for simplicity's sake, but you can imagine this similarly for a significantly larger network of people using automated multilateral exchange credit clearing techniques to facilitate it for each currency network. Trustlines looks and functions in a very similar way to the SardexPay mutual credit network, except starting to use it does not require any onboarding or acceptance by a central authority and the lines of credit can be handled per individual rather than just between businesses. Just like SardexPay, Trustlines can facilitate a mutual credit network for euros or any of the other currency networks.

Another project working in this area is CirclesUBI.[10] Started in Berlin, CirclesUBI uses a modified version of a mutual credit system for making exchanges that also facilitates a universal basic income (UBI) for everyone that is a part of the network. However, to first be a part of the CirclesUBI network and be eligible for the UBI, you need to be trusted by at least three others that are a part of this network on the Gnosis Chain blockchain the application is built on. Usually, people are able to do this by attending either an in-person event with others who are part of the network, or being in regularly scheduled digital events over group video conference calls. This requires someone to introduce themselves in order to find at least three others that are willing to trust them into the system, thus reducing the possibility of bad actors using several accounts on the network to game the system.

Each user in the network issues 1 circle token (CRC) per hour with a 7% yearly demurrage on the money supply.[11] Demurrage is the cost incurred for holding currency over time. So in this case, each CRC loses 7% of its value every year. This system incentivises users to spend rather than hoard their CRC. This also means that the accounting looks more like what we are used to since there are no negative balances. You can only have a positive number of circle tokens in your account. However, this differs from inflation in the fiat money system where most of the new money is handled by banks, because the money is given to everyone. While conversations around UBI are largely focused on how the state can provide a UBI, CirclesUBI is addressing the question of how to provide a basic income without the state as, in an environment where state institutions are constantly failing at providing citizen's basic needs, it's difficult to imagine that they will be addressed at a large scale anytime soon.

But where can you spend your circle tokens? The obvious answer is anywhere that accepts them as payment. Through the face-to-face meetings and video conferences, people begin to build trust and relationships with others who are also interested in something like CirclesUBI and so it becomes easier to find those willing to spend and be paid in circle tokens. In Berlin, the CirclesUBI team also runs a cooperatively-owned café where people can spend their circle tokens. Rather than building a speculative market to create an economic network for transactions like Bitcoin, here they are building a community based on trust for the purpose of mutual exchange rather than personal financial enrichment.

The important, obvious question to address here is, "But why use blockchain? Couldn't this all be done without one?" The answer is, "Yes, of course it could",[12] but there are important pros and cons to consider, just as there are when making any decision around digital technological implementations. What's most important are the social and political characteristics you would like your system to have. This helps to decide whether the global, permissionless and resilient infrastructure that a blockchain provides is useful. Many mutual credit systems have started at small scales for local communities and kept going largely through the involvement of those who were willing to put the most time and effort in. Unsurprisingly, over time, many of these experience scale fail, there aren't enough people to keep it going or they have too many other commitments, while people also need to deal with immediate realities, likely including the fact that they can't pay their taxes in mutual credit.

Political change requires both offence and defence. While we can go on the offence and demand changes to the existing monetary regime, organisations quickly crumble without a defence strategy when capitalist institutions come knocking. Blockchains have proven to be resilient because they were created with the explicit purpose of surviving attacks from antagonistic actors.

Blockchains are secured through a collection of cryptographic primitives and economic incentives that do admittedly fit within a capitalist paradigm, but that nonetheless need to be acknowledged both for their usefulness and limitations. It's useful in that it creates one of the base defences of any larger social structure that utilises it. It's by no means bullet-proof, but it is one of the best socio-technical infrastructural models we have for resilience. Blockchains also provide a more bottom-up approach to starting a digital mutual credit system, which is more decentralised than a system like SardexPay. While SardexPay focuses on B2B transactions, blockchain applications for mutual credit can start at the individual level, facilitate ways for individuals to collectivise, and allow for B2B transactions just like SardexPay but without the company intermediating. Trustlines and CirclesUBI are attempts at a people-powered form of money that doesn't look like money to some, largely because it's so different from our current monetary regime. Both of these projects are working towards the same goal: to create a global mutual credit system that can be used by anyone.

While mutual credit systems are commonly referred to as a form of *complementary* currency, it's easy to see how, similar to the dreams of many bitcoin maxis, mutual credit creates a vision for a future where the power of money does not come from the state or private banks but instead from people trusting their communities. For many who survive off of mutual credit, it is not seen as just complementary but as a real alternative to what has been forced upon them. It also gives the rest of us a peek into what a democratised monetary system could look like, something which would be more likely to solve the problems conservative libertarians point out than creating a new global reserve of money based on something like digital gold.

This Book Is Not About Money

You may think that since this book talks about cryptocurrency, it's surely just about digital money, but that could not be further from the truth. Despite having looked in some detail at cryptocurrencies and their money-like properties, I want to reiterate that money-like is not money, and the ways in which crypto systems are money-like but not money is key to understanding what we will discuss from here on in.

As alluded to in the first Bitcoin white paper, cryptocurrency originated from criticism of the monetary system and in its original conception had the goal of creating some form of digital cash that was independent of government and bank control.

However, akin perhaps to how LSD was discovered by a Swiss researcher's intent to find a compound to relieve childbirth pain, it has since taken on a very different form. While LSD could be used for pain relief in certain situations as some studies have shown, most pains would likely best be treated with something else with less psychoactive side effects.[13] It's always been difficult for people to know with absolute certainty how exactly their new discoveries or inventions are going to percolate through society because it's simply impossible to simulate every future possibility. This is especially true of open-source software, which is inherently open to anyone to iterate on in an endless stream of modifications, updates and improvements. The creation of Bitcoin was undoubtedly an important moment in human history and a technological breakthrough, even if many who are against its proliferation would like to downplay it as a "slow database" yet to find a problem to solve. It has led to a Cambrian explosion of cryptocurrencies and applications for various purposes, many of them revolving around speculation but also including mutual credit, in opposition to the commodity theory of money most Bitcoin proponents adhere to.

It is important to be sceptical therefore not only of those who tell you cryptocurrency and blockchains are the future of money and everything else, but also of those who tell you that they should be ignored and banished either because they don't live up to the ideals originally espoused by their creators or because they do and that's why they're undeserving of your attention. Both are over-promising. Just because most cryptocurrency is not money (even if it is marketed as such by some), doesn't make it useless. It is in fact quite useful for those more concerned with social justice than personal profit.

In order to continue problematising the narratives around crypto, in the next section we're going to look at this technology through the next most common mental model it's seen and understood through — crypto as speculative financial product.

SECTION 2
CRYPTO AS FINANCE

With the introduction of smart contracts by Ethereum, one of the new narratives pushed by crypto marketers was that blockchains, the technology underlying cryptocurrencies, are not *just* about money. Rather, they are about creating an entire alternative financial system — Decentralised Finance (DeFi). Since finance is closely linked to law as an arbiter for private property relations, in order to deal with the contradiction of facilitating finance-like mechanisms through a medium that is meant to exist outside the state legal system, the phrase "code is law" has become an important aphorism. While smart contracts can have properties that are similar to law, software alone does not provide the same functions as law for arbitration and conflict resolution. There have been multiple instances where it has been shown that code is in fact not law on blockchains. Nor is it desirable to uncritically abide by purely software-based outcomes. Even in blockchain-based systems, humans still have a role in accepting the unintended consequences played out in complex crypto financial products. While much of this space is a remake of many of the most capitalistic financial products, representational thinking can limit our abilities to look into the details of these mechanisms and see the realities and potentials of smart contracts and crypto tokens. The differences between the traditional financial system and DeFi are important to understand for developing appropriate strategies that subvert financial systems for ends other than profit.

CHAPTER 4
CODE IS LAW

Liberty in cyberspace will not come from the absence of the state.
Liberty there, as anywhere, will come from a state of a certain kind.
— Lawrence Lessig, *Code: Version 2.0*

To be clear, at this point I quite regret adopting the term "smart contracts". I should have called them something more boring and technical, perhaps something like "persistent scripts". I do think that persistent scripts controlling assets compete with the legal system on some margins, but so do locks on doors. So IMO it's wrong to equate them with a specific philosophy of law privatization.
— Vitalik Buterin on Twitter[1]

Now that we know a little more about how a blockchain works and some of its uses, we can move on to the next question: What does it all mean? First, let's look at three fundamental properties of blockchains that were alluded to in the previous chapter:

1. Blockchains use decentralised infrastructure in the form of a P2P network of computers (as opposed to client-server architecture like most centralised online services) to store a shared database of transactions.
2. All of the data stored on a permissionless blockchain like Bitcoin is publicly available to anyone to view, making it open source, copyable and auditable, ensuring the rules of the protocol are always being followed.[2]
3. As long as blockchains have a sound consensus

mechanism and the economic incentives work, they are very resilient to change directly on the ledger (like a double-spend attack), making them near-immutable.

Blockchains are networks of computers and users that collaborate with one another around a distributed database of (many times, financial) information by reaching consensus through cryptographic (and many times, economic) means. In this light, blockchains are protocols for economic cooperation, of which many types of partnerships are possible, and the design outlined by Bitcoin is just one of them.

Soon after the release of Bitcoin, many different alternative cryptocurrencies were spawned that copied the original Bitcoin source code and made slight alterations to it with different properties. Some cryptocurrencies changed the mining algorithm in Bitcoin to be more resistant to ASICs (expensive hardware specially designed to be good at Bitcoin's mining algorithm) as a way to keep the cryptocurrency accessible to those without the resources to purchase ASICs. Others have changed the max capped supply of their cryptocurrency or even completely removed it, contradicting the narrative originally espoused by Bitcoin about the need to emulate the gold standard digitally.

Some cryptocurrencies were made for specific applications rather than with the intention of being a new global money supply. There was a boom of "altcoins" soon after the creation of Bitcoin, each with different assumptions encoded in them. For example, Litecoin was a **"fork"** of the Bitcoin code that increased the total max capped supply, used an alternative proof of work consensus mechanism so as not to be exactly the same as Bitcoin's, and was marketed as silver to Bitcoin's gold. In software development, "forking" refers to creating a copy of a project's codebase to start a new, separate project that can be developed independently. It's like taking a snapshot of a project at a certain point in time, either starting from the source code or while the projects is live, and then going in a different direction with your own version of the code. This is often done when different groups of people want to work on a project in different ways, or when someone wants to create a new version of an existing project with different goals or features. Namecoin was another fork of the Bitcoin code whose main use has been for creating the censorship-resistant top level domain.bit as an alternative to the Domain Name System .com or .net which is centrally governed by ICANN.

In reality, however, the main use in practice was for speculation on cryptocurrency exchanges based on the "hype" around them and the utopian technological future they envisioned. No matter the intent of the application of the cryptocurrency, the token was almost always acquired through speculative centralised cryptocurrency exchange markets. The centralised nature of these exchanges also caused issues as they became targets for hackers, the most infamous example being in 2014 when Mt. Gox (one of the first popular bitcoin exchanges) filed for bankruptcy under the premise of being hacked for all of the bitcoin held on the exchange.

Up to this point, the main feature of Bitcoin and most of the altcoins has largely been the ability to track or initiate transactions without needing bank or government approval. While there were many attempts at expanding the capabilities of these blockchains, they were mostly just good for that, something admittedly useful in certain contexts. However, only a few years after the launch of the Bitcoin network, that changed in significant ways.

Smart Contracts and Decentralised Applications

Once it was realised that we could create a system of holding some form of digital currency using computers on a P2P network without the need for banks or governments, then hypothetically it should also be possible to program this digital currency as we do with any other computer program. In late

2013 Vitalik Buterin, a nineteen-year-old Canadian college dropout who had previously founded *Bitcoin Magazine*, published a white paper describing a blockchain that could do everything that Bitcoin could as well as facilitate a software development platform for "smart contracts". He called it Ethereum. Like Bitcoin it uses the ether cryptocurrency to pay for transactions on the network, but ether should not be considered to be money either (even though it has money-like properties.)

According to the Ethereum Foundation, the non-profit that stewards the development of the Ethereum blockchain, a "smart contract" is:

> simply a program that runs on the Ethereum blockchain. It's a collection of code (its functions) and data (its state) that resides at a specific address on the Ethereum blockchain.
>
> Smart contracts are a type of Ethereum account. This means they have a balance and they can send transactions over the network. However, they're not controlled by a user, instead they are deployed to the network and run as programmed. User accounts can then interact with a smart contract by submitting transactions that execute a function defined on the smart contract. Smart contracts can define rules, like a regular contract, and automatically enforce them via the code. Smart contracts cannot be deleted by default, and interactions with them are irreversible.[3]

The term "smart contract" was actually first used by computer scientist Nick Szabo in 1994, predicting that the digital revolution would at some point come to automate the same functions as legal contracts. This would facilitate global free markets in which small businesses could compete with large corporations on a level playing field.[4] Buterin, however, popularised the term with his white paper, describing Ethereum as not just as an electronic peer to peer payment system, but as a platform for "**decentralised application**s" which are also commonly referred to as "dapps".

At this point there are many more blockchains that have smart contracts, but to keep it simple, let's stick to Ethereum for now as the others work similarly. An Ethereum smart contract can be thought of as a facilitator of an automatically enforceable event that has many different possible outcomes depending on the inputs of the contract and how other accounts on the network are interacting with it. Like a normal computer program or a script, a smart contract is an IF-THEN statement defined by the smart contract programmer. It waits for certain conditions to be met (IF) which defines the next step in the process (THEN). A major difference with a smart contract compared to a legal contract is that the enforcement of the consequences of the conditions being met is automatic, as it is with any computer program, as opposed to enforcement by a legal jurisdiction like a government or state. However, similar to a legal contract, it can define and have concrete consequences for assets and property in a way that a normal computer program without a link to the state legal system cannot.

In some ways you could think of it like a vending machine which takes in the inputs of your money plus the input of the snack you want to receive and then outputs the snack you wanted plus any change. While a vending machine is largely a physical interaction, a smart contract is largely a digital one. This has had many implications in not only thinking about money or finance, but also politics and democracy.

Here are some simple examples for how a smart contract could be used:

1. **IF** your flight is cancelled **THEN** receive a refund from the airlines
2. **IF** enough ether is raised from investors **THEN** send all of the ether to the fundraisers and a token to represent the proportional stake to investors

3. **IF** the proposal has over 51% of the vote for "yes" **THEN** proceed with the proposal
4. **IF** enough people in the organisation have expressed dissatisfaction with the current leader **THEN** recuse them and start a new vote to choose a new leader

The technical reason why Ethereum is able to handle smart contracts comes from pushing the function of nodes on the network beyond just tracking a single cryptocurrency to assisting in computation more broadly, making the P2P network that secures Ethereum not just a distributed database but also a distributed computer. In one way, you could see Ethereum as one big computer that is made of smaller computers distributed around the world running an Ethereum client that exerts the computational power necessary to track the movement of ether and execute smart contracts. This is often referred to as the Ethereum virtual machine (EVM).

By combining the permissionless nature of blockchains with the Turing completeness of programming languages and the EVM, Ethereum creates permissionless composability for the creation of dapps. If a programming language is "Turing complete", it means it can perform any computation that any other system can perform. It's considered a gold standard for determining whether a programming language or system can be used to solve a wide range of problems. Think of it like a set of building blocks that can be used to build anything you want, as long as you have enough blocks and know how to assemble them properly. A system that is Turing complete can be used to build any kind of software, from simple calculators to complex games and artificial intelligence systems.

In a normal application you have a backend, the code that runs the application, and the frontend, what users see when interacting with the application. For example, the frontend of Facebook shows you your feed, your profile, your friends' profiles, Facebook pages, etc, while the backend of the Facebook application you are interacting with are the databases owned by Meta from which the data is retrieved to show in the frontend.

In a dapp, the blockchain acts as the backend. The main difference from the Facebook backend is that only Meta and its partners are allowed to take advantage of the data stored with it. Whereas the permissionless nature of blockchains open up the backend for anyone to interact with and take advantage of. This also means that anyone can create a frontend for a smart contract that is deployed on a blockchain. Depending on how the smart contracts are designed, for usual backend processes you have the option to potentially not be reliant on a centralised company.

One thing to keep in mind though, when using smart contracts, is that the inputs that the smart contract can look for need to be "on chain". This means that most of the information and data on the Internet cannot be used natively by smart contracts because it is not recorded directly on the same blockchain that the smart contract is being deployed on. In order to get around this, developers use "**oracles**", which are a type of API (Application Programming Interface) that retrieves data from another place on the Internet that is not on the blockchain. For example, if I want to receive a refund for my cancelled flight then the information about my cancelled flight needs to be recorded "on chain". For that to work there needs to be an oracle (or API) that is retrieving that data for the smart contract to execute. At least this is the case in order to have the refund automatically enforced.

We can think of the combination of blockchain and smart contracts as opening up a new *design space* for digital architecture. On the Big Tech Internet, we are used to particular models of interaction and transaction between each other and those who own the infrastructure that we're using. Most people normally need to create an account when they first start on a new platform and provide personal information like their name and email, then agree to the terms and conditions in order to use the platform. These terms and conditions will then give the right to the platform owners, many times Big Tech companies, to package and sell the data that users produce while on their platforms. This has become the dominant model on Internet platforms: offering services for "free" to everyone while also staying profitable. By selling ads and personal information, Big Tech companies become perfect surveillance machines as well. By using a more decentralised architecture and technological stack, it allows us to experiment with entirely new economic models that were technically impossible or very difficult previously. Some of these new economic models will be detailed later in the book.

How are these new designs built more concretely and made to be able to interact with one another? This is largely done through agreed upon standards that are adopted by the developer community, a common practice in software, hardware and elsewhere where sometimes a government body (e.g., The National Institute of Standards and Technology) or non-profit standardising bodies (e.g., Internet Engineering Task Force) helps determine standards (e.g., electrical plugs, TCP/IP, etc.) as generally agreed upon methods and technical configurations. For Ethereum, it's the Ethereum Foundation that stewards this responsibility through EIPs (Ethereum Improvement Proposals) in which a proposal for an ERC (Ethereum Request for Comment) is made by a developer in the EIP community. It starts as an EIP, but once accepted by the community, it becomes an ERC and therefore an accepted standard. This can apply to changes to the Ethereum protocol to smart contract standards. The most widely used standard in Ethereum for tokens is called ERC-20, which helps define the general structure for fungible tokens represented on the Ethereum network.

But first, what exactly is a token and why are they important?

Tokens

A token is an empty representation of something else that only derives value and meaning from the context it is in. When people first hear the word, they may think of arcade tokens used to spend on arcade games. At an arcade, you purchase arcade tokens with normal money based on a set exchange rate. The token is very useful inside the arcade, but if you were to take it outside, it would be useless — the token is only valuable within a certain context.

In the arcade token example, there is a clear link between an arcade token and financial value by way of the exchange rate set by the arcade owners. However, a token does not always represent something of financial value. If we think of the phrase "a token of my gratitude", this is used largely in a non-financial sense. You may have done a favour for me by helping me move without an expectation of receiving anything back, and I may offer you some cold beers after a long day of work as a token of my gratitude. The beer represents my gratitude for your help with moving my furniture and is valuable to you because it shows we have a strong friendship. However, we could also potentially financialise our interaction by trying to give a monetary amount for the work you did and make a contract for me to pay off the work you did over time in five payments at 2% interest, or I can give you an equal amount in monetary value of cold beer, but that would be a strange thing for friends to do.

In a capitalist economy though, many of the tokens that have influence over our lives do have financial value. We could also think of stocks as a type of token that represent ownership rights in a company, or depending on the class of stock you have, as a claim to dividends at the end of the quarter with no say in voting on matters pertaining to the company. A stock almost always has a financial value attached to it, but it could also have a political value too if it gives control rights. In this way we can also say that the vote you have a right to as a citizen of a country is a token of political value that is difficult to quantify in financial value.

A token is a very important "primitive" for Ethereum development, and the ERC-20 token standard is by far the most widely used. The ERC-20 token standard contract is essentially its own ledger that tracks a completely different digital asset than the native cryptocurrency for the Ethereum blockchain, ether. While the Ethereum blockchain is tracking the movement of ether, it is also tracking the state of smart contracts deployed on the network. For example, I can make a token, let's say Josh Coin, that I want to give out to my friends to thank them for all helping me move. I can deploy an ERC-20 smart contract on the Ethereum blockchain with the appropriate inputs (e.g., there are only 100 tokens in supply, give the entire supply to me, you can't send decimal amounts, etc) and then send the Josh Coin tokens to my friends' Ethereum addresses. In order to deploy the contract and send the tokens, I will also need to pay the transaction cost (sometimes referred to as "gas cost" on Ethereum) in ether. Once this has all started, my friends and I can begin to develop together the exact context and system in which we want to use our Josh Coins. That can stay in the form of just a token of gratitude or evolve into something else. One way in which that could happen is by creating new smart contracts that use Josh Coins for other types of interactions. We could use them like a vote, as a representation of ownership over some other assets, or anything else we decide to conjure up. The composability and inherent interoperability built into blockchains and smart contracts makes it easy to create new contexts for a particular token which imbues different types of value.

Financial Tokens

In reality, the vast majority of uses of tokens revolves around financial value in various forms. Throughout 2017 and 2018, when Ethereum was still very new and without much of the infrastructure that exists today, one of the most common ways to use ERC-20 tokens was for Initial Coin Offerings (ICOs), something similar to the IPO of a company listing their stock on an exchange. Here though, there is very little if any regulation to follow in order to list your token, since all you need to do is know the code, which is open source, and pay for the necessary transaction fees. You can see the basis of how the combination of smart contracts for an ICO would work in smart contract example #2 above.

What commonly happened is that a white paper would be published detailing the technical specs of a potential dapp to be built on top of Ethereum which utilised a token in some form. The token could be a representation of voting power on the progress of the dapp or it could be something that users needed inside of the dapp for it to work. The money raised by investors for that token would also be used to hypothetically begin building what was outlined in the white paper. The vast majority of the time, these tokens would use the ERC-20 token standard.

After a white paper was published, there would be a marketing campaign to advertise the new token to potential investors, generally through the Internet, and a time would be set for when the ICO smart contract would become open for investment. Once the ICO started, investors could give ether in exchange for an equivalent amount of the token being offered. The amount of tokens received would usually be set at a fixed price by those organising the ICO. The token would then be listed on an exchange, making the token liquid and the price would change based on supply and demand on the exchange. Usually, the price of a token fluctuates based on news or rumours surrounding the related project, or if a single entity owns enough of the supply of a token, they could manipulate the price.

While the practice of ICOs was already quite common before smart contracts, and Ethereum itself did do an ICO to raise funds in bitcoin to start its development, the bar at which people could start an ICO technically became much lower through smart contracts. In an environment in which there is very little regulation and a lot of money to be invested, it is unsurprising that this became a hotbed of crude scams. Nefarious actors could raise capital solely through a white paper that detailed an application that would theoretically become essential infrastructure for the future without ever building anything simply because there were enough people willing to invest. Often the nefarious and sometimes completely anonymous actors that led these ICOs would disappear along with all of the ether that was raised, leaving investors with a bunch of useless tokens. No context was built for some of these tokens, leaving them empty and valueless.

A study prepared by the ICO advisory firm Statis Group showed that more than 80% of ICOs launched in 2017 were identified as scams.[5] In the report they stated that in 2017 "over 70% of ICO funding (by $ volume) to-date went to higher quality projects, although over 80% of projects (by # share) were identified as scams". Around $11.9 billion in total was raised in 2017 through an ICO, however only 11% of that was given to projects categorised as scams. So while there was a not insignificant amount of scams, the vast majority of the money went into projects that were not considered to be a scam.

However, scams did happen often enough for regulators to take notice. Tokens earned from ICOs were classified as securities by the Securities and Exchange Commission (SEC), the US regulatory agency responsible for protecting investors and maintaining fair and orderly markets, in December 2017, likely at least partially in response to the rise of ICOs as a mechanism for raising capital. SEC Chair Jay Clayton stated it had proved that "a token constituted an investment contract and, therefore, was a security under our federal securities laws. Specifically, we concluded that the token offering represented an investment in a common enterprise with a reasonable expectation of profits."[6] Since then, most ICOs don't allow, or advise against, US citizens investing. The SEC has also since provided guidance for organisations to know whether their ICO tokens should be categorised as a security in their *Framework for "Investment Contract" Analysis of Digital Assets* that shows how to apply the Howey Test, the usual framework for knowing whether something qualifies as a security, to digital assets. Since then, many new mechanisms for raising capital to fund new projects have arisen and become as or more popular than ICOs at the time of writing.

Some of the projects that came about through ICOs did manage to begin building dapps on the Ethereum blockchain. As mentioned previously, most of these tokens were intended to be useful due to their future financial value. The vast majority of ICO white papers were imagining new applications with financial use cases and are now key players in the "Decentralised Finance" or DeFi space. A big contributor to their success was the adoption of standards like ERC-20 which have effectively created protocols that act as primitives for developing on the Ethereum blockchain. While it's true that the dominant form of tokens has been a largely financially speculative one, we should not allow this to restrict the way in which we think about tokens generally.

Pathetic Dot Theory

Traverse the forums, subreddits and other communities around Ethereum and other cryptocurrencies and you may stumble across the phrase "code is law" being used by its proponents. This is understandable considering how intertwined finance and law are in the non-crypto economy. If you are trying to create a financial system outside of the state as much as possible, you will need to have some sort of substitute for the law imposed by the state. Finance requires stable property relations and, historically, these relations are legitimated through the state. In what seems to be a purely digital world, it's easy to think that code can replace law, but the issue is a bit more complicated than that.

While many may only have come across that phrase in the context of some proposed future run by smart contracts rather than governments, the term is actually not new. One of the first proponents of the dictum was liberal law scholar Lawrence Lessig, who wrote about it in his 1999 book *Code and Other Laws of Cyberspace*. His influential argument was that computer code can regulate behaviour in similar ways to legal code, therefore enforcing the amendment of code could be a tool for states to impose regulation, among other things. It came about in a time when the Internet was just starting to really take off and the start of when our lives became more dependent on it.

According to Lessig's "pathetic dot theory", there are four major regulators of individuals (pathetic dots) in the meat space legal system: the law, social norms, the market, and physical architecture. By architecture, Lessig is referring to the facts of life that dictate what is and is not possible biologically, physically, technologically, etc. In his book he equates code to physical architecture but for cyberspace, giving it the ability to constrain behaviour as law does. However, similar to how bitcoin is like money in some ways but not the same, code is like law but not the same, and also like physical architecture but not the same. Cornell law scholar James Grimmelmann wrote in 2005:

> The structures that can be built out of software are so much more intricate and fragile than the structures that can be built out of concrete that there is a qualitative difference between them. You can hack a computer program into destroying itself; you will have no such luck hacking a highway. [7]

According to Grimmelmann, software has three distinct characteristics that differentiate it qualitatively from architecture, as Lessig uses the term. Software is *automated*, in that once it is deployed, it deterministically keeps going without human intervention. It is *immediate*, in that it doesn't wait for an infraction to occur to impose punishment, but it prevents forbidden behaviour from happening once it starts running. And it is *plastic*, in such a way that a programmer can implement almost any system they can imagine and describe in code. These properties produce consequences that make it different from both law and physical architecture, including the fact that one bug can have immediate unexpected effects on an entire system with dire consequences. Grimmelmann suggests that code is instead its own modality for regulation that should be separated from the others.

The same is true for smart contracts, which are run through code, as can be seen in the various hacks of smart contracts since the start of Ethereum and other smart contract blockchains. The most famous one is "The DAO" hack, the first major hack on the Ethereum blockchain. Not to be confused with a DAO, or a decentralised autonomous organisation, which is a loose term for entire organisations that run on smart contracts (DAOs will be covered in a later chapter), The DAO hack was the first attempt at making the idea of DAOs a reality as a collectivised investment firm where those who helped fund it could vote on where to allocate the funds. It launched on 30 April 2016, with an ICO that distributed DAO tokens in exchange for ether over the course of twenty-eight days. Three weeks into the sale, they had raised over $150 million in ether, or about 14% of the total ether supply. Before the ICO finished, however, 30% of the funds in the smart contracts that made up The DAO were hacked and stolen. A group of white hat hackers were able to protect the other 70% of the funds, however the damage had already been done. A very large percentage of the total supply of ether was now owned by black hat hackers and many who had entrusted their money to The DAO were obviously unhappy. This was also a bad start for a blockchain network little more than a year old.

Soon after, an open letter was published by someone claiming to be the attacker, stating that the funds they took were obtained "legally" since "code is law" (which was also a tag line used for The DAO), therefore it was in accordance with the rules stipulated by the smart contracts. As tensions rose, it was proposed by the leadership of the Ethereum Foundation that they "hard fork" the blockchain so that the attacker would no longer have the funds. A hard fork is when new rules or history are introduced into the blockchain code for nodes to follow that are not compatible with the rules of the blockchain's previous code. This can result in the blockchain splitting into two networks, one which operates with the old rules and history and one which operates with the new. After much debate between developers, node operators and exchanges, the hard fork was implemented and Ethereum's history was effectively rewound to before the attack, and all of the ether was reallocated to another smart contract so investors could withdraw their funds.

To put it mildly, this was a spit in the face to those who truly believed in the immutability of smart contracts and that code was law, creating a rift in the community. The more die-hard libertarian believers in code being law stuck with the old chain, now called Ethereum Classic. However, the choice to hard fork ultimately proved its legitimacy and the new Ethereum chain has vastly out performed Ethereum Classic, which has largely become a "zombie chain" with little activity and interest.

This seminal event exposes how smart contracts are deterministic, but only up to a point, and that point has a lot to do with what humans collectively decide is legitimate or not. When bugs are found in smart contracts, just like any other code, they are taken advantage of in ways that are not only unintended, but can be detrimental. There is not only smart contract risk in this regard, but also in the event of protocol updates to the platform the smart contract runs on top of, which could also distort how a smart contract is meant to work. Smart contracts are also limited in their scope to take in inputs, which is why they use oracles, but this makes oracles another dependency and vector for attack. Believers in "code is law" with smart contracts are failing to recognise that smart contracts are just one of many social agents to consider when speaking about blockchain systems.

Unlike the mathematics driven logic of code, law intentionally contains ambiguity in order to allow for applicability to various situations, whereas it is incredibly difficult for code to foresee all of the possible situations in which a law can be applied. This ambiguity allows for participants in a contract to outsource low probability scenarios to the court system if they were to happen. Even ordinary contracts allow for ex-post resolution through courts and arbitration. All contracts are incomplete due to the existence of future uncertainty.

Programmers looking at the legal text of contracts may balk at the (intentional or not) ambiguous logic or unenforceable specifications common to them, but that is a feature, not a bug. "Code is law" ignores that people use contracts as social resources to manage their relations and human relations require ambiguity in many circumstances.

Smart contracts were at first seen as a solution for libertarians interested in doing business over the Internet without the need of the state to mediate relations. They may have correctly seen code as similar to law, in that code can act as an instrument of social control, but incorrect in seeing it in absolutist terms in such a way that code could supersede law and therefore become the law. Szabo, himself a cryptographer, cypherpunk mailing list member and conservative libertarian, intended for smart contracts to remove the human element in contractual obligations. In practice, as we've seen with The DAO hack, this is not what happens. Additionally there are many instances where smart contract hackers have still been persecuted and charged under national legal systems or the fact that many ICOs need to register with the SEC in order to sell their token. In the human world, human social organisation still trumps code.

At first glance this seems surely like an outright

conservative libertarian ideal — to remove humans in order to maximise what is under the control of free markets. They want less governance — as in human discretion — and more free markets. But we will see as the book goes on that this is not exactly what has happened with smart contracts in practice and has ironically diversified and increased the amount of mutual human interaction through the Internet.

The truth is that smart contracts are neither "smart" nor "contracts" in the ways that these two words are most commonly understood — they are more like automated scripts that handle data and code which many times happen to have financial consequences attached. But this is OK — just as bitcoin is not money, but still useful in certain situations, smart contracts certainly have their advantages over standard legal contracts. You can deploy a smart contract to facilitate mutual financial agreements faster than you can probably finish the legal bureaucracy for the first steps. We will be diving deeper into these intricacies throughout the rest of the book.

Decentralised Court Systems

Blockchain is commonly hailed as a new mechanism to escape state regulations in ways that are similar to claims made by early Internet pioneers. The decentralised architecture of many blockchains (like the early Internet) make them resistant towards surveillance and control. This has led to some describing blockchains as "alegal", in that they operate beyond the purview of the law, neither completely legal or illegal.[8] Developers can easily create smart contract code-based systems that do not comply with the law and with little direct reaction possible by the state.

Over the past few years, as cryptocurrencies have continued to penetrate into the mainstream, many projects, even if mainly managed through smart contracts, have sought to play it safe and register as a legally recognised organisation. Legislation has been passed in places like Wyoming, Vermont,

Switzerland and elsewhere to make it easy for organisations building blockchain-based applications that include smart contracts to register as a legal entity. One of the main reasons for this is because the state is able to provide certain assurances that blockchain-based systems still are not able to in the event of a hack or misuse of funds. Many investors and those who engage in these systems are right to be sceptical that smart contracts can protect them, considering the known risks associated. In spite of all this, there will still be some who attempt to resolve these contradictions.

One such attempt is the project Kleros, a cooperative that received funding from the European Commission's Horizon 2020 grant programme, which looks to explore creating a decentralised court system for arbitration and dispute settlement for the crypto economy.[9] In essence, it is a platform that allows individuals to form a variety of mutual agreements that are also accompanied by a course of action and arbitrated by neutral parties in the event of a dispute. Through the use of game theory and cryptoeconomics, the smart contracts can factor in human subjectivity and discourse. This is facilitated largely through the use of their Pinakion token (PNK), inspired by the token used by Ancient Athenians to draw jurors for their popular trials.

Using Kleros, people who enter into an agreement have the option to raise a dispute, for example claiming another party did not fill their end of the deal. Rather than trying to automate every possibility, the agreement can be completely based on text, similar to legal code, and the smart contract code would refer to the agreement text. The smart contracts are used as a neutral social agent to facilitate the arbitration process based on the inputs of all parties involved and require a deposit from the agreeing parties in the event that there is a dispute, although how this is done depends on the agreement. To raise a dispute, the offended party must pay arbitration fees as collateral and a group of jurors will be randomly selected to help make a decision. In order to be chosen as a juror, you must also have provided some PNK as collateral to the platform. The randomly chosen jurors will then vote in favour of one of the parties involved. The jurors who vote in the majority will be given a cut of the arbitration fees, while the minority will not receive anything and lose some of their PNK. If one of the parties still does not agree with the outcome, they can pay even more arbitration fees for a new judgement from even more jurors. This can continue as long as a party is willing to pay arbitration fees, but it begins to get more and more expensive to do so. Once the dispute has been settled, arbitration fees are given to jurors and all of the cryptocurrency locked in the smart contracts is released based on the results of the vote.

There are several different use cases and common types of agreements Kleros is designed to be used for. Their use case list includes escrow, governance, curation and oracles. For example, one way it could be used is as escrow is if Amir agrees to do some freelance work for Benoit and they enter into an agreement through an escrow smart contract on Kleros. This set-up works great since they both live in different parts of the world and wouldn't want to go through the hassle of needing the other's personal information to take legal action in the appropriate legal jurisdiction, let alone the actual financial costs. Plus, Amir is in Iran which is under economic sanctions, making it more difficult to go through traditional legal structures.

Benoit deposits the full payment into the escrow smart contract that refers to the terms of agreement. Once Amir is done, he will deliver the work and if Benoit is happy with it, he will release the cryptocurrency from escrow to be sent to Amir. Benoit can also express that he is only partially satisfied for partial payment or raise a dispute that the work is not satisfactory, which would trigger the smart contract to call on jurors to make a decision. If Benoit wins, he will receive his cryptocurrency back, if he loses, the money will still go to Amir. What is important here is that the jurors take a look through the terms of the agreement and assess whether Amir fulfilled the terms.

Let's take the experiment undertaken by the Kleros team with the public called "Doges on Trial" as another example of how it works in practice.[10] In this experiment, Kleros was trying to gather as many images of a "doge", the famous meme of a Shiba Inu popular on the Internet, from the public. All successfully submitted images of a doge will be given a share of a pot of 1 million Doge Coins (the infamous first meme cryptocurrency) as well as a chance to win other prizes. Anyone who is successful at getting an image of a cat they uploaded through the challenge period will win a prize of 50 ether. Jurors however can challenge any image they feel does not fit the requirements stipulated. If the judgement from the chosen jurors agrees with the challenger in the end, the deposit the image submitter gave with their image is given to the challenger. Since the challenger also needs to submit a deposit, if the submitter wins, they receive the deposit. If no challenge is made during the challenge period, then the deposit is returned to the submitter.

While many adorable and funny photos of the doge meme were submitted without issue, there were a couple of very interesting submissions, including one that was of Leonardo Loredan Doge of Venice, a nobleman who reigned as the 75th Doge of Venice in the 1500s. It turns out that the word doge is also the Italian word for duke. At first the image was challenged and rejected from the list (0 yes and 3 no), however the submitter appealed the decision and revealed the name of the man in the image. After learning the name, the jurors accepted the image to the list (7 yes and 0 no).[11]

Soon after, an image of Paolo Lucio Anafesto, believed to be the first Doge of Venice in the 700s, was submitted to the list. At first it was accepted (3 yes and 0 no), but was subsequently appealed under the argument that the first Doge of Venice was clearly not the doge meant by the intention of the requirements, that it was accepted the first time and should not be accepted again as subsequently everyone should be aware of the requirements. The vote of the second appeal rejected the image (1 yes and 6 no).

What this example shows is that the use of smart contracts does not necessarily remove the human element in the way that Szabo may have envisioned. In fact, they can be created in ways that increase the ability for humans to interact with each other over digital space. The decision to reject the second Doge of Venice image did not come from shared knowledge that was encoded on the blockchain — it was the social fabric and shared understanding of the community that led to the creation of the precedent. At the same time, this flies in the face of critics and gatekeepers who declare confidently that smart contracts have no ability or place in dispute resolution, governance or social coordination.

There are legitimate concerns around the dangers of embedding a token important for dispute resolution in a financially speculative economy like in the Kleros model, but it's likely that from here others can begin to experiment by taking and modifying pieces that make up the Kleros system that can get around its particular token dynamics. It's also important to keep in mind that most justice systems require considerable financial contribution for cases similar to those that Kleros is dealing with. Kleros does not claim to be able to solve the many injustices we live with today.

So, does Kleros's framework complicate the idea of code being law? While it is possible that the results of disputes handled through Kleros could be recognised by various international frameworks, there is no guarantee that interventionist courts would not seek to overturn or not recognise the results.[12] There is also a question of how courts who disagree with a Kleros judgement will enforce their decision on the parties. Only time will tell how legal courts will interpret disputes handled through Kleros, but it is unlikely to be the case that all will agree.

Putting that aside, these examples, and the many more to come, show some of the advantages of using smart contracts.

Smart contracts can give predictability and confidence when using templates that are tried and audited for bugs. They can automate many of the same functions of various types of agreements that people are likely to make with each other without involving more parties. They do not need to try to foresee every single possible outcome and can implement structures that take into account the complex relations that are inherent to agreements between humans. They are certainly not needed or perfect for all types of agreements, but that's OK. Just because code is not law does not make smart contracts not useful. And it is with this grounded understanding we can begin taking a closer look at their many more complex applications.

CHAPTER 5

MARKET-MAKING FOR THE COMMONS

When years have been spent in the development of a theory with considerable power and elegance, analysts obviously will want to apply this tool to as many situations as possible... Confusing a model — such as that of a perfectly competitive market — with the theory of which it is one representation can limit applicability still further.

— Elinor Ostrom, *Governing the Commons*

So, if bitcoin isn't money and code isn't law, how is crypto supposed to replace finance, as the hypemen declare in their speeches at conferences in Miami and in their conservative libertarian books? Money and law are surely two of the primary building blocks of a financial system of any kind.

Many of the innovations that smart contracts have created up until now can be seen as new representations of various financial products. With the token example we used earlier, we can see that many of them, though not all, are similar to stocks in a company, with some clear differences, although many can be categorised as securities. Some may see this and say that therefore tokens are just stocks of a blockchain company, but that would be incorrect because tokens can be many things, even if they are all enabled by the same token standard (ERC-20 in Ethereum's case). If we recall, tokens are a representation of something, or many things at once, that derive value based on the context in which they exist. And the context we live in today is one dominated by financialised capitalism. The incentive systems have been in place for a long time to prioritise profits over everything else. Living under neoliberalism has not only affected our economic policy however, it has also warped our understanding of finance.

If you're on the left, when you hear the word "finance", you'll likely think of a hyper-individualised pursuit of personal wealth, or the power that large financial institutions have had over society, especially in the fallout of the 2008 recession. If you're on the right, you may think of the more "entrepreneurial" aspects we associate with finance as a positive force, or of financial markets as simply a necessary fact of life no matter the consequences, because they are better than a command economy. However, the financial system contains many moving parts and systems working in tandem that take inputs from the economy, including both private and public entities, in order to determine how, as a society, our resources are deployed. Whether it does that well, or in the interest of the majority of people as it stands today, is another story. Through investments of financial capital in certain sectors of the economy, actors with capital are inducing the movement of labour towards their desired projects. The less power that labour has, in the form of a social safety net, unions or whatever else, the more easily it is directed under capitalism.

However, viewing finance as a system of resource allocation in the aggregate, and not necessarily as only something done via capitalism, financial institutions and markets, helps us deconstruct some of the most basic pieces that make it tick. One of those pieces is of course money, or what is really a relative value accounting system to facilitate exchange. In our financial system, we have essentially one type of value accounted for, which collapses information from the economy into a blunt instrument, creating multiple negative externalities leading ultimately to the degradation of our climate.

Much of our economy is facilitated through large international markets of commodities, securities and other financial products that are bought and sold by traders. The markets are commonly facilitated by nationally registered exchanges that allow the trading to happen, or that the state allows to facilitate market activity as long as regulations are met and taxes are paid. The state of the markets, with heavy influence from supply and demand, subsequently funnels (or not) resources in particular directions. For example, shortages of a particular commodity prevent the flow of that commodity to buyers, leading to price increases. At the same time, with various financial products, like options, agents in these markets can also hedge against the risks of these outcomes, creating counter feedback loops that end up helping keep the system in place as long as there is liquidity, meaning the ease at which an asset can be turned into cash without changing the market price thanks to an easily available supply.

Finance can also be done in more democratic ways that rely less on the whims of those with significant control over markets, in order to create more democratic outcomes. For example, the Government Pension Fund of Norway consists of two sovereign wealth funds administered by the Norwegian state, which owns stakes in companies around the world, as well as Equinor, the state-owned energy company with access to Norway's oil reserves. Thanks to the social wealth fund, Norway also has one of the most robust social welfare systems in the world, with one of the lowest rates of wealth inequality.[1] Social wealth funds can be seen as using markets and finance for the pursuit of the common good of the people of a nation state through reinvestment in socially minded endeavours.

While many of the distinct parts of the traditional finance system are held together by laws of private property administered by the state, as we learned from the previous chapter, smart contracts originally come from an attempt at creating a similar but parallel system that meets many of the same functions as the state but with qualitative differences. Moving forward with our understanding that code is in fact not law, let's dig deeper into how to facilitate markets and exchanges via smart contracts so that we can see how it can be deconstructed and twisted to fit ends other than free market fundamentalism and with a more commons-oriented logic.

DeFi Primitives: Decentralised Exchanges

Computer systems contain primitives. You can think of the table of elements as a list of primitives for the creation of more complex materials that we interact with as beings in our universe. By combining different elements together in certain ways, we can create plastics, metals and all the various materials that are required for you to have got up to this point reading this book. Additionally, it could make more sense to view primitives at the compounds layer rather than the elements layer (e.g., H20 vs hydrogen) depending on what you are trying to do.

In a similar way primitives are the building blocks to create more complex pieces of software and architecture. Primitives can be the smallest units of computation available on a given machine, or they can be atomic elements of expressions in a programming language. Each layer of a complex computer system can have different primitives available to system designers that can, depending on the layer being looked at, have smaller primitives inside, allowing for the creation of more complex primitives that are applicable to different layers in the stack.

A protocol is a standard set of rules that allow information or data to be shared between systems. For example, the Internet uses the TCP communication protocol to define the basic rules for establishing a network connection and sharing data between networks.[2] The Hypertext Transfer Protocol, or HTTP (the same "http" you see before almost any website URL), is a protocol that relies on TCP to give specific instructions on how to read and process the data once it's received by a computer. Together they allow computers hooked up to the Internet to share information with one another and create the Internet experience we are familiar with. Without these protocols and standards, it would be difficult for computers to be interoperable enough to make the Internet possible.

ERC standards can be seen as a layer of primitives for building systems with smart contracts on Ethereum. They are the building blocks for creating more complex forms of interaction while also staying interoperable with the rest of the Ethereum ecosystem that follows the same standards. Since so many other dapps use the same ERC standards, they effectively act as open source protocols to help build dapps that talk to each other readily and easily. This type of interoperability is very different to the Silicon Valley platform-dominated part of the web. There is not much interoperability between Facebook, Twitter and Snapchat, for example. They each use their own standards and data formats to share information and data produced on their respective platforms as a way to enclose the data collection of the interactions of its users. This then allows each company to sell ads on the platforms they control. Not all smart contracts are designed with a high level of interoperability in mind, but it is possible, something which is not an option on most corporate tech platforms

The vast majority of building on top of Ethereum has been focused on the creation of dapps for financial use cases. The quickly growing ecosystem of finance-related applications using smart contracts on the decentralised architecture of a blockchain, or DeFi, has championed user-controlled custody of tokens and other assets (as opposed to being under control of a centralised tech company) while still taking advantage of similar financial products that can be found in more traditional financial environments. For most financial products you can think of, there is a DeFi alternative using smart contracts on a blockchain, usually Ethereum, but increasingly on several others.

For example, think of an exchange which has the purpose of allowing traders to make trades for different financial assets, the most well-known being a stock exchange where traders can buy stocks of a company with a bet that the price will rise. There are also foreign exchange markets that allow trade between different national currencies and that help establish exchange rates. If you have ever purchased cryptocurrency, then you most likely went through a centralised cryptocurrency exchange like Coinbase, Gemini or one of the hundreds of others that have been created since the start of Bitcoin.

In order to sign up to the exchange you probably also needed to provide some personal information so that they could abide by the Know Your Customer (KYC) laws of your legal jurisdiction. For most cryptocurrency exchanges, you can either purchase a specific cryptocurrency at the market price or you can set a buying price that will automatically execute when that price is available in the order book. Many also offer more complex financial products like options, swaps, futures and other derivatives that involve leverage and are more difficult to gain access to on normal stock exchanges for most people because of the risks involved. Like any exchange, there are also professional traders or trading bots with complex trading strategies that you would be up against in the markets. You are also technically reliant on the company that owns the exchange on keeping your cryptocurrency safe, and so you would be out of luck if the exchange went bust (something that has happened in the past like with Mt. Gox, QuadrigaCX, FTX), making them the very middlemen the original vision of Bitcoin intended to get rid of. These types of cryptocurrency exchanges are commonly referred to as **centralised exchanges (CEX)**.

The alternative to CEXs, which involves using smart contracts, in DeFi are uncreatively called **decentralised exchanges (DEXs)**. DEXs do not collect any personal information because you don't need to create a profile, instead your pseudo-anonymous Ethereum wallet address is your profile. In a DEX, the functions of what an exchange does is automated via smart contracts to facilitate trades. There are many different ways that smart contracts can be configured to create a DEX. For several years there were actually many attempts to create a DEX, but they failed to offer a good enough experience to get investors and traders to move away from CEXs.

For example, the EtherDelta marketplace brought together buyers and sellers of ERC-20 tokens via an order book, a website displaying order information, and smart contracts that were run on the Ethereum blockchain. With EtherDelta's smart contracts, orders were validated, terms and conditions were checked, paired orders were executed and the blockchain was updated to reflect a trade, similar to how a normal exchange would work. While the dapp provided a familiar dashboard that more advanced traders would be used to, this model still required users to deposit funds into a separate EtherDelta wallet, a point of centralisation, and was unfriendly for new users. Additionally, in 2018, the SEC charged EtherDelta founder Zachary Coburn with "operating an unregistered exchange." This spelled the end for EtherDelta.

The first successful DEX on Ethereum was Uniswap, which was founded in late 2018 by Hayden James, after he had been laid off from his first job as a mechanical engineer at Siemens.[3] Convinced by a friend who worked at the Ethereum Foundation that it was the best thing to happen to him and he was just in time to begin learning Ethereum development, he began to explore the Ethereum ecosystem. In order to have a concrete project to work on to learn more, his friend suggested trying to build something originally proposed by Buterin — creating automated market makers (AMM) on Ethereum, something which has now become an important primitive for DeFi.[4]

Most stock exchanges, CEXs and EtherDelta used an order book model for facilitating trades between buyers and sellers. To facilitate a trade, there needs to be some amount of liquidity. While most stocks of large multinational companies are usually very liquid and can be exchanged for money quickly, trading a house for money can take a lot longer, making it a less liquid asset. Liquidity in a CEX is usually provided either by the exchange itself or by firms that they may partner with to provide liquidity to their markets. For example, one of their partners may be the main liquidity provider for the ether to US dollar trading pair on their platform and are willing to always buy or sell an asset at the current market price to create liquidity. This firm is paid by the platform to provide this liquidity (literally just a lot of ether and US dollars and a willingness to buy and sell) to help facilitate trades more easily. This also means that frequently there are multiple orders for buying and selling made not at market price that execute later or are cancelled. This means an order book model contains a very high number of transactions in order to function, which is not ideal for a blockchain with limited block space (i.e., memory) and fees for any transaction made.

In the AMM model, smart contracts facilitate a "liquidity pool" to make it easy for traders to trade without permission in and out of assets rather than a market of buyers and sellers. In Uniswap, a single liquidity pool will contain a pool of two different assets (either ether or ERC-20 compatible tokens) to create a trading pair. Anybody that is willing to provide both assets in an equal amount of value can become a liquidity provider for a single liquidity pool which is held by the smart contract. When a liquidity provider provides liquidity to a liquidity pool, they receive back a proportional amount of "LP tokens" that represent the share of the liquidity pool that they are providing for. LP token holders can then claim and receive their portion of the fees that traders pay to use the related liquidity pool. Sometimes DEXs also offer extra rewards to particular liquidity pools to incentivise more liquidity into a particular pool. Searching for new liquidity pools with the best incentives attached to maximise financial return is called liquidity mining.

As you can see, in this set-up, there is no direct trading between a buyer and a seller —instead, traders are trading with the pool of funds held by the smart contract. But if there are no sellers and buyers setting a price for their orders, how is a price determined? An AMM uses a deterministic algorithm called a "bonding curve" to always have a known price. In a bonding curve, the relative price of the assets in the liquidity pool are determined by the ratio of supply of each asset in the pool. For example, in a liquidity pool for Josh Coin and ether, if there are two times as much Josh Coin as there is ether in the pool, then Josh Coin is worth half as much as ether at that moment. This ratio would most likely be determined by the creator of a liquidity pool (anyone can create a liquidity pool for two ERC-20 compatible tokens) .

With a very simple equation, a price can always be determined based on the available liquidity of each token in the AMM smart contract.[5] When a trade is made with the liquidity pool, the price will inherently change and could do so considerably if you are trading a large amount relative to the size of the liquidity pool. The price could also change from what is originally shown because other trades are taking place in the liquidity pool that change the price right before you submit your own trade. The change in price while a trade is happening is called "slippage" — the difference between where the dapp signalled the entry and exit price for a trade and what actual average price entered and exited the liquidity pool. In the Uniswap dapp (and most others that use AMMs), you can set your slippage tolerance so that if slippage goes beyond a certain threshold, the trade will not execute. If the change in price in liquidity is large enough, there can be a mismatch from the smart contract and the prices shown on other DEXs and CEXs. This presents an opportunity for arbitrage, or the simultaneous buying and selling of an asset on different markets to exploit the difference for financial gain. AMMs often intentionally rely on arbitrageurs to do this so that prices more accurately reflect the average market price. Using an AMM means that a DEX doesn't need an order book and there is no reliance on a single powerful liquidity provider, although the lack of order book means there is a risk of slippage and a single wealthy liquidity provider could always show up and dominate.

A potential downside of a DEX is that you can't trade your cryptocurrency directly into a national currency to be sent to your bank. In order to do that you'd most likely need to send the cryptocurrency to a CEX. Another is that, with a CEX, your deposits are maybe insured (which is enforced partially with KYC), whereas in a DEX, since you still have custody over your assets (and no KYC enforcement), there is little recourse in the event of a hack. Generally though, CEXs have been much bigger targets for hacks compared to DEXs since CEXs are still single points of failure. Most likely you will need to get at least your first cryptocurrency from a CEX to send to a DEX or any other dapp, although there are lesser known options like physical meetups for exchanging cryptocurrency or cryptocurrency ATMs.[6] So it's difficult to say whether CEXs are inherently better than DEXs or order books are better than AMMs. It's more that depending on the context, one or the other could be more beneficial to use or take part in.

This reliance on CEXs in order to begin to take part in DeFi shows that much of the money and the law are still coming from the traditional financial and legal systems. It also shows how CEXs have become targets for regulation as they are choke points for entering the crypto economy and DeFi. Saying "code is law" in the face of this is difficult to defend, but the most die-hard believers will likely still believe that this is just a transitional step towards our supposedly stateless cryptocurrency future.

Markets and the Commons without Capitalism

Most theories of capitalism were developed in the eighteenth and nineteenth centuries, when markets expanded and the privileges of the nobility were challenged. It was also a period of intense competition between capitalists as they jockeyed for power not only in markets, but also politically. The rise of capitalism also coincided with the rise of the modern nation state, in which political rights were expanded from the nobility to include countrymen (but not women) who owned property. Nation state governments played an important role in codifying the powers of both the noble and capitalist classes, governed their relations and introduced the current legal regime that makes accumulating extensive amounts of private property possible. This truth, however, is normally ignored in liberal and conservative accounts about how capitalism and competition are just "human nature".

Due to this widely accepted mythology, it is easy to equate capitalism with markets, a view that has been re-enforced in the past few decades by neoliberal policies within which markets have increasingly impacted public services negatively through privatisation. Today, capitalism is more and more driven by large corporations, powerful financial actors and platform unicorns such as Meta, Uber and Amazon. The goal of these companies is not to compete on the market, but rather to own it.

Capitalism, however, is not the same thing as markets, which existed well before capitalism became the dominant mode of production.[7] They are universal in recorded history going back at least as far as the origins of urban civilisation. Capitalism is more recent, and is usually imposed from above, mostly via the exercise of state power and the creation of legal regimes that prioritise private property (capital). Marx calls such pre-capitalist market-oriented relations of production "petty production" — when capital concentration has not yet proceeded beyond the limits of individual property. While private ownership of the means of production remains an essential precondition, some historians have stressed that petty production also relied on various forms of commons. In fact, one of the major events that brought forth capitalism in England was termed "the enclosure of the commons", in which land that was legally owned by the Crown but used by local peasants and vital to village life at the time, became subject to newly imposed restrictions by the nobility and wealthy landlords in the 1500s, more closely resembling the way we think of private property today. Many contemporary companies also rely on different commons, like open-source software, commonly held intellectual property with public institutions and the collective intelligence of workers.

There are essentially two definitions of the commons. It can be used to signify a resource that is freely available like water, air or land, at least before private property enforcement was used to prevent local populations from accessing land or water. Alternatively, as the work of Elinor Ostrom showed, it can also be seen as an institution. Ostrom was the first woman to win the Nobel Prize in Economics for her work on how various types of communities have managed common resources like forests, fisheries or grazing land without the need for governments or private companies. In contrast to the "tragedy of the commons", to Ostrom, the commons are an alternative form of property to that of the market or state which permits collective governance of a resource system with some degree of success over a long period of time.

The truth is that the story of the "tragedy of the commons", commonly used to justify the need for capitalist markets and push for neoliberal economic policy, was one made up by the conservative American ecologist Garrett James Hardin.[8] Hardin later retracted his original thesis in response to evidence of historical and existing commons, stating that "The Tragedy of the Unmanaged Common" would have been a better title, but the damage had already been done. What's also problematic is that Garrett was vocal about his white nationalist, hard-line anti-immigrant and pro-eugenics views.[9] There seems to be a noticeable connection between ideological support for neoliberalism and anti-democratic tendencies with a reactive belief that humans can't manage a commons.

The commons are not simply freely available natural resources, however, but are defined and regulated by social systems. Ostrom argues that such social systems, or "communities", enable the commons to be regulated. They define rules of access and norms of common property, and enforce these rules and norms collectively. Based on her research, Ostrom outlined eight principles for managing a commons that most successful communities that have managed a commons follow:

1. Define clear group boundaries.
2. Match rules governing use of common goods to local needs and conditions.
3. Ensure that those affected by the rules can participate in modifying the rules.
4. Make sure the rule-making rights of community members are respected by outside authorities.
5. Develop a system, carried out by community members, for monitoring members' behaviour.
6. Use graduated sanctions for rule violators.
7. Provide accessible, low-cost means for dispute resolution.
8. Build responsibility for governing the common resource in nested tiers from the lowest level up to the entire interconnected system.

Following these principles helps groups solve the free-rider problem, where group members that don't actually participate in the work can nonetheless benefit from the wider collective effort. This is not just a problem for the governance of commonly held resources, but also in organisations like labour unions. I mention labour unions because they are an example of a type of organisation that does not fit neatly into the category of private (with the purpose to make profit in order to survive) or public entity (they are not run by the state). Labour unions are similar to a commons, with the defined group boundary being workers in a certain industry or company. They also take advantage of many financial products that help fund their commons (i.e., pension funds, strike funds, etc).

Using the previous example of bonding curves that help

make AMMs possible, let's see how commons-oriented principles can fit into a blockchain world that generally thinks of finance as an individualistic profit-driven endeavour.

Augmented Bonding Curves: Liquidity for the Commons

Only knowing the example of using bonding curves to facilitate AMMs as shown above may lead you to think that bonding curves are the same as DEXs, or that DEXs are the only use of bonding curves, but this is not correct. Bonding curves are multi-purpose tools that use algorithms to manage a pair or basket of assets held in a smart contract. By doing so, bonding curves act as an automated counterparty that will engage on any side of a trade based on the ratio determined by the algorithm used. Notice that it only makes trades happen when another agent initiates one and does not create trades, hence the reason they are commonly called "automated market makers" but can also be seen as an automated counterparty. This helped solve the problem of liquidity for tokens that may have had low or no liquidity on CEXs as well as not needing to rely on exchanges to have custody of a user's assets.

We can further dissect AMMs into two more specific functions. The type of AMM we have been most focused on here to facilitate DEXs are secondary-market AMMs (SAMMs) in that the assets held in the smart contract originate from somewhere else but are used to trade between them. For example, all of the AMM smart contracts that use bonding curves in Uniswap are all technically SAMMs since the assets in the pool originate from elsewhere. So where do these crypto assets originate from?

While there are many mechanisms used to create new crypto assets, primary-market AMMs (PAMMs) are a popular one.[10] PAMMs are bonding curve mechanisms that issue new assets based on the supply provided in another asset. They are used to determine an appropriate ratio and price of tokens to give to a single person relative to the total amount of new tokens purchased. They can further be used to purchase back the assets they mint at a dynamically fixed price based on the algorithm used. In this way, PAMMs are a primary issuance market that provides an alternative to projects needing to mint a fixed amount of their own tokens at the start to raise money in an ICO while also providing guardrails on the price that make it more stable and less attractive to speculators. PAMMs use the assets provided by buyers to be able to provide liquidity for selling assets back or buyers can move their assets to trade on SAMMs.

The Commons Stack, a development collective inspired by Elinor Ostrom's work on the commons, is building a library of open source component blueprints for helping communities build out what they call a "minimum viable commons" with tools that realign incentives toward the public good. One of the first components they have been building is termed an "augmented bonding curve" (ABC), in which they have taken the bonding curve primitive and adapted it to include a commonly-owned pool of funds through a tax for buying and selling assets held in the ABC. The common pool of funds can then be put towards the collective goals of the community through the use of the newly issued asset as a token for voting over the allocation of those funds. This configuration is also called a Commons Market Maker (CMM), since it does everything else that AMMs do with added fees that help fund the commons. Inspired by systems in the biological world, those from the Commons Stack think of this mechanism like a cell wall which separates the wider capitalist economy from the more localist commons economy by combining tokens, markets, liquidity and a desire to grow the commons. CMMs help enable circular, regenerative flows of value within the cyber-physical commons that promote economic sustainability while also interfacing with the wider economy.[11]

The system is launched in two stages: the Hatch Phase and the Open Phase. In the Hatch Phase, the first contributors to a community start a crowdfund based on set initial parameters (like hatch tribute, hatch price, and exit tribute) for the bonding curve, This allows those without much financial capital to still be able to take part in the crowdfund and the parameters can be set so that those who can only contribute through their labour still receive a share. Depending on the parameters set, a lockup period begins where the initial tokens minted from the hatch are slowly vested to contributors to combat potential early speculation that would hurt the stability of the price. When the Open Phase begins, anyone is then able to take part in the CMM to purchase the new tokens while also contributing to the common pool.

The design space for CMMs is much wider than I can possibly detail here. On the Commons Stack's website, you can simulate the potential results of a hatch with the parameters you've chosen thanks to cadCAD, a simulator built by their research partners, BlockScience.[12] However, to make it more comprehensible, let's look at how the Token Engineering Commons (TEC), the first community to work with the Commons Stack, took advantage of a CMM for their initial fundraise.

The TEC is a collective of people who are interested in token engineering, a cross-disciplinary field of study that combines cryptography, political science, law, economics and cybernetics, to name a few, and in advancing it as a science. It asks us the questions, "What if we could create our own economies? How would we design them if we could do it intentionally together?", while also providing the tooling necessary with blockchains and smart contracts, like CMMs. The TEC is particularly interested in using token engineering for creating the standards and open-source tools for building stable commons-based economies inspired by Ostrom's principles. The purpose of using a CMM to bootstrap its community is to be able to fund projects from within the community that discover, develop and proliferate best practices for engineering safe tokenised economies.

To prepare for the Hatch Phase, members of the community came together and took part in parameter debates in which they discussed what parameters for their CMM they wanted to build to understand the trade-offs and risks. The chosen set of parameters included a Minimum Funding Goal of $800,000 worth of cryptocurrency with a funding period of thirty days. If the goal was not met, all of the funds would be returned to contributors and the Hatch Phase would need to restart. They successfully met the target and raised approximately $1,571,223.57 in the thirty-day period and vested the appropriate amount of TEC tokens over time. The tokens then allowed the hatch participants either to be able to vote on new proposals for the community using the funds raised in the common pool or to be swapped back for some amount of cryptocurrency through the CMM.

What's interesting to note about this example is that against the free market fundamentalist underpinnings of Szabo's idea of smart contracts, the smart contract-based mechanism helps the commons by *reducing* the effects of an unrestricted free market. Where capitalism was birthed from the enclosure of the commons and the imposition of private property legal regimes to create new markets, here we are seeing attempts to reinvigorate the commons using tools that crypto hypemen and gatekeepers will declare are meant only for capitalism. At the same time, the burgeoning field of token engineering blurs the line between markets and economic planning, likely to the dismay of Szabo. The idea of intentional economic design looks more like the experimentation under Cybersyn, the decentralised economic planning system implemented under Chilean socialist president Salvador Allende with the help of famous cyberneticist Stafford Beer, than it does laissez-faire libertarian capitalism. The common pool of funds raised through a CMM also looks more like a non-state-based social wealth fund then it does an ideally libertarian free market.

Looking back at Lessig's framework from the previous chapter, we know that code has similar properties to architecture, but still with qualitative differences. Smart contracts, being not just code but also agents within an economy, whether free-market or commons-based, also have properties similar to the market as a regulator in Lessig's framework. What is clear now is how smart contracts can be used to create the conditions for libertarian free markets but can also be designed in a way that reduces the effects of a free market, depending on how liquidity is designed to be used in the system. Smart contract code is still qualitatively different from law, architecture and the market in Lessig's framework, but nonetheless still useful.

By systematising and creating best practices and methods for token engineering, we can break down the different elements that are needed to create a cryptoeconomy and choose from a library of primitives to build the infrastructure for it. This in turn makes economic design more approachable by more people, and when more people can take part in discussions they can provide more input for collective decision-making. And if a community were given the choice between an economy built for a free-for-all capitalist market and one for treating shared resources as a commons with clear rules for the benefit of all, I'm willing to bet they would pick the second.

CHAPTER 6

THE PEOPLE'S SHADOW BANK

Crypto is the new shadow bank. It provides many of the same services, but without the consumer protections or financial stability that back up the traditional system.
— Senator Elizabeth Warren[1]

The 2008 global financial crisis was a wake-up call for many people, showing that the so-called free market system was far from perfect. It was caused by a number of factors, but one of the key problems was the "shadow banking" system. Shadow banking is a term for the activities of financial institutions that are not subject to the same regulations as traditional banks. This includes hedge funds, private equity firms, investment banks, insurance firms, payday lending and other non-bank financial institutions.

But why do states allow shadow banking to exist? Why not submit these bank-like but non-bank financial institutions to the same regulations as proper banks? A part of the reason is that shadow banking is necessary because it provides credit to businesses and households that would not otherwise have access to it from traditional banks. One of the main jobs of a nation state in a liberal capitalist country is to create the conditions for the economy to continue to grow. Allowing for a more deregulated section of the financial economy provides a way for consumers or businesses to take out loans or engage in other types of financial activity at rates that they cannot get through traditional banks and thereby stimulate the economy. It provides credit for economic growth without the responsibility that comes through regulation.

However, it can be very risky to engage with shadow banking institutions since there is no deposit insurance guarantee from the government, as there is with traditional banks. The trade-off is similar to the difference between products categorised as medicine, which are strictly regulated, versus supplements, where there is significantly less regulation. At the same time, shadow banking is the part of the economy where wealthy elites are able to stash away money and assets for higher returns or find loopholes for paying much less proportionally in taxes than the average person.

One of the by-products of shadow banking is the tendency for these institutions to make loans and then securitise them, or pool them together, to create new financial products that can be traded on newly created markets once there is enough liquidity. It is a way to make illiquid assets into more liquid ones. The most obvious example of this was with the subprime mortgage crisis in 2008, where shadow banking institutions were responsible for securitising hundreds or thousands of mortgage loans (a house being a very illiquid asset generally) to turn them into collateralised debt obligations (CDO), making all of these mortgage loans very liquid. Credit default swaps (CDS) were a counter financial product to CDOs, acting as insurance against default risks with all of the mortgage loans bundled inside the CDO. Once there was a critical number of defaults, enough holders of the CDSs demanded settlement. Since there was no deposit insurance from the government, this led to the collapse of AIG, the largest insurance company in the world at the time.

This collapse led to a series of further financial catastrophes. Many people could no longer afford their mortgages, which created a credit crunch, a sudden reduction in available credit being loaned by banks and other financial institutions, followed by the bailouts and stimulus packages. For many this showed that the shadow banking system was clearly a systemic risk to the entire global economy if not managed correctly. For those looking closely enough, it also showed how shadow banking institutions were able to introduce new credit, and therefore new money, into the economy without the same regulations imposed on normal banks. Once again, this challenges the right-wing libertarian assertion that there being too much money or credit is strictly a consequence of central banks, as a significant amount of money via credit was introduced into the economy through the deregulated private sector (i.e., shadow banking), thanks to neoliberal public policy decisions.

While one would hope that governments would have learned from this experience, unfortunately the shadow banking economy is larger today than it was before the 2008 crash — according to the Financial Stability Board, assets held by shadow banking institutions equalled around $63.2 trillion in 2020.[2] This includes investment firms like BlackRock, with $10 trillion of assets under management as of January 2022, and Vanguard, with about $8 trillion of assets in 2022. Just these two companies own a very significant amount of the mutual fund and exchange-traded fund market, giving them a worrying amount of control.

Although questionable from a prioritisation standpoint, it is unsurprising to see states adopt seemingly appropriate regulations for a growing cryptocurrency industry with a market cap of about $1 trillion by February 2023.[3] One of the loudest voices in US politics to be calling for more strict regulation for fear of expanding the shadow banking system is Democratic Senator Elizabeth Warren, known for her progressive positions on financial regulation and role in the creation of the Consumer Financial Protection Bureau in 2010. Originally a conservative Republican, as she believed they were the party that best supported markets, she switched parties in the mid-1990s in the belief that it was the Democrats who now did.

While certainly not a conservative libertarian, it is clear that Senator Warren believes in markets under capitalism as the optimal system for allocating resources in the economy. Her politics essentially advocate for a slightly more progressive and regulated capitalist economy, a position which would be considered centre-right liberalism in many other countries that are not the United States. From a point of view that is critical of capitalism, a more regulated capitalist economy can still not answer the contradictions inherent to capitalism that lead to regular crises such as the one in 2008.

There are no doubt plenty of reasons to believe that organisations built around cryptocurrencies and DeFi have many similar properties to shadow banking institutions. The systemic risk posed by shadow banking, as shown in the 2008 crash, makes it reasonable to speculate on proposing regulations as a way to limit the risks that could end up being borne by consumers. In order to take a deeper look into the criticisms levelled by Senator Warren, that crypto is a new form of shadow banking, let's first understand a couple more common mechanisms prominent in DeFi.

DeFi Primitives: Lending Protocols and Stablecoins

Smart contracts designed to allow for lending between agents are an important primitive for DeFi. A couple of the most popular ones on Ethereum at the time of writing are Compound and Aave. These protocols function like a money market, which is a market for short-term loans in the non-crypto economy. Similar to the AMM model for DEXs, in DeFi lending anyone can be a lender for a specific token facilitated by a smart contract which can earn them interest, often referred to as an annual percentage yield (APY). Suppliers earn this return from borrowers who take out loans from the pool of tokens held by the smart contract. Borrowers pay back their loan plus their accrued borrower interest rate, which is always more than the supplier APY. Usually in this set-up, every loan needs to be over-collateralised, meaning that the borrower must supply more value of another asset as collateral in order to take out a loan. The excess amount that needs to be supplied is determined by the "collateral factor" set in the smart contract. For example, let's say you want to use ether as collateral for a loan you want to take out, and the collateral factor for ether is 0.75. This means that you can borrow up to 75% of the value of your collateral. So, if your collateralised ether is worth $100 then you can borrow up to $75 of the asset you want to borrow.

This DeFi primitive has become a very popular way for people to earn interest fairly safely on their digital assets. The reason it's fairly safe as a lender is because of the required over-collateralisation of the borrower. If the price of the asset put on as collateral drops below the collateral factor threshold required to back the loan, their collateral is automatically liquidated through the smart contract in order to pay off the loan. In order to determine the real price that the lending smart contract should consider for liquidation, it uses oracles to receive data from multiple other exchanges, taking the average of them so that they are not dependent on a single exchange that could be hacked or manipulated.[4] Additionally, it is sometimes common for these dapps to offer extra rewards as incentives for being a lender for a specific market, making it a part of liquidity mining strategies.

At the time of writing, taking out under-collateralised loans is still not widely available. This makes sense when you're using a medium that can't reliably use your personal information and give it to lenders to make risk assessments on its own. One way that Aave allows users to take under-collateralised loans is through a technique called "flash loans". Here, a user can take an under-collateralised loan as long as the loan itself is paid off in the same block that they are taking out the loan on the blockchain being used.[5] If the loan can't be paid off in the same block, then the loan isn't made. At the moment it's largely used for very niche scenarios and has been a common weapon for DeFi hackers to try to manipulate markets and as a way to steal money from smart contracts. In this environment, it makes sense that the vast majority of loans require at least an equal amount in collateral to the loan, but plenty of people are trying to find out ways to make it work through third-party risk assessments and credit scores.

But why would you want to take out a loan with an equal amount of value of collateral on the line? This is not so different to when people use their house as collateral for a loan from a bank, but as an active trader of different cryptocurrencies, you may want to have exposure to a different asset without completely losing the collateralised asset, similar to getting exposure to cash without necessarily losing your house. By doing this you take a risk, but you can get exposure to more stable assets while holding on to your riskier ones. It could also occur that unexpected expenses come up that require you to pay for something denominated in something more stable, like US dollars. This brings us to another DeFI primitive, **stablecoins**.

A stablecoin is a cryptocurrency whose price is pegged to a usually more stable asset like the US dollar, a commodity like gold, a basket of different assets or even to another cryptocurrency in order to prevent its price being too volatile. This is not only an extremely useful thing for traders so that they can move in and out of volatile positions, but for anyone who would want to use cryptocurrency without needing to worry about big changes in price relative to the underlying asset being pegged. Stablecoins most commonly try to stay pegged to the US dollar. There are a few different ways different stablecoins are able to keep their peg.

The first way proposed was by Tether Ltd and their Tether US dollar stablecoin (USDT). Started in 2014, it is currently the largest stablecoin by market capitalisation. Each USDT is meant to be pegged to $1, with the intention that there is an equal value in assets being held by the company to back each token. However, recent investigations have shown there is reason to believe that Tether Ltd likely doesn't have an equal amount in assets to back each USDT in circulation most of the time, and uses its position of being able to create USDT to help its sister company Bitfinex, a CEX. A case was settled in February 2021 forcing Tether and Bitfinex to pay $18.5 million and share quarterly reports of Tether's stablecoin reserves for the next two years.[6]

Tether Ltd holds their assets with Deltec, a bank held in the Bahamas that holds US dollar deposits as part of the shadow banking system, since it's based outside the US. This means that their dollar deposits are not federally insured like traditional banks in the US.[7] US dollars existing in financial institutions outside of the US are commonly referred to as "eurodollars", even if they don't reside in Europe, making Tether's USDT backed mainly by eurodollars, if indeed they have any backing at all. An entirely separate book could potentially be written on the shady practices of the company and team behind Tether. Because of its position in relation to financial law and its ability to mint new USDT tokens, it is considered a potential future choke point and risk for crypto markets. Many will claim, however, that because Tether and other similar stablecoins like USDC, which is operated by the company Circle (owned by Coinbase), are centrally controlled, they should not be considered as DeFi, but we can't ignore that USDT and USDC are accepted tokens in many DeFi protocols.

An alternative and more decentralised stablecoin approach is the one taken by the MakerDAO protocol, in which they intended for the system to not need to rely on a centralised authority to function, like with Tether. Their stablecoin is called DAI, which is also meant to be pegged to the US dollar, like USDT. To create the peg, they utilise DeFi lending smart contracts that allow users to use ether (or some other assets on the Ethereum blockchain) as collateral to withdraw, or really create, DAI, which is meant to be worth roughly $1. By giving collateral, a user creates a vault in which they can withdraw approximately two thirds maximum of the value of their assets in collateral. Like other DeFi lending protocols, if the value of the collateral falls so much that the value of DAI taken out is worth more than the threshold, the smart contract will begin to automatically liquidate the collateral. Additionally, over time, a borrower of DAI will need to pay interest, or in this case the stability fee, on their loan.

While in other lending protocols the interest rates are determined largely by market dynamics and supply in the money market, the stability fee in MakerDAO is determined by those who hold the MKR token. MKR is also known as a governance token, because with MKR you can vote on what the stability fee should be for MakerDAO. The earnings from the stability fees paid also goes to the MKR token holders. This system is meant to incentivise MKR holders to not set the fee too high (or else no one will use it) but not too low, so that they are still able to earn from it. Similar to a stock, investors can purchase MKR (as well as DAI) on DEXs, and therefore their voting power is proportional to the number of tokens they hold and are willing to lock up in the voting contract.

It's very important to note the clear differences and implications to the approaches to creating a US dollar stablecoin taken by Tether and MakerDAO. Similar to CEXs, Tether relies on a centralised for-profit corporation to administer all of its duties, complete with a CEO and shareholders to answer to. For MakerDAO, the functions of the organisation are facilitated by smart contracts and decisions around the stability fee and earnings are determined by MKR token holders. While there's no doubt that many if not all MKR token holders are motivated by profit, it is very different to how Tether makes decisions. At the same time, USDT, DAI and MKR are all using the ERC-20 token standard.

What all of these DeFi protocols show is the flexibility of the composability of smart contracts with interoperable standards, that has characterised the development of software, especially open source software. It can be seen as similar to the way Lego pieces follow a particular standard to allow other Lego pieces to stack on top of each other and make it easy for the pieces to be combined to create larger structures. For better or for worse, the open-source primitives and protocols on blockchains are readily available to potential developers and systems designers to create complex economic systems.

However, at the same time, there are also certain dangers that come with this low-friction and interoperable economic infrastructure. The increasing complexity of financial products built on decentralised architecture opens up the potential for there to be bugs in the smart contract code that can be exploited by hackers. In order to limit potential losses, many times the creators of these DeFi dapps add admin keys that can turn off certain parts of the system in an emergency, however this adds a centralisation risk that becomes worse if the admin keys are stolen by a bad actor. This is one of many examples of how blockchain projects need to choose between security and usability.

It is worth acknowledging that stablecoins received bad press throughout 2022 as one of the largest stablecoins suffered an extraordinary crash and ended up being worth almost nothing. Terra was a smart contract-enabled blockchain created largely to offer a collection of different stablecoins pegged to different national currencies, including the US Dollar, called UST. The system used a mechanism where, to buy UST, you need to burn (equivalent to destroying a cryptocurrency) LUNA, the native cryptocurrency for the Terra blockchain. In return a user receives the market rate amount of UST. This means the supply of LUNA decreases and theoretically its price increases. The mechanism also went in the other direction where a user can mint LUNA, by burning UST. This theoretically results in an increase in the price of UST.

This mechanism made UST an algorithmic stablecoin, or one that keeps its peg purely through smart contact-mediated economic incentives without any collateral to back the stablecoin. This means that, unlike collateralised stablecoins, there was no floor price to secure the peg if there was severe volatility which could lead to a downward spiral as people lose confidence. This is what happened in 2022. LUNA saw its price drop from over $100 to less than $1 within forty-eight hours, starting on 11 May 2022. The significant crash of nearly 99.9% meant a huge loss for token holders and a record drop in the crypto industry. This also meant that UST, which required LUNA to be burnt in order to be created, also saw it severely de-peg from $1 to become effectively worthless.

This issue does not exist in collateralised stablecoins to the same degree because during this type of situation, the stablecoin can be converted back into the asset used as collateral. In the future, it is guaranteed that algorithmic stablecoins will be utilised by scammers again as it is the holy grail of scamming in crypto for its creators. It allows them to essentially print money for as long as the scam stays alive. While I'm not one to give any financial advice, in this case I am willing to say that readers should stay away from these types of stablecoins at all costs, or at the very least accept the very high risks they involve.

Shadow Banking Was the Point

For some, including Senator Warren, cryptocurrencies and DeFi are a new arm of the shadow banking system. Mimicry of various lending and credit-creation mechanisms with little to no regulatory oversight has no doubt helped fuel the recent speculative bubbles around cryptocurrencies that have popped, hurting many who invested their fiat money into crypto. This has put pressure on the United States Securities and Exchange Commission (SEC) Chairman Gary Gensler to begin creating recommendations and proposals for new regulation specific to companies dealing with cryptocurrency in the name of investor protection.[8]

One of Senator Warren's campaign slogans in the 2020 Democratic primaries was "capitalism without rules is theft". One could equally infer from this slogan that capitalism is thus theft with rules. Progressive capitalism may be more desirable over a less regulated neoliberal capitalism, but it doesn't solve the inherent contradictions of capitalism itself (and neither does crypto or any similar technology, for that matter). Part of the solution to limiting potential damage done to everyday people could be by increasing regulation on shadow banking, but at the same time this just changes the rules of theft.

Regulating shadow banking institutions in a way similar to that of traditional banks has been discussed for a long time, with little to nothing to show for it. This is largely because the US has a toxic and dependent relationship with shadow banking. The shadow banking system is crucial to keep the economy moving and stimulated when more regulated, traditional banks can't service everyone. At the same time, shadow banking is one of the loopholes used within the traditional financial system by wealthy elites to avoid paying taxes and preserve their wealth. This dependency makes federal insurance a double-edged sword, treading the line of limiting systemic risk and moral hazard. The tendency for the state to bail out financial institutions intentionally encourages risk-taking, but also increases the probability of later panics and crashes, leading the state to have to undertake a bailout again.

Within the current paradigm, the cycle won't end. While the right may blame the spending of states for economic crashes, it looks more like states understand who the ones with the real power are and create policies that favour them, leading to greater financialisation. While shadow banking certainly creates systemic risk for markets, there are much deeper systemic contradictions to the capitalist system itself that make the state necessary. As lender of last resort, it needs to prop up the financial institutions it is dependent on or else risk complete economic meltdown. It is too limiting and dangerous to assume that we can trust the state to regulate capitalism in a "fair" way with new rules. All that does is change the amount and direction of theft that capitalism relies on.

One of the ways that states try to appear to be doing something to deal with the contradictions of capitalism is through regulation by surveillance. The clearest example is through Know Your Customer (KYC) regulations that require financial institutions to have a copy of their customers' personal information in order to comply with the anti-money laundering (AML) and counter terrorist financing (CTF) regulations, which largely came into effect in the intensive form they take today after 9/11 as part of the Patriot Act. CEXs must comply with these types of laws in order to do business with American and European customers legally, which is why you need to give your information to these entities in order to begin using them. What this means in turn is that these financial institutions (including CEXs) are honey pots for hackers wanting to steal all of the personal information that they are required to store by law and which can be a cumbersome thing to protect. At the same time, very few studies have been done to actually measure the efficacy of these regulations in stopping crime. One of these few found that AML policy intervention has less than a 0.1% impact on criminal finances, with compliance costs exceeding recovered criminal funds by a hundred times, and banks, taxpayers and ordinary citizens are penalised more than criminal enterprises.[9] Don't take this as a defence of financial institutions, but it's important to recognise the failures of these regulations. What they end up doing is creating more dependencies that still don't solve the problem.

The other option being proposed by many states are central bank digital currencies (CBDCs), another potential financial privacy nightmare. While the exact architecture and technology to be used for proposed CBDCs in different countries is unclear at the time of writing, the reasons are obvious as to why states have been interested in the possibility of creating a form of digital cash that is controlled neither by private banks or in the more elusive way that cryptocurrencies are. The main difference between your digital money held at a private bank and a CBDC is that a CBDC would be a liability of the central bank.

While states are already largely used to asking financial institutions for transaction history on their customers when desired, CBDCs can potentially enable states to have real-time access to financial transactions made in the CBDC. This is however not a guarantee, as there are plenty of technical decisions that need to be made first before declaring that would be the outcome. CBDCs also theoretically offer an option for the unbanked and an alternative for people interested in cryptocurrencies. The left-liberal Senator Warren has been one of the most vocal CBDC-supporting US lawmakers on the premise of helping the unbanked.[10] However, less tech-intensive proposals for helping the unbanked, like allowing for postal banking, as proposed by the democratic socialist Senator Bernie Sanders, have not received the same amount of attention.[11] China has so far progressed the furthest along in introducing a CBDC digital renminbi, with several pilots in different cities across the country, suggesting that there is a kind of geopolitical race happening. It's important to note as well that China's shadow banking system has grown rapidly over the period since 2008.

In the left-liberal mindset, it's reasonable to think that one should use the power of the state as it exists to try to bake guarantees to consumers and investors into the law. From an optimistic view of the state, CBDCs could offer more granular monetary policy that would protect everyday people. Some degree of surveillance is likely necessary to do this, but surveillance is also like a bright light from above that shines down on us revealing what we're doing. This may be fine for those who do not have any powerful enemies or fear being discriminated against, but shadow banking in the form of cryptocurrency is the only avenue for those deemed enemies of the state. It is exactly through this mechanism that Wikileaks, Sci-Hub, sex workers in the US and those living in sanctioned countries can have basic financial rights, for better or for worse a necessity under our current form of capitalism.

The alegality of blockchains will also make it very difficult for lawmakers to try to apply regulations on the most decentralised financial protocols. The only way to do so would be to massively increase the surveillance state, something which would, in the long run, hurt progressive movements the most. Regulators are most likely to try to target centralised entities that handle cryptocurrency like CEXs, Tether Ltd and others residing within clear legal jurisdictions as they will be easier to reach. The applicability of the same regulations on what are essentially immutable smart contracts available to anyone will likely prove to be much more difficult as there aren't clear centralised choke points to target. You simply can't force a smart contract to ask its customers to provide personal information so as to comply with KYC, AML and CTF laws.

The obvious answer to surveillance would be for it to be better regulated to not hurt the most vulnerable, but there's little reason to think that this change will come about any time soon, rendering moralistic arguments against the use of crypto because it resembles shadow banking weak. The legitimacy of the struggles being fought by the most vulnerable should not be subsumed into paternalistic calls for legal clarity and submission to surveillance in the name of protecting investors.

The original intention of cryptocurrency was to subvert the state through regulatory avoidance and technical resilience. This is obviously a double-edged sword. If you trust the state and feel it can do an adequate job at regulating society, you will be outraged by that attempt, but grateful if you think differently. The Pandora's box has been opened and instead of trying push all of the evils back in, the only reasonable way to continue is to adapt, creating a new world with the useful parts of the demons we can tear off. Calls for global bans on cryptocurrency are moralistic and ignore the totalitarian surveillance required and the dangers that poses to those who have no other viable alternative. Vulnerable people don't have time to wait for action from a state that considers their existence a threat when useful alternatives are already in front of them.

Shadow Banking for the People

Assuming that shadow banking is likely here to stay, how can the open financial tools afforded by the technology be used in socially positive ways? One attempt at this is Popcorn. Popcorn is the name of a project that is utilising protocols built on DeFi to let investors push a portion of their yield-generating assets towards social impact organisations. Crowning itself "DeFi for the People", Popcorn tries to bake "social good" into a decentralised finance protocol. Novel, yield-generating DeFi products can be created where a small fee is levied for the benefit of public benefit organisations without adding any additional friction to the user. With Popcorn, users would benefit from a yield-generating financial product, while also contributing to public-benefit initiatives.

The organisations that receive a portion of the yield are voted on by those that hold their POP governance token. Popcorn originally did a token launch auction, which was a two-and-a-half-day event near the end of 2021 where the general public were allowed to purchase POP tokens, starting from a high price with a specialised bonding curve. This disincentivised bots, front-running and speculation, then automatically decreased the price over time using the fancy math in the bonding curve with the collateral provided in the smart contract for the auction.[12]The cryptocurrency raised for the auction was then stored in the Popcorn Treasury, a smart contract controlled by POP holders who could then vote on how the funds are allocated.[13]

Popcorn offers automated asset strategies for generating yields to make it easier for users to not have to actively trade.

A portion of the yield is then given to the organisations voted on by POP holders. The more one interacts with Popcorn's smart contracts, the more POP tokens they are also given. To make an analogy to the traditional financial system, it's like an investment firm, which would be a part of the shadow banking system, that allows for slightly more democratic decision-making on where their social impact donations go to.

While this setup may sound nice for many and a good compromise, it clearly still does not have a vision for creating a new economic system that deals with the contradictions of capitalism. It still relies on generating a significant profit for users who are satisfied with slightly less return. While within the currently existing economic framework this can potentially still be a net positive, depending on the social impact organisations benefiting, it can also be used similarly by giant financial institutions for green-washing and good PR. This type of limited thinking is endemic in our current ideological moment in Western capitalist countries and especially found in many crypto projects that put on a progressive veneer. It is as if the only way to do something good in the world is to include an individual profit motive, ignoring the vast majority of human history in which our economic systems were not ruled by profit.

Since so much of our lives are dominated by profit due to the totalising nature of capitalism, it can be difficult to imagine a viable alternative. It can feel like we live under structures that will never change in our lifetimes because they are so entrenched. It seems contradictory to idealise an imagined post-capitalist world when the one we live in comes nowhere near that ideal. What's interesting about building on blockchains in this regard is that we can now move beyond just imagining our ideal systems and begin to prototype them in consequential ways.

Once I realised this after discussion with a group of others in the crypto leftist online communities who thought similarly, we decided to begin creating the infrastructure that could help facilitate such projects and initiatives. We wanted to begin creating the dapps that could help deal with the contradictions of living under capitalism while also attempting to germinate the seeds for a post-capitalist system. We called the project Breadchain, named after the book *The Conquest of Bread* by anarcho-communist Peter Kropotkin.

Breadchain Cooperative is a loose organisation and federation of blockchain or DLT-based projects that are working to advance a post-capitalist vision for this technology and its effects on society. The primary goal is to challenge the largely conservative and outdated economic models and assumptions which many cryptocurrency and DLT projects are built upon and demonstrate that an alternative, more cooperative framework is possible. Part of this means collectivising resources while also keeping the necessary independence needed to pursue the goals of an individual project.

In order to accomplish this, Breadchain Cooperative adheres to four principles to guide the development of projects in the network:

Economic Democracy: We strive for an economy in which resources are allocated democratically rather than solely through market forces.

Mutual Aid: We are only as strong as the weakest among us which is why everyone should be entitled to the things they need to live a dignified life.

Transparent Governance: Everyone should be able to have a say and those given power by the community must be held responsible for their decisions for all to see.

Dual Power: We must build parallel institutions from the grassroots using the tools we have because technology without direct social intervention only favors those in power.

All of these principles sound nice in theory, however the difficulty with trying to explore post-capitalist systems is that we still live under capitalism, and that means you need capital to pay people to continue working and afford the things they need to flourish. In order to deal with this issue while also taking advantage of DeFi tools, we developed the Breadchain Crowdstaking Application. This is essentially a smart contract on Ethereum that forwards Crowdstakers' DAI, the US dollar-pegged stablecoin, into an Aave lending pool in which all of the interest earned on the DAI goes to the Breadchain multi-signature wallet (you can think of it like a joint bank account) which is controlled democratically by Breadchain Cooperative members. In return for giving DAI, Crowdstakers mint and receive a token called BREAD as collateral in the same quantity as they gave in DAI. The BREAD token acts as both a form of collateral from the cooperative and a digital local currency for the Breadchain ecosystem.

It acts as a form of collateral not only because it represents the exact amount of DAI provided by the Crowdstaker but also because Crowdstakers can burn their BREAD token to receive an equal amount of DAI back. In this way, Crowdstakers are not donating any of their capital (although they can do that too if they want to) but are instead giving Breadchain the permission to take the interest generated through the Aave DeFi lending protocol on their DAI which will then be used to fund the operations and future projects from Breadchain. This means that as a Crowdstaker you have two choices, either mint BREAD (fund the cooperative) or burn BREAD (defund the cooperative). You can think of it as a decentralised cooperative bank where the bank uses its money for funding decentralised cooperative projects.

Since the BREAD token is given in the same quantity as the DAI provided and can be redeemed 1 for 1 at any moment, BREAD is also therefore similarly a stablecoin pegged to the US dollar, like DAI. The implications of this are much deeper than they may seem on the surface. If we consider the Breadchain

Network as a type of digital town in which the citizens are people who align with the Breadchain principles, than the BREAD token serves as the basis of a digital local currency for a town which can democratically decide what to build on top of. BREAD can be transferred and traded just like any other ERC-20 token but keeps a stable value of roughly $1 according to the current price of DAI.

The Breadchain Crowdstaking Application acts like a membrane for building a post-capitalist economy within the confines of present-day capitalism. With the combination of 24/7 access to burning your BREAD for DAI and a clear price point, it is easy for the Breadchain Cooperative to protect the token from speculators through a managed liquidity pool using Arrakis Finance. With Arrakis, Breadchain can create a liquidity pool on Uniswap via smart contracts for anyone to provide DAI and BREAD in equal amounts as liquidity for traders, but only at a price range at a fraction of a penny below and above $1. The liquidity pool allows anyone to trade any asset for BREAD if needed without risking large price swings while netting additional revenue for the co-op and other liquidity providers in the form of trading fees.

The revolution will not be funded by the current rulers of the economy, but if we are going to try to live with the contradictions inherent to building the new in the shell of the old, funding during this awkward stage will certainly not come from the state-regulated banking sector. Only by creating bonds of solidarity and networks of mutual aid for cultivating dual power will we reach true economic democracy and freedom, and doing that will likely include engaging with some parts of shadow banking in a strategic fashion. BREAD is not a governance token like a stock in a company or some other speculative financial product, and it is not just a stablecoin. It is a form of economic expression that shows support for a vision of post-capitalism. The Breadchain Crowdstaking Application can be seen as many different things depending on the lens you use, but most of all, it is an engine for funding efforts that explore post-capitalism on the blockchain.

Relying on shadow banking can be seen as a reaction to the failure of the state to regulate financial flows. However, the trade-off must be made clear. Regulation requires more surveillance and those at the top will always have loopholes at their disposal. Regulation is not just a tool for the state to dampen the most extreme exploitation, but also a handy legitimation tactic for capitalist organisations to further entrench their power. Some may be led to think that DeFi is just a new digital space for more financial speculation, and while there is no doubt much of that, it is also a new terrain of political struggle, just as the larger amoebic surface of financial capital should be seen.

State regulations have historically served as a way to legitimate power relations through private property regimes that favour the accumulation of capital over the benefit to society, with occasional concessions for workers when the material conditions are right. But we live in very different material conditions than the industrial capitalism of the 1800s and early 1900s, when basic labour rights were won by the brave men and women who put their lives on the line. Our form of capitalism is more reliant on finance than ever before, while much of the world's most vital industries are exploiting the local populations in the Global South, through institutions under the ownership of shadow banks in the Global North. Through pooling capital collectively and strategically to support progressive efforts that improve labour rights and make structural economic changes, autonomous zones of post-capitalism can spring up and stay resilient, like the villages of artisans and tradesmen that challenged entrenched noble powers when feudalism was the dominant mode of production in Europe.

CHAPTER 7
DIGITAL SCARCITY VS FEASIBLE ABUNDANCE

The spectacle is not a collection of images, but a social relation among people, mediated by images... Just as early industrial capitalism moved the focus of existence from being to having, post-industrial culture has moved that focus from having to appearing.
— Guy Debord, *The Society of the Spectacle*

On 11 March 2021 Mike Winkelmann, a digital artist also known as Beeple, sold an NFT (non-fungible token) through the auction house Christie's for $69 million in ether, by far the most expensive NFT ever sold at the time.[1] He was originally known for creating a piece of art every day, starting on 1 May 2007. Beeple's sale of his piece *Everydays: The First 5000 Days*, which was a collage of all of the five thousand images he had created, catapulted NFTs into the mainstream, seemingly out of nowhere for most. Soon after, every corporate brand and their mother needed an NFT collection and a **web3** or "metaverse" strategy. It was just the beginning of NFT mania in which digital images, popular Internet memes or historical moments were being sold for seemingly outrageous sums of cryptocurrency. Images of "cryptopunks", "Bored Apes", various Ethereum-related memes and the original nyan cat video of a pixelated cat shaped like a poptart were bought, sold, flipped and traded on platforms like OpenSea.

For many, this just didn't make sense. How could a digital image, something that could be theoretically reproduced infinitely, be sold at such a high price, as if it was an actual physical thing? How can you sell a meme or a historical moment that nobody can actually own? And what in the world is an NFT? Along with the media frenzy came the backlash from many prominent artists, calling it all an outright scam and something other artists should not get into. Or claiming that minting an NFT was one of the worst things someone can do for the environment (more on that in the next chapter). Many critics claimed that NFTs are the ultimate attack on the inherent digital abundance of the Internet by imposing financialisation and artificial digital scarcity.

It also didn't help that Beeple's type of art became the face of NFTs for a time, with incredibly detailed phantasmagoric 3D renderings of Donald Trump, Hillary Clinton, Elon Musk and various cartoon characters against dystopian backdrops. However, that didn't stop the growth, with NFT trading spiking up by 21,000% to more than $17 billion in 2021.[2] While the media focus on NFT market speculation has slowed down at the time of writing, and whether or not the general public will ever truly understand what it is, it's very likely that NFTs are here to stay. And if that's the case, it's important to understand not only what they are, but also why they have been such a polarising force along with some of the trends that surround them and the science fiction that inspired them.

NFTs and the Metaverse

In 1992, Neal Stephenson's dystopian science fiction novel *Snow Crash* was first published. Telling the story of Hiro Protagonist, a hacker and pizza delivery driver, the novel is set in a dystopian twenty-first century where hyperinflation is everywhere, caused by overprinting of money by governments and tax avoidance as more people use untaxable encrypted electronic currency. Also something called the Metaverse has replaced the Internet. In the book, the Metaverse is a virtual reality-based environment that's a lot like the real world, including corporations that own vast amounts of real estate. The book has very obvious libertarian and anarcho-capitalist undertones and is an influence on many Silicon Valley founders and investors. It was the main influence for the term "avatar" for a graphical representation of someone's profile as well as the most recent re-emergence of the idea of a metaverse in large part inspired by the rise of NFTs.

While the idea of a metaverse was a dystopian one in the novel, this has not stopped crypto hypemen from pushing the narrative. It's ironic that many seem to think that an improved Internet would be one with open standards for digital private property through "digital scarcity" — proposing interoperability for enclosure and rent-seeking in a medium with theoretically limitless abundance. One of the main enablers of the rise of NFTs was the creation of the first NFT standard on Ethereum, called ERC-721, which was able to be used to represent a unique asset on the blockchain, an idea that was tried previously on the Bitcoin blockchain but never caught on and had several technical limitations since there is no native smart contract support.[3] There were also attempts on Ethereum before the creation of the standard, but these were largely customised and therefore not easily accessible in the way that the standard allowed for.[4]

Similar to the ERC-20 standard that allowed for the creation of interoperable (fungible) tokens on Ethereum, the ERC-721 standard allowed for people to be able to buy, sell and trade their unique tokens between each other through NFT marketplaces that adhered to the standard, like OpenSea, Rarible, Foundatio and many others. However, it was first used for an Ethereum-based collectible game called CryptoKitties.[5] In the game players could buy digital cats with unique traits called "cattributes" that included their eye colour, mouth, fur, base colour, etc, which they could "breed" with other cats to make new ones that would have new and different traits with associated rarity. The rarer ones are generally more expensive than the ones with more common cattributes. Interestingly, these types of cryptographic trading cards were described by Hal Finney, one of the early cypherpunks and potential identity of Satoshi Nakamoto in the cypherpunk mailing list back in 1993 (one year after *Snow Crash* was published).[6]

So, what exactly is an NFT? You may have already consumed many different pieces of media that try to explain it, but let's first quickly understand the concept of non-fungibility. Fungibility refers to the property of an asset being interchangeable with another asset of the same type. Money especially needs to have this property to be considered good money. For example, when you withdraw money from the ATM, you likely don't mind that these aren't the same dollar bills that you deposited. Also if you have five $1 bills, you can get one $5 bill and both arrangements would be equal to each other. Of course, this gets more complicated if for example you're trying to launder money through cash and people know the exact serial numbers to look for on the bills, but let's not complicate things too much yet. But the property of fungibility can be applied to a lot of commodities more broadly.

As an example of non-fungibility, when you pick up your child from day care, you likely won't accept it if they give you any random child back. This is because your child is non-fungible, they have a unique value which is not exchangeable. So, in short, a non-fungible token, or NFT, is a representation of a unique thing in the form of a token on a blockchain. Similar to the ERC-20 standard discussed in previous chapters, the thing that is represented through the ERC-721 token, what it means and how it's valued, can take many different forms based on the social context that surrounds it. Although the lead author of the standard certainly had the intention of applying the standard to physical objects as well, it is much easier to represent digital files, especially images and text, through tokens on a digital medium like a blockchain. This made digital art, memes and gaming seemingly the perfect first use cases to propagate NFTs.

The way that these types of NFTs commonly work is that,

in the smart contract standard, there is a space for the smart contract creator to add metadata, or data about the data of the NFT smart contract. In other words, metadata is additional data that structures, identifies or describes a core set of data, in this case the smart contract deployed on the blockchain. For example, common pieces of metadata associated with a digital file would be file size, file type, format, length, data created and so on.

In the case of Ethereum, transaction fees depend on how much data you wish to add to the blockchain, as well as the complexity of the functions that you are using. If you recall from the earlier chapters, blockchains have very limited memory space, so metadata is extremely useful in the context of blockchains. Let's take the example of a picture of a cartoon ape in the Bored Ape Yacht Club, a collection of ten thousand similar cartoon apes. Within it will be, among other things, a list of the associated ape's traits in text, including a URL link to where the digital image of the ape is stored. This URL can be from anywhere, but the most common standard for those making NFTs is to store the "original" image on a decentralised file storage solution like IPFS or Interplanetary File System.

This is an important thing to note because HTTP (Hypertext Transfer Protocol) is the most common and foundational protocol for data transfer on the Internet. One of the issues with HTTP is its centralised client-server approach to data transfer, which means that if the centralised server is down, so is the data. The reason IPFS is considered a decentralised alternative to HTTP is because it uses a P2P approach to data transfer, which means that multiple nodes that are part of the IPFS network would hold all or parts of the data being stored. IPFS can also be used for hosting entire websites in a decentralised fashion without relying on the centralised infrastructure of HTTP.

At one point during the NFT media frenzy hype cycle, there were claims that many of the NFTs that people had purchased were simply gone or led to bad links.[7] The main reason for this was likely because many of these early NFTs used an HTTP link which was subsequently not upkept. This issue does not exist to the same extent with IPFS since multiple servers host the data. As long as there is a node hosting the data, then it can be accessed without permission, but there can be instances where there are no nodes hosting an IPFS link for an NFT of some crypto art piece. This is similar to other types of art preservation expected of art collectors in the traditional art world. While art preservation for a canvas painting may involve protecting the material or restoring it if much older, with NFT crypto art, it could be ensuring the IPFS link is still hosted. A piece of media should always be hosted by multiple IPFS nodes to ensure redundancy, since if nobody hosts it on IPFS, the media will disappear.

In the case of the Bored Ape NFT, the decentralised image hosting and NFT smart contract combine to provide collectors with a "community" in which they can verify ownership in order to get exclusive access to a digital space called "The Bathroom", as well as a private discord group. There have even been in-person private events and parties like "Ape Fest" in New York City. Many athletes, celebrities and other famous people including Stephen Curry, Mark Cuban and Snoop Dogg have bought an ape in the collection.[8] Both Paris Hilton and Jimmy Fallon awkwardly announced and showed their apes to a seemingly confused audience on his show. According to the Bored Ape Yacht Club site, collectors also have commercial rights over the use of their cartoon ape image, which is not the case in most art purchases. Pairing the ownership verifiability through cryptography on the blockchain, commercial rights and exclusive access to spaces where celebrities might also be hanging out, attracts a particular collector clientele. The shallow and materialist nature of it being a "Yacht Club" are obvious.

Thinking back to the example of the Metaverse in *Snow Crash*, the need for something like NFTs and IPFS becomes clear. In order to create a universally accessible and playable video game environment, there needs to be decentralised and resilient forms of storing data about assets that would be a part of the game. The line between art and gaming has already been blurred with NFTs as it is not uncommon for collectors to display their collected pieces in virtual world game environments like Decentraland where they purchase virtual land to build their own galleries. Through Decentraland, people can walk around with their avatar as in any MMORPG, view NFT art pieces and potentially even buy or bid on NFT art.

As alluded to, many crypto art-related NFTs contain attributes in their metadata that are largely meant to express the degree of rarity of the individual piece in a collection. However, it's easy to see how this can also be used for items in a video game that tracks multiple attributes of that item. For example, a sword with ten attack power and weight of 1.2 digital kilograms. This video game asset can then be bought, sold and traded without needing a centralised gaming company like Activision or Steam to allow the trade. In fact, it's not uncommon in many very competitive MMORPGs like *World of Warcraft* for players to attempt buying and selling items and entire profiles for real money in black markets, even though this is prohibited by most companies. Being caught doing so can lead to a permanent ban, with the player losing all of their progress and potential profit along with it.

A common response from Blockchain sceptics is something along the lines of "OK, wow, so you're telling me an NFT is just a link to some digital art that you can speculate on?" One of the biggest issues with the way that people learn about NFTs and what they are, is that the accounts are largely written by journalists who have likely had very little time to research under the hood. How they report then shapes popular understanding of NFTs, and this can be extended to cryptocurrency, blockchains and new technologies in general. As the media largely focuses on price fluctuations of digital images in NFT marketplaces, this has given the impression that NFTs are only speculative financial vehicles disguised as net art. Focusing so much on trying to define what NFTs are in their essence, through limited representational models that are understandable by a lay audience, impedes a proper understanding by the general public. It is important in any conversation about NFTs from this point on to bear in mind that NFTs are not simply art on the blockchain and in fact have many different use cases that extend much farther beyond it.

One of the biggest things that is missed when talking about NFTs is actually one of their most popular uses. The Ethereum Name Service (ENS) is similar to the Domain Name System (DNS), which is where people can register to own specific domain names on the Internet for their websites. For example, I purchased theblockchainsocialist.com, which redirects you to my site, where you can read my articles, listen to my podcast, sign up for my newsletter and all the other normal Internet things you expect. DNS is convenient because without it we'd have to know the numerical IP addresses of the websites we want to visit. Since at least 1985, DNS has been an integral part of the functionality of the Internet.

ENS does something similar, where instead of someone needing to know your Ethereum address (a random string of numbers and letters) to send you ether or some other Ethereum-based cryptocurrency, they can instead send it to your ENS name. For example, I own theblockchainsocialist.eth that I bought cheap since, perhaps unsurprisingly, no one else wanted it. People can send Ethereum-based cryptocurrency to it instead of needing to copy and paste my full public address. All of this runs on NFT smart contracts because each name is non-fungible in order to function and therefore the name is tokenised. Similarly to DNS, those who own an ENS name have to renew their name registration once it expires.

What was at first a discussion largely about creating decentralised digital cash has expanded tremendously. NFTs, whether they are a picture, a meme or an ENS name, bring up important questions about property rights in a digital space. Discussions about the role of property over a digital space however are not new. Many who pay attention to the digital rights movement are well aware of the fights with large multinational media corporations and their imposition of digital rights management (DRM) software for ensuring no one is allowed to copy their content (among other things) under their intellectual property (IP). While the implementation of property preserving software through DRM has been an ongoing issue, it seems that the introduction of NFTs has elicited a much larger reaction from the general public. The larger issue is that the discussion keeps being framed as purely an issue of imposing digital scarcity, but taking a closer look at NFTs shows that this framing is incorrect.

Art as the Research-and-Development Arm of Capitalism

Before the term "content creator" there was, and still is, "content marketing", which is the practice of companies giving free "content" to potential customers in the hope this will lead them to buy their product or service. Before the Internet this included the magazine published by John Deere called *The Furrow* which tells stories of farmers who use the company's tractors, or the *Michelin Guide* that offered drivers information about car maintenance and travel recommendations to encourage people to drive their cars and thus wear down their tyres, meaning they would need new replacements more often. It's believed that US founding father Benjamin Franklin was the first to use this strategy when he published the *Poor Richard's Almanack* to promote his printing business. This type of marketing strategy was not very common, but the introduction of the Internet changed all that. Now on the Internet, "content is king" and companies regularly produce content that could lead a potential customer to want to purchase their product based on search queries

The Internet has effectively been enclosed for most

users through platforms that make the majority of their money by financialising our attention via advertising. The attention economy approach of treating our attention as a scarce commodity to be fought over by advertisers and tech platforms has had profound socioeconomic effects. The incentive structures of capitalism along with the socio-technological medium of the Internet has allowed for the relationship around content marketing to be reversed. Rather than a company making content for potential customers to find their products, companies can make deals with content creators and influencers who are ostensibly customers of theirs to advertise the company's products to their audiences. The influencers can make tens of thousands of dollars or more per piece of sponsored content, making what they do a lucrative endeavour. But even though being a content creator or influencer has grown to be one of the most sought-after careers by young people,[9] very few actually succeed in making it their full time source of income.[10]

What was once just the attention economy has produced what is now the creator economy, or the ability for "creators" to earn revenue through platforms like Instagram, YouTube, Twitch, TikTok, OnlyFans and many others. There are about fifty million creators in the creator economy, approximately 2.3 million of whom earn enough to make it a full-time job, but the revenue is far from evenly distributed. The "middle-class" creators are almost non-existent, beyond the lucky few who earn a comfortable living. Only 2% of creators on Patreon earned the US federal minimum wage of $1,160 per month in 2017, while on Spotify it takes 3.5 million streams for the equivalent of a full-time US minimum-wage worker's $15,080 a year. Content creators are essentially working for free for platform owners, who pocket billions of dollars in advertising revenue each year while also often having other commercial rights over the content shared on their platform. Additionally, content creators are dependent on the very algorithms created by the platform operators in a black box that are used to display information on users' feeds. The reasoning given for this opacity is that if the algorithm was public, it would be gamed by advertisers, though in fact it is already gamed through search engine optimisation strategies.

Many of the trends that we've seen in the creator economy have mirrored what has happened in the arts. The arts have long been dominated by an awkward relationship between cultural institutions largely controlled by wealthy elites with occasional state support and a class of precarious artists in the fringes of culture producing the most innovative works. Platforms like YouTube and others have become sites of cultural production similar to Hollywood but with much more ubiquitous and plentiful content. It's not a stretch to say that artists are a type of content creator. Many content creators use similar digital tools to create particular audio or visual aesthetics that require some artistic talent, even if its aim is more explicitly commercial than many more artistic attempts.

Traditionally in the fine arts, artists are commonly dependent on either wealthy patrons, a well-funded public arts program from the state or being well known enough to be able to sell their art through auction houses and galleries. Before an artist is able to accomplish any of these things, they are largely in a very precarious position. This usually means that there is some amount of accommodating the tastes of the dominant cultural institutions in order to survive as an artist. It isn't uncommon for artists to critique the situation many find themselves in through their art and especially through the use of new mediums for art, like the Internet.

"Internet art" is a term that encompasses many artistic movements, including net.art. net.art is the use of the Internet as a medium to distribute art that circumvents the physical galleries and museums that many artists are dominated by. In the introduction to the German art critic Tilman Baumgärtel's book *net.art. Materialien zur Netzkunst*, he describes net.art as having "connectivity, global reach, multimediality, immateriality, interactivity and egality".[11] The net.art movement started in the 1990s in the wake of the fall of the Soviet Union, the rise of dot com companies and the tech stock bubble, a time in which the narrative that the Internet was inherently a democratic tool to fight state and corporate control was widespread. Net artists, however, questioned the structures that undergirded the Internet to show that it was in fact heavily controlled by corporations like Microsoft and Netscape. The movement was also a critique of the art world as a business itself.

The Internet presented the art world with a central problem: how can you sell a piece which is digital and infinitely reproducible? There were a number of responses to this. Russian net artist Olia Lialina created an online gallery for showcasing and selling net.art through its "original" URL in the 1990s using her web platform Teleportacia.org. The owner could control the location address as a way to limit access to the piece. The project was subverted by artists Eva and Franco Mattes who cloned the site with the same quality as the original. This moment seems now like a foreshadowing of the creation of NFTs and its critics' "right click save as" strategy as a way to subvert NFT art. While it seems that no piece was purchased from Lialina's experimental satire, in May 1999, Teo Spiller sold his work Megatronix to the Mestna galerija Ljubljana for approximately $500 through a sale negotiation hosted on an open online forum. As a result, Spiller was one of the first net.art artists to sell an "original" piece to a gallery or collector.

Fast forward a few decades, however, and there are still few options for digital artists to make a stable living outside of the traditional cultural institutions. Some may make a living from selling prints of their work or requests from those in niche digital communities who want customised avatars or banners, but it's rarely sustainable. Before Beeple started selling his work as NFTs, the most he had ever sold a print for was $100. Although he amassed a large audience from his digital work, he still needed to work for large corporate clients, as many digital artists do. The contradiction between a capitalism predicated on the idea of living with a scarce amount of resources, paired with a new globally connecting medium with a theoretically infinite amount of resources, since all it is, is information, had not been addressed. The introduction of NFTs however was a first step toward helping to resolve this.

NFTs of digital art created a way for artists to sell something which was infinitely copyable without having to restrict who gets to see it. The artist makes money and the collector gets something that is authoritatively theirs through the record on the blockchain, and anyone is still able to view the piece of art if they go to the smart contract or URL where it is stored. This point and its implications are critically missed by both critics and hypemen of NFTs alike. On one side, it's not uncommon to find hypemen on Twitter claiming their NFT is their personal property thereby barring others from using or saving the image they purchased, forgetting that code is *not* law and private property is enforced by law. On the other side, many who are anti-NFT can be found online claiming to "right-click save" NFT pictures on to their personal computer as a way to violate the NFT hypemen's property rights. The Australian artist Geoffrey Huntley "right-clicked" many of the most popular NFT art projects and mirrored all of the images on a separate site called NFT Bay, an allusion to The Pirate Bay, a common P2P file sharing torrent site, as a way to "steal" the NFTs. However, this attempt at subversion only in fact exposes the same basic misunderstanding of NFTs' relationship to art and property.

In her essay "My Collectible Ass", McKenzie Wark details a funny story about how a famous performance artist sold a piece of their work in which the collector would receive oral instructions on how to perform it, with a verbal contract in the presence of an army of lawyers and witnesses.[12] One of these pieces almost went on the secondary market, where art is sold by the current owner of an art piece and not the original artist, a peculiar thing for a performance art piece since nothing physically exists. The logistics for something like that would presumably be incredibly difficult. Wark then proceeded to try to convince a few collectors who liked that particular artist that her ass was signed by the same artist via a tattoo and asked if they wanted to see it. They did not take her up on the offer. Upon further reflection, she notes that similar "to any other financial instrument, the artwork in a collection gains and loses value at the volatile edge between information and noise". Her attempt to make her own collectible failed because there was not much noise around it. She further notes that paradoxically, an object whose image is very widely spread is in itself a rare object in the sense that few objects have their images spread widely. This can be exploited to create value in art objects that are not rare and singular in the traditional sense. The future of collecting may be less in owning the thing that nobody else has and more in owning the thing that *everybody* else has. This helps explain the attraction for collectors of "purchasing a JPEG" through an NFT even though it is still copyable. The fact that it is copyable is actually a good thing for collectors who understand what they're getting into, and attempts at debunking and subversion like The NFT Bay actually assist those who are collecting NFTs by propagating the images and by creating backups of them for later provenance.

In her blog post "Welcome to the Dessert of the Real", Rhea Myers, one of the first artists to start using blockchain and cryptocurrencies as a medium for art, explains how art, especially when in the form of "high culture", is also an exploration of new property regimes for capitalism.[13] Capitalism is always interested in finding new ways to enclose art pieces as property for private collectors as the art market proposes potentially new property regimes for other types of commodities.

In a discussion between Wark and Myers, the explicit connection was made that art is like the research and development arm of capitalism for new property relations.[14] A big part of the backlash, especially from artists, who have historically had a contentious relationship with cultural institutions and property well before net.art came about, is a reaction to this new and seemingly abrupt change in property relations that brought in a lot of money from a new social class of collectors who are perhaps more kitsch in their artistic tastes, open about their intent to speculate by (incorrectly) treating it as a commodity, and an overall confusion around both this and the highly technical nature of it all. It looks as though, with NFTs and digital art, there is no longer a way to do art online without commodification. But this perspective depends on mental models based on other types of commodification. It seems lost on many that similar to other types of art, the existence of an NFT of a particular digital image does not take away from the ability for others to enjoy it.

So why then is there so much focus on NFTs when DRM is an actually existing mechanism for creating digital scarcity? DRM prevents you from doing things like screenshotting a Netflix show, uploading copyrighted music on YouTube, or the iTunes store limiting the amount of devices that can store your purchased music. NFTs don't do this.

In an article written by artist and researcher on technical and ethical protocols Mat Dryhurst titled "Digital Scarcity Feasible Abundance and the Shock of the Nude", he pushes back against the claim made by critics that these technologies arbitrarily introduce scarcity to digital media:

> Digital media has always been scarce, because there is a rights holder conferred by law unless that rights holder renounces those rights with a license... No scarcity is being imposed on media, existing scarcity is being surfaced and experimented with.[15]

The truth is that the real scarcity lies in the realm of the law and how rights over digital media are recognised. Although platforms make money off of the content created by users, the rights to that content is still owned by the user, even if not formally registered.[16]

The financialisation of digital media has been happening for a long time at this point, mainly through advertising in order for big tech platforms to make revenue as users largely don't want to pay for digital media. For Dryhurst, "NFTs represent an elegant proposal to attempt what I would describe as feasible abundance, i.e., how can we make free media fair for the people creating it?" Tech platforms are essentially black boxes where we know financialisation happens, but we don't know all of the particular details since they are often considered business secrets. "Public blockchains, through making visible latent forces such as financing, unequal returns, or scarce and valuable ownership, are bringing long existing dynamics to the surface to be scrutinised. These forces are not new, they are nude." And so, similarly to the moral panics from social conservatives about nudity or other forms of sexual expression in media, critics of NFTs seem to be uncomfortable with viewing the naked truth about digital media.

Platform Risk vs Hyperstructure

While part of the distaste from the critics seems to also stem from their subjective feeling that NFT art lacks taste, this alone can't be the reason for the strong reaction NFTs have provoked. To understand this more deeply, we need to understand the incentives that the Big Tech platform economy runs on.

When content creators publish on any Big Tech platform, there is almost always a check using automated software for DRM, looking for anything that is under the IP of giant media conglomerates like Disney, Warner Bros, MGM, major music labels, etc. This has been a standard practice since well before NFTs ever existed. At the moment, becoming a content creator, similar to many other forms of work, is like making a deal with the devil. You may be lucky enough to amass the following that nets you enough in advertising revenue and sponsor deals, but you are beholden to the policies of the platform in terms of the percentage of ad revenue it shares with you, the DRM policies you must follow, its black box algorithm for showing your content to users, and, if the platform fails to make enough money for its shareholders or you are suddenly removed from a platform, it could also mean an end to sustainable income. Platforms, like any other business, like to privatise gains and socialise losses. This creates platform risk for all types of creators, pushing many of them to use multiple platforms at once in order to be shielded against the possibility of removal or the platform losing popularity. The inertia that goes along with joining a platform and finding your own followers also makes it difficult to bring a following to a new platform, creating even more inertia.

Part of what these platforms have done, similar to all capitalist businesses, is create mechanisms for people's labour to be fungible through the commodification of attention. Users' attention is commodified while creators' content is commodified through advertising. This system promotes having users engaged on platforms for as long as possible through weaponised and gamified emotion inducement. What at first was the promise of removing middlemen like record labels and studios has actually created more alienated artists, creators and users while platforms and their shareholders take in the profits, just like the cultural institutions that the net.art movement sought to criticise in the 1990s.

Similar to the first uses of tokens in crypto as (bad) money or equity in a barely existing crypto project via ICOs, the trajectory of NFTs has followed a similar path of popular use within a narrow mental model. The main reason is that using already existing models or concepts in important ways makes marketing and creating systems easier. In other words, the quickest to market are those with the simplest language and mental models that are accessible to an already existing large clientele. Continuing the trend of financial speculation and already existing libertarian ideas, JPEGs, but with auction houses that act as a membership card into an exclusive club, was an easy concept to sell. It also made it easy for media and critics to write and opine about it at the expense of more interesting examples that foreshadow new systems and create new types of relationships.

The typical process in the world of video games is for a central company to create a video game with in-game assets that are only relevant for the game in which they originate. The eight thousand NFT collection Loot is attempting to reverse that relationship by creating NFTs of a plain text list of randomised adventurer gear generated and stored on Ethereum. Each "loot bag" is one NFT that contains eight items: a piece for an adventurer's chest, foot, hand, head, neck, ring, waist, and weapon. For example the items could be a Short Sword, Leather Armor, a Pendant, a Heavy Belt, a Gold Ring of Power, etc. The stats, images and other functionality are intentionally omitted from the NFT to allow for others to build on top of the NFTs to create their own worlds and lore with it. Since its release in September 2021, multiple derivative projects have sprung up. These allow those who have a Loot NFT to purchase a generated image in various styles with the NFT loot bag inventory items on them and others that offer quests for your characters to go on.

Unlike the typical video game, Loot has no parent company and no way to gatekeep decisions made by others who build on top of it. It is a permissionless smart contract that can be used as long as the blockchain keeps going and therefore an infinite amount of games or derivative projects can be built from it. Many of these derivative projects also let people create their own bags of loot without the costs associated with the original Loot and only require the payment of the gas fee for using the Ethereum blockchain. No single company is able to ban players or control the future development of the game, at least without legitimacy, since their smart contracts would be open source and copyable, allowing access to anyone. This starts to get close to what Jacob Horne, co-founder of the NFT marketplace Zora, has termed "hyperstructure".

In his blog post "Hyperstructures", Horne outlines a new mental model to describe how crypto-enabled protocols can create new resilient public infrastructure.[17] More specifically, a hyperstructure is a protocol with some specific properties that runs on blockchains. It must be unstoppable (it runs for as long as the underlying blockchain exists), free (besides the gas cost), valuable, expansive (built-in incentives for participants in the protocol), permissionless (universally accessible and censorship resistant), positive sum (it creates a win-win environment for participants) and credibly neutral. So, while all hyperstructures are protocols, not all protocols are hyperstructures. What this highlights is the major difference between using a platform versus using a protocol. With smart contracts it is now possible to create public economic infrastructure as protocols that can run forever and for free, something a platform controlled by a centralised company is not able to do.

For an NFT to go to auction or on sale, it needs to interact with a separate smart contract that facilitates the listing and the type of market or auction the seller prefers. On many of the most popular NFT marketplaces like OpenSea, the platform takes a 2.5% fee from sales made using their smart contracts (much less than the 30% taken by Apple). Horne's conception of hyperstructures stems from his work on creating Zora, which differs from most other NFT marketplaces in that it takes no fees from sales. The Zora smart contracts for creating NFT markets is a type of hyperstructure that would continue to exist even without the presence of the Zora companies, which allows for other entities to make new frontends for artists or collectors. This is a different paradigm for content creators used to thinking about platform risk.

The implications of hyperstructures were tested when the largest NFT marketplace on the Tezos blockchain (a blockchain similar to Ethereum in that there are smart contract functionalities but using a different programming language) called Hicetnunc was abruptly ended by its founder. While in most cases this would have likely meant the end of all of the work that was created from their smart contracts, as was assumed by many in the beginning, within hours of the discontinuation of the website over fifty mirror sites went live where artists could continue to browse, mint and collect NFTs originally from Hicetnunc. Building protocols as hyperstructure helps alleviate many of the problems around platform risk for creators.

This potential to move away from platforms to using protocols on blockchains allows for new economic models that don't rely on the alienating dynamics of the attention and creator economy. While platforms like Patreon introduced a new way for creators to be paid by their most supportive fans via subscriptions, each creator needs to have their own separate page and do marketing for themselves. A very individualistic endeavour. Since Patreon makes money from transaction fees that patrons pay to creators, the incentives around the platform don't align with allowing creators to more easily collaborate by combining payments. Wanting to take advantage of the affordances of blockchains and its potential for a more collaborative form of content creation and funding, and realising they had overlapping audiences, the podcasters from Interdependence (co-hosted by Mat Dryhurst), New Models and Joshua Citarella, started Channel.

Essentially, Channel is a token-enabled RSS feed that gives access to all of the podcasts, including paid premium episodes that listeners would only otherwise receive through Patreon.[18] An RSS feed is a standardised content distribution method that is common for many types of media including newscasts, blogs and podcasts. Since it's standardised, it is interoperable in a way that can syndicate multiple media sources into one feed so you don't have to manually look up each separate source of media. Listeners who are interested in the offer from Channel can purchase an NFT that includes a digital artwork, and through verifying that they have the NFT on the Channel website they can get access to the RSS feed that syndicates all three podcasts. So, in this context, the NFTs are not just media, they are also content distribution and a direct connection between the premium listeners and the podcasts. At the same time, the podcasters are able to collectivise without necessarily losing the autonomy of their own show. They form a collective or "squad" that doesn't need to compete for the same group of listeners who would likely enjoy all three podcasts, greatly reducing the alienation between creators. Along with the RSS feed, those who purchased the first NFTs to be released can also directly interact with the team behind Channel to make suggestions and steer the direction of the project, in turn reducing the alienation between the listeners and the creators.

The ultimate goal of the project is to build it as a hyperstructure that stores subscription data and functions as a pseudonymous community registry. Assuming that it's successful, it's not difficult to see how this type of setup could be used for other types of content creators or artists to squad up in collectives rather than trying to compete according to the rules set by large tech platforms. It can be a way for creator communities to be portable, interoperable and durable in ways that are impossible using existing legacy platforms and payment processors.

For my own content creation for *The Blockchain Socialist*, while I use Patreon for fans to support my work through normal means, I also offer an alternative using crypto. People can access my podcast episodes through most podcast platforms, but occasionally I release bonus episodes available only to those who support me financially to thank them. While Patreon works for me most of the time, I know it is a centralised service which could at any point remove me from their platform. To not be dependent on a single centralised tech platform for monetisation, I also use Unlock Protocol so that fans can purchase an NFT to access bonus episodes directly on my website (theblockchainsocialist.com) through token gated posts.

The NFTs are unlimited supply and so non-speculative and can be purchased by anyone for a single monthly subscription price. The NFT is stored in the wallet of the user who purchased it and when visiting a token gated page, my website can check their wallet to see if they own the NFT. Once the NFT ownership is confirmed, the visitor can access the bonus content. Just like Patreon, in order to have access to the content, they will need to have paid the monthly subscription to the NFT. It's a way I've found to give myself more resilience from platform risk while also giving fans an alternative to use the tools I often talk about on my show and in my writing.

While hypemen try to onboard new people into NFTs using limiting mental models of speculating on art, digital scarcity and the Metaverse, and gatekeepers criticise those very incorrect representations of what NFTs are as a reason to stay away from them, it's clear that the story is not so simple. By deconstructing what NFTs are able to do and the implications of their being built on top of a resilient blockchain paired with crypto protocols as hyperstructures, we can begin to see that, while influenced by dystopian ideas about the Metaverse from *Snow Crash*, there are positive alternatives to that vision being built. Alternatives that focus on answering real problems for artists and content creators with the potential to change our currently existing toxic and alienating relationship with an Internet dominated by centralised tech giants.

SECTION 3
CRYPTO AS
COORDINATION

The least problematic representational model used to understand this space. Comparing crypto to a system for coordination has recently become popular as interest has grown in applications for blockchains that are not purely financial. Many already see money and finance as means to coordinate in the modern economy, with blockchains now able to complement or provide alternatives to legacy systems. Through the affordances of blockchains, technologists and artists have become interested in blockchain-enabled decentralised organisation like DAOs, as well as more traditional forms of decentralised organisations like cooperatives. A meta-critique of the status quo of crypto systems has led to the burgeoning Regenerative Finance (ReFi) movement, which is looking to combat the climate crisis through alternative financial systems that attempt to account for environmental externalities. While many of the most well-meaning people in the crypto space like to use the coordination metaphor, it commonly overlooks the importance of power relationships embedded in these systems. If those who are believers in crypto as a technology that can improve the world for the better are serious, then it's not just about coordination but being able to enact change. This means engaging in politics and using the technology to not only enhance democratic systems, but also to enable forms of political resistance when inevitable pushback comes from those who want to keep the sinking ship of the status quo afloat. Only then can one be considered a Blockchain Radical.

CHAPTER 8

DAOS AND DIGITAL COOPERATIVES: DECENTRALISING THE WORKPLACE AT SCALE

Robert Owen's was a true insight: market economy if left to evolve according to its own laws would create great and permanent evils.
— Karl Polanyi, *The Great Transformation: The Political and Economic Origins of Our Time*

"Socialism" became an English word in 1827, when Cooperative Magazine described Welsh reformer Robert Owen (1771–1858) as a socialist — an advocate of the view that industrial wealth should be owned in common, on a cooperative basis. Owen was the first Briton to grasp the meaning of the Industrial Revolution.
— Gary J. Dorrien, *Social Democracy in the Making: Political and Religious Roots of European Socialism*

Decentralisation is an old question that can be viewed through many lenses. In terms of government and politics in Europe, the quest for decentralisation can be traced as far back as the 1600s and into the 1800s, as multiple kingdoms suffered civil and revolutionary wars internally and in their colonies. These conflicts, led by the rising middle class and often supported by commoners, questioned the "divine right" of the royalty to rule. In a society that was moving further away from its feudal traditions, should the king still have as much centralised control? Or should power be more distributed through a governing body of many people? Does royalty deserve their centralisation of wealth over those they rule? These were important questions for the masses, who began recognising their collective power in limited ways as seen in the English Civil War and the French Revolution. One of the common arguments given against decentralisation was, and still is, about the difficulty in coordinating people and resources without centralised power, but over time the monarchists lost, leading to more republics and parliamentary democracies.

Jumping ahead to the present, it is easy to say that these conceptions of the nation state were flawed, as they led to the oppression of those who did not fit within its model, and they were the driving forces of atrocities committed during the First and Second World Wars, to give but two examples. However, today we do not find ourselves in such a different situation from those that led to the transition from divine kingdoms to nation states in Europe. In 2019, in the United States, it was reported that income inequality was the highest it had been since the Census Bureau started tracking it in 1967. Since the Great Recession, one of the drivers for this is wage disinflation for the middle class and asset inflation in the portfolios of the top 10% of earners due to the enactment of particular monetary and fiscal policies.[1] Although there has been a growth in movements to try to overturn and disrupt these policies, there are several barriers inherent to the American political landscape that need to be removed before significant changes are likely to occur.

The Internet and digital technologies are one of the more popular ways of promoting decentralisation abstractly without seemingly getting caught up in traditional politics. Decentralisation was important especially for the cypherpunks, as it was seen as necessary to decentralise the Internet to prevent it from becoming a surveillance dystopia that allows states to listen in on the private lives of citizens. Looking back now, it's easy to say their fears have been confirmed, but there were contradictions within many of the cypherpunk's approach, as they also advocated free market fundamentalism without acknowledging that capitalism itself tends toward monopoly and centralisation. Over time, without significant mechanisms for redistribution, capitalism centralises wealth and power in the hands of those who own capital. And there's little reason to believe that those who are in the upper echelons of power will not fight any attempt to regulate this process. Given this, even if redistribution can happen intermittently, because of the process of centralisation that capitalism entails through the profit incentive and capital accumulation, inequality will only increase over time as the rich get richer. In this way capitalism is a centralisation machine.

Some are able to reach extraordinary levels of power through the social relationships that define capitalism. This relationship is defined by the ability of the minority who own the companies, infrastructure and private property to coerce the majority of people who do not own any of these. This relationship is not just an economic one, but a power relationship that exists not just within one company, where owners are essentially miniature dictators by design, but also in aggregate throughout society. Those who do not own significant capital are thus exploited for their labour; profit thus represents the wages that are not paid to the workers who created the value of the products sold or services that were rendered by the company. If someone relies on their labour to make money to survive, they also have very little choice but to succumb to "agreeing" to being exploited, because it's better than starvation. Welfare and unemployment benefits may help some, but they vary by country and globally and we have been seeing the trend of once social-democratic countries undergo repeated bouts of austerity after each crisis, in which the social safety net is the first thing gutted, pushing the cost of the crisis onto the least well off.

So while the cypherpunks had good reason to promote decentralisation of digital infrastructure to bake privacy into the Internet, this should be supplemented with the decentralisation of the ownership of private property itself, so that the people who actually work can democratically manage the economy and society together, rather than leaving it to the collection of (some not so) mini dictatorships we call corporations and their billionaire owners. Even if the term often is misappropriated, decentralisation is an imperative in the blockchain world, and this obligation has created space for other areas of centralisation to be questioned. And one of the largest sources of centralisation in most people's lives is their 9-to-5, or the place people spend forty or more hours per week.

Cooperatives: Decentralisation within an Economic Organisation

Spurred by the need for remote work, COVID-19 caused working people to question the pre-pandemic habits around the spatial relationships between employee and employer. This is far from the first time the nature of work has been questioned. By the 1800s, capitalism had become the dominant mode of production in England, and joint-stock corporations, like the East India Company, accounted for at least half of the world's trade. Due to the disproportionate increase in wealth for those who owned the corporations versus those who worked in them, a movement to create an alternative form of organisation came about through the work of Robert Owen, William King and the Rochdale Pioneers; the cooperative, or coop.

The International Cooperative Alliance (ICA) defines coops as "people-centred enterprises owned, controlled and run by and for their members to realise their common economic, social, and cultural needs and aspirations". While a standard corporate hierarchy can be pyramidal, with the stock holders at the top making all the executive decisions and the workers below, in a worker cooperative structure, all workers own a share of the company and have a say and vote in the governance of the firm, with each worker having the same amount of votes. Cooperatives are to corporations what democracy is to a dictatorship. However, this is not the only type of cooperative. Consumer cooperatives are businesses that are owned and managed by the people who use their services. R.E.I. — which sells outdoor sporting equipment — is the largest consumer coop in the United States, and all credit unions are forms of financial consumer coops.

It's been proposed that worker ownership could save small businesses under the threat of closure due to worsening economic conditions while also protecting the employees, thanks to the likelihood of lower rates of internal inequality as workers decide jointly on rates of pay. For example, the Mondragon Corporation, based in the Basque region of Spain, is one of the largest and most successful cooperative enterprises. It is a federation of ninety-six worker coops employing more than 81,000 people, and selling in more than 150 countries in four industries. Mondragon coops have a CEO-to-line-worker pay ratio, ranging from 6-to-1 to 9-to-1, compared to the European average of 129-to-1 and the US average of 339-to-1.[2] Mondragon coops have also been less affected by economic downturns compared to standard hierarchical corporations.

Another good example is Emilia-Romagna in Italy, a region which is known for having one of the highest quality of life indices and lowest rates of unemployment in the country, partially because coops make up 30% of the region's GDP and involve two thirds of the population as members.[3] In the United States even, there has also been a major increase in trailer parks converting into community-owned coops to provide alternatives to the encroachment of private equity-funded parks that seek to maximise rent fees and minimise investment into infrastructure.[4] Even the global financial system that was criticised by the creator of Bitcoin is facilitated by a coop. SWIFT, the entity that enables banks around the world to send and receive information about financial transactions, is a cooperative society under Belgian law, owned by its member banks. Some of the largest banks and agricultural businesses are also coops, like Rabobank, Desjardins and Groupe Crédit Agricole.

Sceptics who may have never come across cooperatives before may ask, how can you coordinate a business, which is already difficult, by complicating things with democratic ownership? Surely you can't stay competitive enough if everything you do needs to be democratically decided on? Well, yes that's probably correct, but that's not how the majority of cooperatives are run.

Having every single decision made only through a majority vote by an entire organisation, especially a large one, is usually not a great practice. There are many ways to run a democratic organisation that don't require constant consensus and voting, something which can lead to burnout or make the process too slow to function effectively. While there are many different types of governance structures and philosophies in cooperatives, one that is becoming more popular among newer coops is called "sociocracy". In sociocracy, decisions are made through consent rather than consensus. Sociocracy does not expect or require full agreement for a decision to be made, but instead makes sure that there are no objections by the group. The point is that if it is good enough for now, it is at least safe enough to try. Members of a sociocratic organisation are able to vote on whether they fully consent to a decision, whether they object or whether they disagree with the decision but are able to live with it for now. This allows for a more granular type of political expression than is commonly allowed in democratic organisations focused on consensus.

While blockchain protocols commonly rely on consensus between all individual nodes to agree on the current state of the ledger, this is a much more difficult thing to achieve for human-based organisations. Consensus is simpler when what you are agreeing on is mathematically determined through cryptography. So, while blockchains are a kind of decentralised technological infrastructure that seek to get out of the dictatorial spaces owned by banks, governments and Big Tech, coops are a decentralisation of the workplace and the social relationships within it. Consensus for coops requires a process of social reasoning and deliberation designed to produce a shared culture and commitments, which is inherently more time-consuming than blockchain consensus.

The most recent evolution of the coop, made for a digital and connected world, is the platform coop, an alternative to venture capital-funded and centralised platforms, that puts stakeholders before shareholders. The term was first coined by New School professor Trebor Scholz in a *Medium* article in 2014 that criticised the sharing economy.[5] The sharing economy was represented by quickly (at the time) growing centralised platforms like Uber, Airbnb and Taskrabbit, that were able to tap into digital technologies to create new business models based on their platforms.

Platform coops were proposed to give workers that relied on work provided by these platforms ownership in the business and direct governance of the platform that directs their work, and to provide employee benefits that centralised platforms don't. For example, Proposition 22, recently passed as a referendum in California, exempts ride-sharing companies from treating drivers as employees, limiting workers' abilities to receive health insurance through the gig work platforms that provide for their income. It was reported that Uber, Lyft and DoorDash spent over $200 million on the "Yes on 22" campaign, which advocated in favour for these platform companies to not have to consider their drivers employees. Uber and Lyft drivers in California filed a lawsuit to try to overturn the bill, claiming it "illegally" excludes ride-hail drivers from the state workers' compensation program.[6]

Additionally, social media platforms are facing increasingly difficult choices on moderation and censorship, as research shows social media as an enabler of "fake news" that continues to have negative impacts on democracy. The growing trend for alternatives to platforms like Facebook and Twitter show that consumers want more decentralisation, privacy and choice in digital marketplaces, however the lack of success in creating them demonstrates the tremendous inertia created once a platform has solidified its place. They should be considered private monopolies in digital space that do everything they can to maintain their positions of power.

Some existing platform coops have been able to fill gaps in the market with success in various industries. Some examples include Stroudco, a platform coop based in the UK that helps farmers sell their products online, now also part of the thousands of food cooperatives around the world that make up the Open Food Network. Equal Care is a social care platform coop in the UK that uses a multi-stakeholder model (supported members, advocate members, investor members and worker members) to improve social care work conditions without increasing the cost of social care. Stocksy is a platform owned by photographers that sells stock photos at a fair price and practices fair profit-sharing with around 980 photographer shareholders. The Drivers Coop is a ride-hailing platform coop based in NYC which is similar to Uber except the drivers own part of the cooperative. Ampled is a platform coop, a mix of Patreon and Bandcamp, that focuses on musicians, where they are owners of the platform as well. While platform coops are often healthy businesses, they have serious obstacles in competing with their venture capital-funded start-up counterparts because the current policy environment for financing favours venture capital. However they do prove the upside of decentralised ownership in business for more democratic forms of work.

Decentralised Autonomous Organisations

In their 2016 book *Blockchain Revolution*, entrepreneurs and early blockchain hypemen Don and Alex Tapscott ask the question, "Why do you need a $60 billion company called Uber" when most of the processes centralised by Uber could be automated through smart contracts, reducing the costs for upkeep of the platform? With a blockchain, you could instead automate the administrative processes with smart contracts, and allow the drivers to own the platform themselves, similar to The Drivers Coop mentioned above, but with more automation. To some extent these entrepreneurs advocated a business model which was against their own interests. This was one of the early examples given to describe the potential impacts of a "decentralised autonomous organisation" (DAO) on a blockchain.

So what exactly are DAOs? If you search around, in common with other complex and emergent concepts, you'll likely encounter many, often divergent definitions. DAO is a term for an organisation using smart contracts to facilitate its own governance. It is sometimes simply defined as an online community with a joint bank account, but this is contested as many people have different ideas about what constitutes decentralisation, autonomy and even organisation. Since the experiment with "The DAO" (one of the first attempts at a real DAO), in which millions were stolen due to a bug in the smart contract code as discussed in a previous chapter, the ethos and expectations have changed significantly. The original term was Decentralised Autonomous Corporation (DAC), which focused on how a company could be run entirely on smart contracts, but Vitalik Buterin suggested changing the C to an O since corporations are far from the only type of organisational structure able to be impacted by smart contracts.

In a "A Pre-History of DAOs", Kei Kreutler goes through the many evolutions of what a DAO was imagined to be and the many different emergent forms it has taken since its first experiments.[7] She notes the overlap some DAOs have with the foundational ideals for the operation of cooperatives, the Rochdale Principles, including autonomy, open membership, democratic member control and others. But are DAOs digital cooperatives or another form of platform cooperative? The quick answer is neither.

Organisations can come in many different shapes and

sizes, with just as many types of goals and purposes in mind, which dictate how humans inside those organisations interact with one another. The same can be applied to what people are calling DAOs. If you hear about DAOs in the media, it will most probably be a DAO that tries to raise enough capital to purchase something as a group, often resulting in what can only be described as a financial frenzy. For example, ConstitutionDAO was an effort in November 2021 to purchase an original copy of the US constitution in a Sotheby's auction, in which they raised around $47 million in ether. They ended up losing the auction, likely because of the transparency of the amount they raised through the Ethereum blockchain made it easier for another bidder to know the exact price that would be out of reach for the DAO. After the bid was lost, those who gave to the DAO were refunded what was left, although much was lost in transaction fees.

This type of DAO is focused on joint investments and ventures. Founded by investors and basketball fans, Krause House DAO is trying to buy a professional NBA basketball team. If they were to succeed at some point, members of the DAO would take part in decisions affecting the operations of the team, including general management, ticketing, merchandising and partnerships. This is perhaps not unlike how cooperatively owned sports teams like the Green Bay Packers or FC Barcelona are owned. This type of collective capital-raising model for DAOs can be applied also for philanthropic purposes, as in the case of UkraineDAO, which was created to use crypto to raise money for the war efforts in Ukraine against the invasion from Russia. The crypto raised was used to fund organisations working on the ground in Ukraine, providing supplies.

Many of these types of DAOs could have instead just done a crowdfunding campaign on GoFundMe, but what DAOs offer that regular crowdfunding campaigns don't is a way to govern assets in many different ways with real value across borders, thanks to multisignature wallets or multisigs. You can think of a multisig as a joint bank account represented through a smart contract. Normal wallets native to a blockchain are largely meant for a single person. Multisigs, like a normal wallet and all smart contracts on Ethereum, have a public address that holds crypto assets for a group of wallets. You can encode the number of confirmations needed from other wallets that are part of the multisig in order to make a transaction, e.g., three out of five owners are required to confirm a transaction. The most common multisig contract is the one developed by Gnosis Safe, and at the time of writing has never been exploited by hackers.

There are also DAOs, that govern over entire protocols, especially those involved in DeFi. For example, MakerDAO, mentioned in a previous chapter, has a protocol for creating DAI, a stablecoin pegged to the US dollar through over-collateralisation with other crypto assets like ether. The management of those vaults, the interest rates and voting on proposals put forth to the community are handled through the MKR governance token. The more MKR someone has, the more power they have over voting for changes to the protocol, in much the same way that voting shares for a corporation work. This is usually referred to as token governance. Since holders of MKR can receive part of the fees generated by the DAO, the point of the MKR token is to align incentives around creating a system that people want to use (i.e., reasonable fees), but that also makes MKR holders money in fees. Vote for fees that are too high and fewer people will want to use the protocol. Too low and you won't make money from MKR.

While many of these DeFi protocols were the first types of organisations to start working toward becoming a DAO and thus the first to start experimentations around governance, it shouldn't be surprising that many took a skeuomorphic approach and tried representing something like a voting share with these tokens in order to decentralise governance. It may look to some like a token is just like a stock in a company, but as we recall from the earlier chapter on tokens, we need to keep in mind that they derive value and meaning based on the social contexts in which they are formed. It should always be remembered that governance on a blockchain is an open design space and many influential people, including Buterin himself, are critical of token-based governance, where one's degree of power is related to the amount of tokens one holds. When tokens are always sold on open markets through DEXs, anyone with a lot of money can always hold power over such a protocol, which isn't much of an alternative to the world we live in today.

While venture capital has undoubtedly taken a very keen interest in DAOs (particularly in the form of owning a significant amount of governance tokens in the newest and largest DeFi protocols), there is little reason to believe that this is a desirable thing. While there are certainly many who gladly take venture capital as a way to bootstrap and legitimise their DAO, in the DAO community there is a large emphasis on community ownership and opinions are divided on the role of external capital. This makes it unsurprising that many in it are also interested in the platform cooperative movement, proposing an alternative to the stereotypical venture capital-backed tech platform.

There are other projects out there that are focused on making it easy for people to deploy a DAO with customisable properties that allow them to determine how they want their DAO to be governed. Projects like DAOhaus have smart contract templates for DAO-based, multi-party ownership structures, governance processes and user interfaces for interacting with them on the Ethereum blockchain. You can choose to use one of their templates. The one best suited for worker cooperatives is called a Guild, or you can go "Hard Mode" and customise all of the settings yourself. Spinning up a DAO will also typically cost less than incorporation in most legal jurisdictions.

Of course, deploying a DAO doesn't give you the people

who would ultimately make up your DAO, but it does form the potential basis for your new or even already existing organisation. Lately there has been a lot of interest in cooperatives by those who first came across DAOs as they share many of the same issues around organising humans towards shared goals with minimal conflict. If DAOs reach the mainstream, they will likely have a profound effect on labour and how we coordinate with and relate to each other in the future, in either a dystopian or post-capitalist mode depending on how we react to and build out DAO tooling.

Social and Technological Relationships: A False Dichotomy

While for some it may be disconcerting to think about using a technological medium as a basis for socially relating to each other as humans, humans have been using technology as a mediator for our social relationships and as an extension of our selves for millennia. The Internet has been an extension of our ability to communicate with one another, just like the telephone, telegraph and writing letters on paper were before it. Sometimes those who take a default tech-critical or pessimistic view like to proclaim that "technology can't solve our problems" and that it's all about social relationships around the means of production. While this sentiment is understandable and not untrue in and of itself, it can lead to the idea that social and technological relationships are somehow completely separate from one another. It's not about social versus technological relationships, but about socio-technological relationships in which both interact with one another.

If we recall from the first chapter, most platforms and services we use over the Internet run on a client-server model for IT architecture. Within this technological arrangement, users must use clients or applications that can interact with centralised servers owned by large corporations. The technological relationship between the computers, devices and servers facilitates a particular social relationship in which there is clearly a hierarchy between the company who owns the data, including much of your personal data, and you as a user.

P2P architecture helped facilitate a new kind of social relationship, as seen with file-sharing services like Napster and Limewire where anybody could use their computer as a server to share files without permission with anybody else who wanted to download them. Even though the programs were shut down after long legal battles with media companies who wanted to control their intellectual property, decentralising music distribution still had a profound effect on the music industry.

According to the Recording Industry Association of America, from the 1980s to about 1999 (when Napster was released), the music industry was growing in total revenue at a steady pace, peaking at about $20 billion.[8] The emergence of Napster, however, triggered a steep decline, cutting music revenues in half within the next fifteen years now that people didn't need to purchase overpriced CDs to get their music. Over time the market responded with the iTunes Store and Spotify, which took the basic premise of Napster (access to limitless music), but with a better user interface for a monthly subscription and no fear of being charged for downloading music illegally. At the same time, this has changed how musicians are able to release music, are treated and paid. Artists only received an average of approximately $4,370 per one million streams on Spotify in 2022.[9] Here we can see how new technical structures can create new possibilities for facilitating social relationships that were not possible before, whether for better or for worse.

We can say that this relationship also exists in the opposite direction. The structure of a standard corporation is usually very hierarchical and like a pyramid, compared to a cooperative, which is much more flat hierarchically (and in wage differentials). The way that people in the two different organisations relate to one another is different, given that cooperatives require more democratic participation. At the same time, for many industries, in order to be able to compete, the use of digital technologies is a necessity for any number of functions. However, the vast majority of software meant for businesses is created with the social relationships of corporations and not cooperatives in mind, making it difficult for cooperatives to find the appropriate tools. This is because technological relationships help facilitate social ones. This was observed by the New Zealand-based cooperative Enspiral. Based on their experiences as part of Occupy Wall Street, they realised that there were few if any software tools out there that could allow for democratic deliberation, voting and so on. In response they developed a tool called Loomio which helps facilitate democratic participation in organisations. It's now become popular among many types of democratic organisations, including cooperatives who wish to take advantage of the digital while staying true to their principles. What this highlights again is that social and technological relationships cannot be cleanly separated from each other. The technological and social are intertwined in such a way that it makes more sense to refer to the totality of the system as socio-technological relationship.

Exit to Community

This framework can thus be broadly applied to the technological architecture of a blockchain and the social relationships it is able to facilitate. A big difference between blockchain-based identity versus your identity on legacy tech platforms with client-server architecture is that a company does not own your identity or the data that is produced from your account (your wallet). This means that the assets that you would own on a blockchain medium are yours to control, compared to client-server-based mediums that require a company to give you access to your assets. Let's use the example of "Exit to Community", a term first created by Nathan Schneider, journalist and Professor of Media Studies at the University of Colorado, who wrote extensively about his experience at Occupy Wall Street and collaborated with Scholz in organising the first platform co-op conference.[10] He wrote the first book mentioning platform cooperatives, *Everything for Everyone: The Radical Tradition That Is Shaping the Next Economy*, in 2018.

Exit to Community was first proposed in September 2016 by Schneider in an article in the *Guardian* calling for Twitter to be converted into a platform coop so that the most active users would have the ability to vote on things like how their data is monetised and community moderation.[11] As it stands, most start-up founders have two choices in order to get a pay-out for building a digital platform: IPO on the stock market or a buy-out from a larger company. Exit to Community is an alternative strategy in which founders can give or sell ownership shares of the digital platforms to the community that uses it. Users can purchase the shares in small amounts rather than selling most of their business to venture capital firms as many platforms have done.

There were many different reasons why the campaign for Twitter to undertake an Exit to Community wasn't successful, although there was little reason to believe that it would be. The article was largely meant to be a way to use a moment when Wall Street was hesitating on the platform to share the idea of an alternative ownership model. The transactional costs that were needed to organise all of the current investors as well as all of the users of Twitter to become stakeholders of the platform, and the highly complex legal apparatus needed to coordinate with users in various countries, would be too much.

Likely to the surprise of Schneider, the place where Exit to Community has seemed to take off the most is in crypto. One interesting example was the "airdrop" of the UNI token, a governance token used for the DEX Uniswap. On 16 September 2020, this DEX on the Ethereum blockchain created the UNI governance token to be used by token holders to vote on the direction of the project. 60% of the total supply was allocated to users based on their use of Uniswap, and a user that had used the platform only once could claim 400 tokens, worth over $1,000 at the time. The reason they were able to do this was because Uniswap was able to collect the addresses that were interacting with their smart contracts on the Ethereum blockchain.

Another example was the airdrop of the ENS token, a governance token used for the Ethereum Name Service mentioned in a previous chapter, as possibly the largest NFT project in existence. When the protocol was first released, it was stewarded entirely by the original ENS team, meaning anyone could start owning ".eth" names, but doing so meant you trusted the team. As the project was not decentralised, the team owned the protocol. For it to become a neutral public good, it needed to decentralise its ownership, and why not towards its most active users? Based on a combination of factors like the age and expiry dates of their ".eth" addresses, 25% of the tokens were distributed to users, 50% were given to a community treasury that can be influenced by those who hold the ENS tokens and a little less than 20% was given to core contributors. ENS token holders then choose to delegate their token votes to anyone who nominates themselves to be a delegate. The delegate can then vote with the total number of tokens they've been given towards proposals that have been made. Essentially, a very fluid form of parliamentary democracy governs this crypto protocol. While these two projects largely followed a token governance approach, with voting power being directly tied to the number of tokens one owns, as we have discovered this is not our only option, and we'll see some other governance models soon.

Thanks to the affordances of blockchains, we are starting to see the seeds for collective autonomous collaboration at a scale never before thought possible, and airdrops have been an important enabler for rudimentary forms of Exit to Community in the space. Some may be quick to say that it's the decentralisation of blockchains that enable this, but it's important to understand that decentralisation has many implications for relationships depending on the layer that is being decentralised, since describing something as being decentralised without context means very little. Something cannot be decentralised in its essence. In the article "Decentralize What?", Francis Tseng provides a compelling analysis of this claim, specifically with regard to the conflation of architectural and political decentralisation, especially in computer networks and systems. He makes the case, for instance, that architectural decentralisation, which blockchains have, can also be a desired property of the state surveillance apparatus. When the NSA controls all of the computers in a peer-to-peer network, it can be said to be architecturally decentralised but obviously still very politically centralised.

The important part here is that what is being decentralised in these examples is ownership. This was possible because of the combination of different layers being (de)centralised. While a blockchain is architecturally decentralised (comprised of many computers), it is logically centralised (it uses one monolithic data structure). This is the essence of a shared or distributed ledger. This combination of (de)centralisation creates the affordance of making something like Exit to Community possible, which in turn can help bring about political decentralisation through decentralised ownership over protocols that run on a blockchain.

Worker Cooperatives on the Blockchain

Some may be surprised by the influence of cooperativism in the blockchain space, but for others it was an obvious connection. In the early days of DAOs, during and even shortly after the infamous hack of "The DAO" on the Ethereum network, there were very few, if any, accepted software tools and smart contract standards for actually starting a DAO. Even during the ICO boom of 2017, there were very few dapps built out for people to use their ether cryptocurrency other than for investing in ICOs. This was the case for Ori Shimony in 2019 when he first co-founded dOrg.

While most attempts at DAOs before it were largely attempts at "decentralised" investment firms, dOrg was the first attempt at creating a DAO that provided services as a business. dOrg is a full-stack development collective that's helped build some of the largest crypto applications on the market today and it works similarly to a workers' cooperative. Every official employee at the company owns one share of the company's Vermont LLC. It was also the first legally recognised DAO in the United States. By completing projects for the company, you accumulate tokens and can use them to vote on company decisions. In a world where venture capital is everywhere, dOrg has managed to never need to raise any money, preventing any dilution of ownership that would otherwise have occurred.

Although he co-founded the organisation, Shimony holds no official leadership title and instead prefers taking a more fluid approach to positions in general. When a project is commissioned, a call is made internally in the DAO to see who, with the skills needed, is available to work on it. Once the people have been decided on, they create their own multisig for collecting payment from the commissioners of the project and for paying out those who are working on the project, with a percentage of the revenue also sent to the DAO. Depending on the project, people can assume different roles, and although there are no bosses, there is a natural hierarchy based on merit and skills where anybody could potentially step up as a leader depending on the situation.

All salaries and budgeting are publicly on the blockchain, so all payouts are visible to the entire organisation, making it transparent. Work hours and locations are flexible, but salaries are paid according to skillset no matter where the participants live. This has been a boon for many who work in countries with lower salaries and costs of living who are used to having large companies push for them to be paid less than their peers for the same work. Submitted work hours are approved by peers and paid out at the same time for everyone at each payment cycle.

Those who work on specific projects can often choose to get paid in either stablecoins or in the governance tokens underlying the projects they're working on. Additionally, workers can choose to either be paid out more when it's time to get paid, or receive more of what's termed a "reputation token" that gives them a larger share of the profit sharing that happens at the end of each quarter. This way one can choose to be paid more at once with less share of profits later or vice-versa. The reputation token is then also used to vote on important matters regarding the DAO.

The system provides a level of autonomy that can never be achieved in traditional corporations. In this type of social arrangement, mediated by the technology but not dominated by it, workers "own their projects". The autonomy of the small subgroups increases the democratic input that workers are able to impart while maintaining their ability to work internationally with their own level of commitment. This is possible not because they are trying to turn every process into a smart contract, but because there is an intentional design of interactions based on the needs of the people involved.

Another example of coops built using decentralised technologies is the Distributed Cooperative Organisation (DisCO) Coop model. The DisCO model presents itself as an alternative to the DAO model and takes a carefully planned approach enabled by blockchain technology in order to create value in ways that are cooperative, commons-oriented and rooted in feminist economics. The first cooperative to use this model was the Guerrilla Media Collective, a commons-oriented translation agency started by activist translators who wanted to combine voluntary translation work for activist causes, which provides translation and general communication services on a paid contractual basis. DisCOs allow members of the collective to be valued for the pro-bono work valued by its members as well as fairly compensating members for their paid translation work.

The DisCO model adds a post-capitalist complementary critique to the more general idea of what a DAO is that tries to keep the social aspects in the forefront. It is a framework that does not necessarily require a blockchain, but allows the space for one to be used to track value being generated by the coop. It focuses especially on trying to bring value to care work, which is commonly undertaken by women and often invisible and unpaid.

In regards to compensation, there are two valuable tools that are worth mentioning that have enabled novel ways for DAOs and open source communities to value labour: SourceCred and Coordinape. With SourceCred, groups can allocate tokens to contributors based on a customised algorithm that determines how much value they added to a project overall measured by how others in the group have been interacting with each other's work. This could be based on reactions received on platforms like Discord and GitHub contributions, similar to how Google's PageRank algorithm pushes sites with lots of references to the top of search results. The difference here is that the algorithm can be democratically determined. With Coordinape, each member of a group manually allocates tokens to other members based on how much they believe the other user has contributed. For example, everyone may be given one hundred tokens to allocate to everyone in their group for contributions made in the past two weeks. Once everyone has done so, this creates a visual social graph about what is most important and valuable to the community based on the flows of tokens being allocated. Everyone in the community can also see who is working on what and find opportunities for collaboration or to reduce duplication of effort. While it doesn't make much sense in most cases to rely solely on Coordinape for all types of labour and compensation, it can be a good supplement to encourage group cohesion and goal-directed work.

More Cooperatives on the Blockchain

Considered the "Delaware for cooperatives", Colorado is the home of at least three DAOs that are handled like cooperatives. The first is SporkDAO, which is the group that organises the ETHDenver hackathon and conference, one of the largest blockchain hackathons in the world hosted annually since February 2018.

ETHDenver's SporkDAO represents its evolution from a wholly owned, centrally controlled entity into a member-owned cooperative. Members are owners of the event and community activities, giving them an opportunity to develop connections with those who want to play an active role in building the community. On 26 June 2021, they created the SPORK token which was given out to previous attendees, speakers, sponsors, volunteers and artists that helped with events they hosted. As well as governing SporkDAO through voting on proposals, SPORK serves as the unit of account for the calculation of patronage to SporkDAO members when a profit has been made.

While SporkDAO is one of the few DAOs that is tied to a physical location, contributors to DAOs rarely live in the same place that their DAO is legally registered, if it is. There are also many that take a flexible approach to their work and may work part-time for several DAOs at once. This type of freelancer spirit makes it difficult for DAOs as places of employment to offer the usual benefits of a salaried position. This is especially difficult for Americans who usually have their health insurance tied to their place of work. Opolis is a digital employment cooperative that pools the resources of these workers together to provide health insurance, dental, vision, retirement accounts, disability and automated payroll, helping to bridge the gap for crypto natives who still need these basic benefits. It is also a DAO and uses its own token called WORK. Similar to SPORK, WORK is a unit of account for patronage distribution for members of the cooperative as well as giving voting power. The token is given to members when they use the payroll services, refer new members, help build the technological stack behind Opolis and so on.

What you might notice about these examples is that they use the blockchain-based tokens as a parallel system of ownership where tokens are equal to votes. This presents us with a potential issue since the technical definition of a cooperative under the principles of the ICA includes having a one member one vote system. So how does a DAO adhere to this principle of the ICA on a technological medium that was created to allow anyone to make as many identities as they want?

At the time of writing, Jonathan Mann has published a new song to the Internet every day for the past fourteen years. Also known as the Song A Day guy, there's a good chance you've heard one of his songs at some point since many, including "Baby Yoda Baby Baby Yoda", "The Hillary Shimmy Song", remixes of Alex Jones rants autotuned into a song and a duet he sang with his now ex-girlfriend about breaking up, have gone viral on platforms like YouTube.[12] His experience of being part of one of the first waves of creators on the Internet, becoming aware of the issues that came with relying on Big Tech to host and share his music, as well as being an avid collector, meant that after, learning about them in 2017, "he became interested in NFTs as a possible new tool."[13] After years of exploring and through his podcast *Digitally Rare* he figured out how he wanted to apply the technology to his music, while keeping the ethos of a cooperative and the principle of one member one vote.

Essentially, he turned all of his previously published songs from Song A Day into NFTs for anyone to collect. At the launch on New Year's Day 2022, a single wallet could only mint up to five songs and the collector could not know beforehand which song they would get.[14] Each song is accompanied by a piece of artwork created by one of many collaborating digital artists, and everything is stored through IPFS, the decentralised file storage solution and alternative to HTTP mentioned previously. Once all of the songs were collected, the NFTs could be traded and sold as the owner wanted. Now, every single day, Jonathan still shares a new song, which is put up for auction for that day for anyone to collect. This formed the basis for the creation of a larger project called SongADAO, which is a coop by Colorado law, where members own the copyrights, royalties and auction revenue from all of his music.

There are three levels of participation inside of the DAO. The first level is called "Listener", in which you've collected one of the NFTs of his music but are not part of the coop. To move to the next level, you need to verify your identity through an application called BrightID, a social identity platform that is able to verify that you don't use multiple accounts for different applications. It does this by asking you to attend "connection parties" where you meet others who want to get verified face to face over a video conference call. In that way many random but real humans are inspecting each other, making sure the other isn't a bot or some incredibly intelligent AI. Once you have several verifications under your belt, you're considered officially verified and a "Voter". At that point you can vote on what happens with the treasury from the revenues collected; for example, commissioning an artist to make art for the DAO. The highest level is "Builder", in which you sign a coop membership agreement so that you can be compensated legally from the coop for any work that you perform for the DAO/coop. You also don't necessarily need to spend money in order to join the DAO. In the spirit of doing something every day, every month a cohort of people can propose to do something every day for a month. If they pull it off — they will have to show photo evidence of it on Discord — they will be given one of the NFTs that were not sold in an auction and can join the DAO. Since there is no additional governance token, each member still only has one vote, no matter how many NFTs they hold, as long as they have verified their identity.

Those who are more familiar with the traditional cooperative world still may not be convinced by crypto projects that call themselves cooperatives, feeling they are not living up to the true meaning of the term. This is a long-standing conflict within the cooperative movement. There are those who want to be more restrictive about what is called a cooperative and others who think this is holding the cooperative movement back and is why it has not grown as much as it should have. Trebor Scholz, one of the most prominent academics on cooperatives and the creator of the term platform cooperatives, has this to say about the crypto world's growing interest in cooperatives:

> Many businesses have been eager to adopt the label of "cooperatives" or "community-owned businesses" in recent years. However, without corresponding economic and educational support, these proclamations are little more than empty gestures. True social enterprises are built on a foundation of democratic values and principles, with a commitment to giving workers a voice in decision-making and ensuring that everyone has an equal opportunity to succeed. Without this commitment, businesses will quickly revert to their old ways of doing things. So, while it is heartening to see more businesses in the crypto space adopting the label of "co-ops", we must also push for them to put their money where their mouth is and make the necessary investments in economic and educational support. Only then will we see lasting change.

Based on my own observations over the years, there is a significant number of people working in the DAO space with sympathies towards anti- and post-capitalist political tendencies, even if they don't feel like they have a mastery of all the seemingly difficult to grasp concepts and jargon, or don't necessarily embrace words like anarchist, socialist or communist. So why are so many people becoming seduced by the promise of DAOs? My theory is that the concept of DAOs represents a potential to decentralise one of the most centralised aspects of most people's lives — the workplace.

What's interesting about many definitions of DAOs is

how closely they brush up against collectivist tendencies and the political goals of community-ownership, transparent governance and direct democratic organisation, all of which are relevant for the left. However, while DAOs are an interesting, novel tool for coordinating over digital space, they don't have a clear political movement behind them to define the trajectory. There are seeds of a politics that is interested in decentralisation in one form or another, but this lack of clear political messaging is a reason why it's been so easy for Silicon Valley venture capitalists to co-opt DAOs through what gets dubbed the "Ownership Economy". This means that for many people, the first time they are exposed to the term is through the lens of venture capitalism. This makes it difficult for more progressive-minded people to take the idea seriously when these types of attempts only seek to give a "feeling of ownership" rather than ownership itself.

While DAOs are difficult to define concretely, cooperatives seem to be a good fit for what many well-meaning people would like DAOs to be if they are truly meant to be a real alternative to work in the current system. DAOs are not inherently cooperatives, but they can be adapted to co-operative principles. In 2021, half of the tech workforce expressed interest in joining a union and a new record for tech worker unions formed was achieved. Additionally, many technologists quit their Big Tech jobs for DAOs, having perhaps misunderstood them as being the same as cooperatives. People are looking for new ways to relate to their work, and the left should also be occupying this space to help explicate and maintain standards to be expected as worker-owners, and the cultural expectations in autonomous organisations. The left should see DAOs as a new space of exploration and experimentation, as many older unions and coops have fallen into decline.

CHAPTER 9

CLIMATE COLLAPSE: THE COORDINATION PROBLEM OF OUR LIFETIME

It is clear that we are unsure as to what our long-lived pollutants are doing to our environment; however, there seems to be no doubt that the potential damage to our environment could be severe.
— E. Robinson and R.C. Robbins, *Sources, Abundance, and Fate of Gaseous Atmospheric Pollutants*, final report to the American Petroleum Institute, 1968

In the fall of 2003, British Petroleum (BP), one of the largest non-state-owned oil companies in the world, began a very successful advertising campaign, pushing for people to start measuring their own personal "carbon footprint".[1] The commercial begins with the question, "What size is your carbon footprint?", after which a series of people (likely actors) explain what they believe the term "carbon footprint" means, guiltily implying that their lifestyle choices were hurting the environment. The last third of the commercial includes the line, "We can all do more to emit less", along with a description of how BP was working on projects to reduce its own emissions. On the surface, the purpose of the campaign was to get people to visit BP's "carbon footprint calculator" website, but digging deeper, it's clear that the intentions were much more sinister.

What was the purpose behind legitimising the term "carbon footprint"? Since the campaign, the term has exploded in use and our understanding of climate change and what we need to do in order to prevent it has been framed by the idea of climate change as a personal failing. We each need to be allotting ourselves a budget of carbon, and if you go above that, climate change is your fault. This type of framing plays on well-meaning people's sense of personal responsibility and downplays systemic issues in regard to greenhouse gas emissions. When you live in a community that has no public transport or bike lanes and you need to travel long distances, how can you as an individual be blamed for wanting a car? At the same time, while the individual citizen is supposed to worry about the emissions quantified in their carbon footprint, large oil companies have been funding lobbying efforts to prevent cities from building infrastructure that would allow for less carbon-intensive modes of transportation and energy use in order to justify pumping more fossil fuels. The campaign was an early example of "greenwashing", a marketing trick to convince the public that a company's practices, policies and product are environmentally friendly. It obscures the need for systemic solutions that solve the issue at its root, instead forcing you to make "better" consumer choices within a range of options in which you can largely only choose the least bad.

One of the largest funders of climate disinformation in their attempt to prevent action on transitioning away from fossil fuels has been the group of fossil fuel corporations, lobbyists and politicians known as "Big Oil". Reports have shown that as early as 1968,[2] one of the largest oil and gas companies in the world, Exxon, already knew that climate change was happening due to the burning of fossil fuels and would continue to have detrimental effects on global natural ecosystems.[3] That year, leading pollution-control consultants for the oil industry suggested that carbon dioxide produced from burning fossil fuels deserved the same attention as smog and soot, warning that "If CO_2 levels continue to rise at present rates, it is likely that noticeable increases in temperature could occur", and "Changes in temperature on the world-wide scale could cause major changes in the earth's atmosphere over the next several hundred years including change in the polar ice caps". However, instead of sharing the results of the report to the world, Exxon kept them hidden and funded campaigns for climate change denial.[4] Looking back, it's clear that they were very successful at delaying climate action by sowing doubt in the public sphere.[5]

The ugly truth is that, under capitalism, it will almost always be more profitable to keep the existing system in place than to change it for the social good. For the thousands of companies that make their money from the extraction of fossil fuels, it is in their financial interests to pollute rather than change their practices to become more sustainable in the short term. This becomes more insidious when you consider that all of these oil companies also do extensive modelling in order to predict what effect climate change will have on the environment and on their ability to extract even more oil and gas in the future. Knowing all of this can make one feel like there is simply little to nothing that can be done. In fact, many climate scientists express feelings of depression due to the inaction on climate change.[6] The framing of a personal carbon footprint has exacerbated the issue, pushing many well-intentioned and liberal-minded individuals to think that they can eat organic or voluntarily pay extra while buying flight tickets to offset their carbon emissions, and that therefore those who do not do so are simply not doing their part. Of course, people should make better choices for the environment when they can, but this cannot be considered a viable strategy for systemic change, and this type of individual-moralistic thinking has bled heavily into discussions about cryptocurrency as well, particularly with regards to its energy use.

This is one of the most common critiques of cryptocurrency, leading some to call for a global ban on it. However, while there are understandable frustrations and many legitimate criticisms, often these attacks come from a misunderstanding of the crucial socio-technological aspects of blockchains. The solutions proposed, like a global ban, paint with too broad a brush, besides the likely infeasibility of such a proposal. In many ways, ameliorating the worst of the climate crisis that has already begun is an issue, and to ignore or ban a technological infrastructure that allows for coordination in ways that were not easily possible before would be a mistake.

A Recap of Proof of Work

As you may recall in the first chapters, Bitcoin uses a consensus mechanism called proof of work (PoW) in order to get nodes on the Bitcoin network to agree on the current state of the Bitcoin ledger. To quickly recap, the consensus mechanism is necessary in order to solve the double spend problem, which states that for a digital currency without a centralised authority to be possible, someone cannot be able to spend their funds more than once. The first step in solving the problem is to build a decentralised network, but this poses the Byzantine general's problem, which is a generic problem in distributed computing where a concerted strategy is needed to avoid catastrophic failure of the system, but some of its actors are unreliable. The name of the problem is taken from an analogy in which a group of generals and their armies are surrounding an enemy fort and in order to successfully take it, they must coordinate together such that all of them attack at the same time. There is a chance though that some of the generals are traitors and may lie about attacking the fort. For a peer-to-peer network like a blockchain, this problem is solved by all of the nodes following the specific rules of the protocol to come to agreement in a coordinated fashion.

In the protocol, miners compete with each other to solve a difficult and provably random maths problem using cryptography. Miners are essentially participating in a game of probability where their odds of winning increase if they can make new guesses faster than others. The game is played through the use of cryptographic hashes. A hash is the output of a hash function that has received a string of data as an input. A hash function is one-directional and its hash output is random and always the same size. It is always impossible to guess what the input of a hash output would be and similar inputs create drastically different outputs.

In Bitcoin's PoW, miners are competing to create a hash starting with some number of zeros with 1) the inputs of all transactions recently sent to the network, 2) the hash created to make the previous block, and 3) a random number called a nonce. If they guess first, they can "mine" the next block of transactions to add to the blockchain. Miners are incentivised to solve this problem because they also win newly created bitcoins. Winning miners are also given the transaction fees paid by people to get their transaction added to the new block. This means the more you pay for a transaction, the more likely you are to get your transaction verified by a miner sooner.

On the surface, hashing is a useful way to hide information, but in PoW, Bitcoin makes an unholy alliance between cryptographic hashing and free market competition. Since 1 and 2 are inputs that cannot be changed, the only way a miner can make new guesses is by changing 3, the nonce. Combined with the logic of profit-seeking under capitalism, this means that miners are also incentivised to use specialised hardware that is really good at doing one thing, guessing. The faster you can guess, the more likely you are to create a hash with the appropriate amount of zeros at the beginning. The more zeros needed, the more difficult the competition is, which is adjusted so that a block is created around every ten minutes. This in turn creates an arms race for the fastest guessing machine, and the more you have, the greater your chances of making the right hash and earning a profit. On top of that, these machines use a considerable amount of energy.

How quickly a miner is able to make new guesses for the winning hash is called its hashing power. Therefore hashing power is a direct way to quantify and compare the strengths of different miners. The total hashing power of all of the miners combined also gives us a relative idea of how secure the network is from direct attacks. The original logic behind the PoW algorithm designed by Satoshi was to ensure the safety of the system from bad actors that wanted to take the whole thing down and to make it impossible to cheat. It should be very difficult for one mining entity to reach over 50% of the total hashing power as that would give them enough power over the network to corrupt the system.

It's important to note that Bitcoin's PoW was the first successful attempt at creating a Byzantine fault-tolerant algorithm for a digital currency that was built on a decentralised network. Since its inception, there have been very few modifications to the protocol, in part because many in the bitcoin maximalist community find it a feature and not a bug that the algorithm works this way. Similarly to those who take holy texts written thousands of years ago very literally, any changes to the word of the messiah, Satoshi Nakamoto, represented though the code, is akin to heresy in the bitcoin maximalist religion.

Additionally, it's crucial to understand that the largest miners of bitcoin are businesses. They want to increase revenue through rewards and decrease costs by paying as little as possible for electricity. This means that they are stuck in a feedback loop of buying more and stronger equipment when prices increase and tend to set up in places where electricity is cheap. Many places with cheap electricity get much of it from renewable resources like hydroelectric or geothermal, however this is not always the case. In Iran, for example, since mosques are not obligated to pay for their electricity use, some have set up bitcoin mining operations inside of them, and Iran produces most of its electricity from its own oil reserves.[7]

While many of the largest entities mining bitcoin are actually pools of many different miners sharing their hashing power, they still fall under the centralising effects of capitalism. Capitalism, an economic system that centralises wealth over time as more competitors lose on the market, has led to fewer bitcoin mining entities and the ones that remain are quite large.

Some people argue that bitcoin miners are helping grow the renewable energy market by incentivising the manufacture of more renewable energy infrastructure, however, even if that were true, it is wrong to classify renewable energy mining operations as either carbon-free or entirely environmentally-friendly. Some of the renewable energy claims about Bitcoin stem from the fact that many miners have congregated around places with hydropower from dams, but there are arguments around whether hydropower is clean energy due to its environmental effects.[8] Building solar panels and the batteries needed to store the energy also requires a significant amount of lithium which requires traditional mining of the rare metal in places like the Democratic Republic of the Congo, which has also suffered extensive environmental damage due to this extractive industry. The issue is multi-faceted and complex. Due to an inability to price in externalities like environmental damage, climate action cannot be coordinated within the logic of capitalism.

Moral Panics and Brandolini's Law

In 1999, at the height of the tech boom and rise of the Internet, an article in *Forbes* by Peter Huber and Mark Mills raised concerns that the Internet was using 8% of all US electricity, and that by 2020 it would take up nearly 50%.[9] At the time, the information technology industry had captured the imagination of American society as a force that would transform consumer lifestyles as well as business practices. It was therefore plausible that such an important part of the US economy would use a lot of electricity, which is why the statistics were reported so widely. However, creating credible estimates of information technology electricity requirements can be difficult. Data underlying the research are not known with precision, empirical data are limited and the most useful data are often proprietary, while the technology changes so rapidly that even accurate data becomes obsolete very quickly. Nonetheless, within these limitations, estimates have been made, though they've received different degrees of media attention.

A subsequent study by Koomey et al found that Huber and Mills' estimate for the power use of the Internet was at least a factor of eight too high, however, by then it was already too late.[10] The narrative stuck, and those who could benefit from such incorrect data did. When California entered into an electricity crisis in 2000 and 2001 and rolling blackouts became common, some were insisting that the issue was California's growing computer and Internet culture. What had actually happened was that traders from firms like Enron, which would go bankrupt by the end of 2001, were manipulating the market, increasing the price of electricity by decreasing supply, and this Internet energy use narrative was a convenient weapon to sow doubt about the role financial actors had in the crisis. Dr Jonathan Koomey, who has now been recognised as one of the leading experts in understanding the environmental effects of information technology and measuring the energy use associated with it, co-wrote a paper titled "Sorry, Wrong Number: The Use and Misuse of Numerical Facts in Analysis and Media Reporting of Energy Issues". It covered four different incidences where incorrect data about energy use and consumption were uncritically published by the media (including the Huber and Mills example above) and summarised the issue:

> The claim that information technology uses large amounts of electric power proliferated quickly, driven by a superficially plausible story line and a high-profile crisis in the California electricity sector. *Forbes* itself lent credibility to the argument simply by publishing it. The trade press and the popular media repeated the key claims in the *Forbes* article, often without citing a source, thus enshrining the erroneous statistics as common knowledge. Leaders in

business, government, and academia were misled by this barrage of media attention and cited the statistics widely, thus ensuring their proliferation.[11]

It was only after the bankruptcy of Enron, the recall of the California governor, and years of peer-reviewed research that the situation was properly understood. In this example, we can see how misinformation can cause moral panics, where an often incorrect fear spreads, exacerbated by mass media piggybacking on legitimate fears of climate change.

Things like carbon footprint estimations of new technologies are also quite difficult to discuss publicly because they are deeply technical processes. It's hard to have conversations with laymen about the technicalities of how to choose the appropriate assumptions for the estimations made, and so instead the general public have to rely on whoever is designated an expert, something which is by extension determined by the media they consume.

A similar dynamic is at play when it comes to estimating the energy usage of proof of work cryptocurrencies like Bitcoin, where it is not uncommon to find estimations that Bitcoin uses the same amount of energy as a small-to-medium-sized European country. Before late 2018, almost all estimates of Bitcoin electricity use in the media relied heavily or exclusively on estimates from the website *Digiconomist*, which was started by Alex de Vries, a Dutch economist.[12] de Vries summarises his estimates through a "Bitcoin energy consumption index", which includes a line graph that calculates the estimated daily terawatt-hours (TWh) of energy used by Bitcoin using a formula with several base assumptions and inputs that can be fed by publicly accessible information. Through his methodology, he used inputs from 31 July 2018 through 19 November 2018 to claim the Bitcoin network used 73.12146 TWh/year for the year of 2018.

In May 2019, Coin Center, a non-profit advocacy group focused on public policy around cryptocurrencies, commissioned a research report by Dr Jonathan Koomey (author of the "Sorry, Wrong Number" paper discussed above[13]) to review the various studies on the energy use of Bitcoin.[14] Not a crypto advocate himself, but using similar methodologies to previous studies, Koomey found many issues with the numbers published by *Digiconomist*, which was one of the studies included in the review. He noted that while the approach has the advantage of being tractable using available data, it relies on error-prone assumptions about economic parameters and bitcoin miner behaviour (e.g., optimal allocation of mining resources) to estimate physical characteristics of the technological system. He states:

> Real economic systems may tend toward optimality, but they often don't get close because of transaction costs, cognitive failures, and other imperfections in people and institutions. In addition, the assumptions used by *Digiconomist* (like 60% of Bitcoin revenues equalling electricity costs and 5¢ US/kWh being the electricity price) are so simplistic as to make any careful analyst wary.

In fact, the 73.12146 TWh claimed by Digiconomist for 2018 is a highly questionable estimate, given that the price of bitcoin, an important input for the stated methodology because prices influence how much energy miners will use, fluctuated by over 40% during the period. There was also no clarity over which periods the average price of bitcoin was taken to lead to the estimate.

Koomey also pointed out many other issues with the estimations and assumptions in this widely reported source, making it difficult to conclude that the method used could be a reliable indicator of Bitcoin electricity use. Of the six studies reviewed in the report, Koomey found that three of them were credible estimates that agreed with each other and the other three had serious shortcomings, including the one from *Digiconomist*. Based on one of the credible studies, the Bitcoin network used five gigawatts of power on 30 June 2018. To make a comparison, one gigawatt is equal to about 364 utility-scale wind turbines.[15] Converting the five gigawatts to annual electricity consumption, that would equal 44 TWh, almost half of the claim made by *Digiconomist* and equal to about 0.2% of global electricity use.

Digiconomist also reported on the electricity consumption of Ethereum before it switched to Proof of Stake (PoS) and was using PoW for its consensus mechanism. Based on recommendations made by Koomey in making estimates for PoW cryptocurrency networks, artist and developer Kyle McDonald performed his own analysis of Ethereum and produced similar criticisms of *Digiconomist*'s findings. To summarise the issues with estimates made by *Digiconomist* for Koomey and McDonald, they take a top-down approach to calculations, rather than a bottom-up one. Instead of starting from the bottom, understanding the energy usage of the machines involved in PoW, *Digiconomist* starts their inputs from the top, assuming a fixed portion of mining revenue is spent on expenses like electricity and hardware. They estimate what miners must be spending on electricity, and how much electricity they are using, by working backwards from their mining revenue. McDonald performed his own analysis and concluded that the energy use and carbon emissions of the Ethereum network were closer to the "minimum estimate" from *Digiconomist*, quite a bit lower than the estimate that is often quoted in the media.[16] The study suggested the total electricity use for 2018 was 9.9 TWh, while *Digiconomist* put their estimate at 20.8 TWh.

These rebuttals and critiques of course have not reduced the media attention and subsequent moral panic around energy use of cryptocurrency networks. The rebuttals were in no way defences of the energy use of cryptocurrency, but they are simply likely to be more accurate based on the methodology used. One of the issues crypto and blockchain advocates face is that energy use is a difficult topic to discuss with any nuance because it is filled with complex technicalities that to a laymen may seem to not matter, but in reality are highly consequential. And of course, for the media companies, nuanced conclusions are not compelling headlines to sell to readers.

The issue can be summarised by what has been termed "Brandolini's Law", which states that "The amount of energy needed to refute [nonsense] is an order of magnitude bigger than to produce it".[17] Unfortunately, debunking misinformation necessarily always lags behind the creation of misinformation, and in the world we live in today information can spread across the globe in an instant. Peer review attempts to fix this, but is slow in comparison. Ideally, analysts and the media would show restraint before pushing partial narratives. However, the attention economy works against this, and it is often only the prospect of reputational damage that can persuade analysts to exercise caution. But what is reputation when the next controversial factoid is released the next day and the conversation has moved on?

Another issue with current discussion around energy use being framed so heavily by cryptocurrencies is how it restricts the scope of energy use scrutiny, thereby slowing the rate at which we can properly identify feasible routes for climate action. It's attention-grabbing when headlines claim a single Ethereum or Bitcoin transaction uses up the same amount of energy as hundreds or thousands of European households. However, it ignores the fact that the largest polluter in the world is the US military and that it is the might of the US that backs the power of the US dollar around the globe.[18] We also have very little information about the energy use of tech corporations like Google, Amazon or Meta that have massive data centres all over the world, since that information is behind closed doors. The estimates that we can make on cryptocurrency networks are based heavily on data that is inherently publicly available, unlike with corporate or military infrastructures.

This is not a defence of the high energy use of cryptocurrencies, but an attempt to be honest and accurate about the current state of the discussion in much of the popular media and many progressive circles. Similar to the effects of the framing developed by BP on carbon footprints, trying to measure the amount of carbon per transaction puts the blame on the individual and misunderstands the roots of the energy consumption. McDonald states:

> The Ethereum network is a bit like your home network router. When you turn on your home router, it uses a fixed amount of energy whether you are streaming high-resolution movies or just sending emails. Ethereum also uses a fixed amount of energy regardless of how many transactions are on the network (at least, during normal activity). Because there is no direct marginal increase in energy from additional use, this makes the question of responsibility a philosophical one rather than a technical one. Clearly the responsibility for the emissions should belong to those who are investing in and profiting from the system. But dividing the total emissions per day by the total transactions per day might give a sense of scale, but it could be more misleading than helpful.[19]

For those who are concerned about the environment, their anger would be better directed at the institutions that have been delaying the transition away from fossil fuels for half a century, rather than artists exploring NFTs for their artistic practice. Instead, we should be digging deeper to identify the systemic issues that are leading to increased energy use across the globe every year as we face the prospect of climate collapse within much of the population's lifetime. What are the patterns of behaviour that are being socially reproduced to prevent swift climate action and how do we reverse them? What does it say about us as a society that it is so profitable for people to be mining supposedly useless cryptocurrency? Would a global ban on cryptocurrency get us any closer to reaching climate goals, or would the unintended consequences be too severe? Is there an alternative to energy-intensive PoW?

The Merge to Proof of Stake

Much of what people have said about PoW energy use on Ethereum has become obsolete at this point. While it's unlikely that Bitcoin will ever move to a different consensus mechanism, and the implications of that for electricity use should certainly be studied and scrutinised, the second largest cryptocurrency by market cap has moved away from PoW, as was planned since its launch, to Proof of Stake (PoS).

PoS is where a blockchain network is secured by stakers who "stake", or lock, some of the native cryptocurrency, in batches of 32 ether in the case of Ethereum. The more someone stakes, the more likely they are to be randomly chosen by an algorithm to validate the next block on the blockchain. If a chosen staker is found to be attempting to cheat the system, they can be "slashed" or lose the cryptocurrency that they have staked, enforcing the rules laid out by the protocol. The hardware needs of a staking node are a fraction of what's needed for a mining node and can be as little as a Raspberry Pi or any other miniature portable computer. All that's needed is sufficient memory to hold the full state of the blockchain and maybe at least eight gigabytes of RAM, depending on the requirements.

PoS has been around for several years now, with many of the newest blockchain networks like Cosmos, Cardano and Tezos using some version of it without any serious security breach to their chain. Since Ethereum started before much research into or real-world examples of PoS existed, it had the difficult task of creating a completely new consensus mechanism at the same time as allowing their PoW chain to continue, analogous to trying to fix an aeroplane when it's already in the air. The way it did this was by creating a parallel blockchain called the Beacon Chain that performed the task of the PoS. Once the Beacon Chain was connected to the Ethereum mainnet while it was running PoW, the entire network officially moved to PoS, making Ethereum miners obsolete in the process. This process was dubbed "the Merge" by the Ethereum Foundation.[20]

In this setup, the two chains work as one to provide all the features that the PoW Ethereum chain offered while now securing it through PoS. The Beacon Chain did not replace the function of executing transactions, but instead only focuses on coordinating stakers for facilitating the consensus mechanism. Hence why it's sometimes referred to as the "consensus layer". The original Ethereum mainnet chain continues to process transaction and smart contract interactions. Sometimes this chain is referred to as the "execution layer".

Even according to *Digiconomist*, the Merge reduced Ethereum's energy consumption by at least 99.84%.[21] To put this into perspective, if we compare the relative energy use of Bitcoin with the two versions of Ethereum, using height as an analogy, Bitcoin would be equal to the Burj Khalifa, PoW Ethereum would be equal to the leaning Tower of Pisa and the PoS Ethereum would be equal to a screw. While some may try to downplay the significance of the technical achievement of massively decreasing energy consumption and the carbon emissions for a decentralised network currently in use, there are few if any other examples of something like this being achieved. There has not been a single corporation or government agency to publicly announce plans to reduce their emissions by such a large factor, actively communicate on its progress, have constant real-time information to confirm the claims and achieve it without being forced to by any other institution. Will the media coverage shift when it comes to reporting on Ethereum energy use? It's hard to say at this moment, since little has been said about the event in mainstream media, but it's likely that many critics will still not be sold.

Criticisms will likely shift towards the pitfalls of a PoS system. Does PoS still produce inequality? Yes, because it still follows the logic of capitalism, and PoS was never posited as a fix for capitalism. Ironically, many of the progressive critics are in agreement with right-wing Bitcoin-maximalists that PoS is a "rich get richer" scheme, since those with more wealth to stake earn more rewards. The bitcoin maximalist position for PoW over PoS claims that stakers are able to compound their wealth which only comes from owning the native cryptocurrency, whereas in PoW anyone can buy mining equipment. What this claim misses is that miners are able to take advantage of economies of scale inherent to the physical operations of mining operations. Wealthy miners are able to buy equipment in bulk and have access to cheaper electricity than poorer miners, while a cryptocurrency itself will cost about the same for everyone. While those who bought the cryptocurrency early are more likely to receive more benefits from staking than those who come later, a similar dynamic is at play with miners as well. As it stands, it is very difficult for the general public to begin mining bitcoins without significant capital up front. We have seen the centralisation effects of capitalism on Bitcoin today where the majority of mining power comes from organised operations and rarely from hobbyists in their bedroom. Considering the significantly lower costs for equipment as well as need for electricity for stakers, engaging in staking is much more attainable, especially with the creation of staking pools which allow people to pool their crypto together in order to reach the 32 ether minimum needed to begin staking.

A study by chainleft.eth compared the centralising forces of PoW against PoS assuming much higher operating costs for PoW, equal living expenses, a 2% annual depreciation on mining equipment, a 10% annual reward base for both and a 5% economies of scale effect on operational and equipment costs.[22] The model showed that wealth inequality between rich and poor miners increased by 6.2% within the PoW system, whereas the number was 0.9% for PoS. The wealth gap between the rich and the poor increases much more in a PoW network than in a PoS network according to their estimate. The conclusion to be drawn is that while both are centralising-over-time, PoS at least does not centralise faster than PoW does.

Still, some may claim that neither are good enough and that all cryptocurrency networks should still be banned at a global scale. We've alluded to the reasons why this is problematic for activists but we will go into more detail later.

The Emergence of Regenerative Finance

Discussions around energy use in the face of climate collapse often tend towards a moralistic judgement of what is and is not worth doing. When some estimates say we have only a few years left to dramatically decrease our carbon emissions to prevent the worst from happening, it's easy to look at the way cryptocurrencies are reported on in the media and conclude that a decentralised network dedicated to gambling isn't something that should exist. This is a reasonable position to take and it is distressing seeing masses of pseudo-anonymous investors using this new global coordination technology in order to risk their life savings on some of the most ludicrous financial products one could think of. In crypto speak, these types of people are referred to as "degens" (short for degenerates).

With the pandemic and lockdowns that began in 2020, people began looking even more to the Internet in order to pass the time. As a result, the technology and user interfaces for DeFi applications built on Ethereum became friendlier for new users, and extra spending money became available through government support programs. It was a perfect mix of conditions for DeFi to grow. Total value locked in DeFi was $690.9 million on 1 January 2020, growing to $11.73 billion by November 2020.[23] Even in mid-February 2023, after a crash that has seen prices get cut by more than 50%, the total value locked in DeFi on Ethereum is approximately $45 billion.[24] Needless to say, although it does not come close to the size of the US financial services industry, which is well into the trillions of dollars, DeFi has become significant. For context, Apple had a market cap of about $2.5 trillion in May 2022. The growth in DeFi was a result of hype and speculation led by crypto marketers, hypemen and scam artists for people drawn into crypto by inflated promises of getting rich quick through dog memes. It was clear, however, for those who have more idealistic goals for the development of the technology and the culture behind it, that this was not a good direction to be going in.

One of the attempts to shift much of the resources and capital going into crypto towards climate-related projects has been termed Regenerative Finance, or ReFi. ReFi projects generally involve attempting to account for and regenerate what is normally considered a negative externality, especially when it comes to nature and climate. That sounds laudable, but is this just another form of greenwashing?

Many of the first projects to adopt the ReFi banner have been focused on carbon credits in one form or another. Existing carbon markets generally run on a "cap and trade" system where government bodies or a voluntary third-party system set a cap, or maximum amount of carbon dioxide that a single company is allowed to emit. That is then divided into credits that companies can use as their allowance for carbon emissions. If a company uses up all of their credits, they will then need to purchase credits from another company that has extra. As the maximum decreases every year, the credits should become more expensive for companies that choose not to decarbonise their business. While in theory this sounds like a good idea for pricing negative externalities, the issue so far, according to some economists, has been that the system has failed because the prices of carbon are much too low, as are the fines that companies face for not complying to environmental regulations.

Two of the projects that have sought to ameliorate the current issues with carbon markets by making it easier to purchase carbon credits through tokenisation are Toucan Protocol and KlimaDAO Toucan, launched in October 2021 as the infrastructure provider behind Base Carbon Tonne (BCT), a carbon reference token. Each token represents one tonne of carbon from the Verra Verified Carbon Unit (VCU) registry. Verra is a major voluntary carbon credit issuer and each VCU in their registry represents emissions savings that have been measured and audited by independent third parties. Toucan tokenises VCUs as BCT on a blockchain and because BCT is a fungible ERC-20 token it can be directly integrated into any DeFi application. KlimaDAO launched the first application to use BCT on their platform. BCT achieved $2 billion in trading volume through KlimaDAO within the first month of launching.

For those who believe in carbon markets as a viable strategy for pushing for reform around climate action, the higher the prices for carbon credits, the more successful they become. And so, while for a short time KlimaDAO pushed the price of BCT to just above $8, starting from approximately $5 in late 2021, the price fell to nearly $1 by December 2022 and has continued to fall since. Even more strikingly, the price of KLIMA, the token that governed KlimaDAO and was backed partially by participants in the DAO that purchased BCT, went from a high of around $3,600 to $3.50 by June 2022 — needless to say, a major loss for those who took part. Although it does feel strange to judge a climate-based project based on financial return, there are actually other reasons to be critical, especially regarding the types of complex financial mechanisms utilised to promise high returns for investors which inevitably didn't pan out.

It's important to note that these protocols are buying credits on the voluntary market. Voluntary markets are not backed by any government standard or mandatory goals, but on specific organisations certifying that emission reductions have environmental integrity. These types of markets have had issues before, such as many of the credits being found to not be very credible after investigation, including Verra, with some claiming that 90% of their rainforest credits are worthless.[25] Even with government-enforced carbon markets, regulations differ (or may not even exist) between countries, something which incentivises businesses to move to countries with more lax rules. Governments need to be both very strict and aligned to prevent companies from gaming the system or finding loopholes.

While carbon credit markets have been growing over the years due to pressures on companies to have a corporate social responsibility policy, they still follow the logic of carbon footprints. Many new blockchains that have started since 2018 have claimed to strive for being carbon neutral or even carbon negative. This trend can be seen in many other industries, however the main way that these entities justify their claims to being environmentally friendly is through showing the carbon credits that they have purchased to offset their emissions. The truth, however, is that offsetting through carbon trading is a way to avoid the problem and is essentially a continuation of "greenwashing" by corporations. It limits the framing of the issue, much as the idea of a carbon footprint does, in that it again obscures the need for systemic solutions, focusing instead on specific choices that each corporation makes. Are there ways to move beyond this frame?

From Degen to Regen

One of the most vocal projects to attempt breaking away from the "degenerative" culture of DeFi into something more socially beneficial is Gitcoin. Founded by open-source development advocates Scott Moore and Kevin Owocki, Gitcoin is a platform that leverages the Ethereum blockchain to enable open source developers to monetise their work. Not unlike blockchains today, open-source code, or code that is publicly available for anyone to copy, modify, or share, started off as a seeming fad for many in the 1990s but has since become extremely important for the development of many products that millions of people and businesses now depend on, like the Linux operating system, or LibreOffice, the suite of tools similar to Microsoft Office which I used to write this book. Notoriously though, open source development is difficult to make money from unless there are enough good, willing people wanting to donate, or a large corporate that uses your software prepared to give you money for your work. Gitcoin has come up with a way for open source developers to be paid from donations using crypto protocols through their platform and we will cover how Gitcoin does this in the next chapter.

What is interesting about the Gitcoin project is how they have explicitly attempted to push those who take part in degen activity (e.g., financial speculation without any regard for externalities) towards the social good by propagating new memes. For example, one is a call for using profits made from crypto for funding public goods, which in economics refers to a commodity or service that is made available to all members of a society. This frames open-source software, the foundation of much of our digital infrastructure, as a public good in the digital world.

Regen refers to someone who engages in ReFi. For Owocki, ReFi is a "cultural preference for the funding of community and the public good over (or in parallel to) projects that are expected to produce a return for the funder."[26] Owocki expands on these memes again by encouraging degens to take the "greenpill", a play on the famous scene in *The Matrix*, and become regens instead.

One of the overall goals of Gitcoin is to use aesthetics to create a shift in perspective and culture. While the pessimistic may feel that we're careening towards a future of cyberpunk authoritarianism and eventual collapse, Gitcoin is trying to create a "solarpunk" vision of the future. Opposing cyberpunk's grey and degraded, highly technologised corporate authoritarianism, typified by films like *Blade Runner*, solarpunk proposes a world where technology is instead used in a utopian fashion so that we can more readily interrelate with the natural world. It is an optimistic vision focused on local sustainability and collective human thriving. However, one of the obvious things that need to be addressed for a crypto-based organisation intent on building a solarpunk future is how to engage with the world beyond their computers, the blockchain and crypto markets.

The Regen Network is a sovereign, PoS blockchain built to verify claims, agreements and data related to ecological states, and according to their white paper, you can think of it as "living capital accounting".[27] The project was founded by Gregory Landua, a long-time advocate and social entrepreneur of regenerative agriculture who has worked with several agricultural cooperatives and permaculture initiatives. Landua has described the project as trying to "align short term economic gain with long term ecological health".

The Regen Network is meant to be foundational infrastructure on which other projects can build their own climate-focused endeavours, but it has already started helping those who are already engaged in carbon sequestration practices to onboard to their protocol, even if they have not been verified by an existing carbon market. The Regen Registry is a voluntary carbon credit market that is interoperable with several other already existing carbon credit registries. The Regen Network also has its own rules for farmers and others to make claims about their ecological work. This is helpful for many small farmers, since getting accredited by many of the existing organisations can be time-consuming. The Regen Network blockchain is used to verify the provenance and quality of ecological data claimed and payments for ecosystem services, and employs smart contracts that automate the necessary administration based on verified changes in ecological health. The Regen Registry maintains high standards by combining remote sensing technologies with satellites, sensors or ground observations. This makes it easier for small farmers across the world to sell credits, so that they can also benefit and not just larger agricultural organisations.

REGEN is the native cryptocurrency token, and is a way for users to pay transaction fees, secure the blockchain through PoS and governance over the protocol itself, meaning that it is governed by token holders. Many of the tokens are given and paid to the projects that are sequestering carbon for carbon credits, who thereby gain voting power over the network so that it can be developed in ways that are beneficial to them. While the blockchain is meant to reward and track positive changes to ecology, on its own this could be problematic in that it could induce the use of exploitative mass production practices for the creation of carbon credits. To avoid that, Regen works closely with these organisations and has dedicated staff that help them onboard to the technology and register their carbon credits. They have also explicitly recognised the important role that many black, indigenous and people of colour play in stewarding the Earth and have committed to equity and inclusion for these communities through dedicated funds. Although Regen Network does focus on voluntary carbon credits, they go beyond just facilitating trade for trade's sake.

Kolektivo is a ReFi project focused primarily on the Caribbean island of Curaçao, with the aim of finding solutions to many of the economic and sustainability issues island-nations face by creating a complementary economic system driven by social impact.[28] The hope is that Curaçao will be the ground-zero for building a framework for regenerative economic solutions that others can build on. Founders Luuk Weber and Andy Kirchner, natives of Curaçao, saw the problems already endemic to the country exacerbated by the COVID-19 pandemic, which slowed down the tourism the island is dependent on.

One of the first projects they embarked on was the creation

of a regenerative alternative to traditional farming called a food forest, which involves planting a diversity of edible plants that require little water and resources once established.[29] Food forests are a way to provide food security, conserve water and provide local employment in a resilient way, and it was funded through selling forty unique NFTs for 250 DAI each for a total of $10,000.[30] Each NFT represents 1% ownership of the forest and therefore 1% of the yield from the harvests, something paid out in CuraDAI, a local stablecoin pegged to the local currency, the Antillean Guilder, that Kolektivo created using PoS-based blockchain Fuse. This can be used to pay for products or services, exists in parallel with the official currency and is already accepted at local grocery stores. The benefit of CuraDAI is that the payment is received within seconds, even if a user is in another country. Since many of the native island inhabitants either live or have family abroad, it facilitates the easy sending of money across borders.

The vision is the creation of a regenerative economy that works with local people, puts local products on the market, and accepts local payments. Kolektivo hold workshops about blockchain and cryptocurrencies, partner with local businesses to educate the community, and gather data about the food production of the food forest in order to continue expanding in a regenerative way. What the experiments by Kolektivo are showing is that by combining digital technologies like blockchains with real in-person human coordination in particular combinations, we can begin to think about larger scales of coordination for climate action that the affordances of a blockchain enable. However, it's important to remember that the issues around climate change are not just about coordination failure, but are also a power struggle against the largest polluters in the world and the defeatism they often engender in wider society.

We need to be careful with the issues we push forward when it comes to climate change in order to address it the best we can, given the circumstances. For example, the story of how oil companies intentionally tried stopping the development of electric cars might lead to the conclusion that we should be supportive of billionaire-owned electric car companies like Tesla without even considering the other option of building more and better public transportation services, something which would produce significantly less greenhouse gases than simply replacing gasoline-based cars with electric ones as well as removing the reliance on roads that destroy natural habitats. Supporting these billionaires adheres to the same logic as that of the carbon footprints, because it wrongfully attributes the flow of power that is behind inaction on climate change. The solution will not be found in making better individual consumer choices or backing one billionaire over another, but through collective action against those who profit from extraction of the Earth's limited resources. We should not waste time shaming others for making the wrong consumer choice when their options are limited, but instead be trying to build systems that satisfy people's basic needs.

CHAPTER 10

RETHINKING POLITICAL SYSTEMS AND ACTION

As the powers of states fade... efforts to pluralize and socialize the rights of property must look beyond the public to other means of support.

— Michael Hardt and Antonio Negri, *Assembly*

On paper, most "Western" countries are liberal capitalist democracies where every citizen has the right to vote, and therefore theoretically the outcomes of elections and the legislations that are passed into law are democratically determined. In practice, however, this could not be further from the truth. In many countries, but particularly in the United States of America, bribery is essentially legal, it's simply referred to as "lobbying".

In 2014, a Princeton study by Martin Gilens and Benjamin Page investigated which groups, including average citizens, had the highest likelihood to have their preferred policies made into legislation by the US government.[1] They concluded "that economic elites and organised groups representing business interests have substantial independent impacts on US government policy, while average citizens and mass-based interest groups have little or no independent influence." They found that the opinions of the bottom 90% of income earners have essentially no impact at all on the government policy passed by their representatives. Hardly a democracy by anyone's standards.

A favourable policy only costs a fraction of what wealthy economic and business interests earn from it, making lobbying a profitable endeavour. The growing influence of capital on politics can be seen in the political campaigns of the majority of senators and congressmen and women. Elected officials commonly spend 30-70% of their time in office fundraising for the next election. They become dependent on the money needed to defeat their opponent, pressuring them to pass laws that are preferred by their donors. A few, like Bernie Sanders, have been able to overcome this barrier by running campaigns that prioritise engaging as many of their constituents as possible.

It's no surprise therefore that voting rates in the US, even compared to similar Western countries, are so low. When your opinion doesn't matter to those that represent you at the highest levels, why bother to express your political preferences? The largest political constituency in the country is non-voters, and is generally made up of those who are working pay check to pay check and simply may not have time to vote on a weekday afternoon.[2] The country appears stuck in a downward spiral; political institutions are unresponsive as people grow more apathetic and thus the institutions become even less responsive in turn. This trend has been seen in many developed countries, and it's this dynamic that has led to the rise of populist governments and parties, and has increasingly pushed people into fringe, extremist ideologies that flirt with fascism.

The default left-leaning techno-pessimist's conclusion is that the only future that can be created with blockchains is an ever-more oppressive technocracy, but this would ultimately be defeatist and ignore the full design space. While not a solution by themselves, when designed and used in intentional ways, blockchains and what they enable can help us envision and create political futures that are more democratic and politically expressive in ways that were not possible before.

Understanding DAOs through Cybernetics

One of the biggest issues facing many Western democracies is that they have calcified, becoming slow, bureaucratic and poorly adapted to contemporary conditions. While conservative libertarians may argue that this is the natural state of "big government", the more likely cause has been the increasing power of capital over the government itself, spearheaded by the same economic elites and business interests that lobby those who enter into the highest levels of government with donations, through which they are able to keep the system that they benefit from in place using legalised bribery. Many of the institutions of these countries were designed in a time that looked very different from today, and while there is often space for some adaptability, it is well-known that, in America's case, the Founding Fathers also encoded already existing inequalities into the original Constitution, from keeping the practice of slavery intact to the creation of the Senate and disallowing the right of anyone who was not a land-owning white man to vote.

This system of current government institutions, however, is not the only one that we live in. There are a number of systems and subsystems that overlap and interact with each other which can best be explained through cybernetics. Cybernetics is a transdisciplinary field of study and framework for understanding systems of all kinds, including ecological, technological, biological, cognitive and social systems, and Artificial Intelligence is itself an evolution of cybernetics thinking. Cybernetics can be a way to understand how we design, learn, manage organisations, speak and more. The way it does this is by abstracting the similarities of all systems into categories like sensors, controllers and feedback loops, to name but a few, that describe how a system is able to sustain itself and be autonomous, or otherwise. Self-governing systems include biological systems, such as plants and animals, computer systems, and institutions, including corporations and governments.

One of the most famous cyberneticians was Stafford Beer, an ex-captain in the British military who served in World War II and became a pacifist. In his book *Brain of the Firm*, Beer details what he calls the Viable System Model (VSM), starting off what would come to be known as management cybernetics, or the application of cybernetics to all types of organisations. VSM represents the organisational structure of an autonomous system that is able to adapt to changes in its environment in order to fulfil its purpose. Autonomy in this context refers to a system that is self-governing.

In the VSM, there are five interacting subsystems that operate on a progressively larger spatial and temporal scale. Systems 1 and 2 are related to day-to-day primary functions and aligning those activities with the collective purpose of the organisation. System 3 refers to the rules and structures that support the activities of Systems 1 and 2. System 4 is the parts of the system that are looking outward to the environment to monitor outside influences that may require adaptation. System 5 is what governs the policies of the overall body of the organisation to balance the demands from the various other systems.

While at first glance this may seem merely an academic or intellectual exercise, it has real-world application. For example, VSM was being used in Chile in the early 1970s as part of Project Cybersyn — that was before the US-supported fascist coup that killed the democratically elected socialist president Salvador Allende and installed the dictator General Augusto Pinochet in his place. The purpose of Cybersyn was to create a control centre that allowed for decentralised management of the economy, taking inputs from the workers and businesses in order to make appropriate real-time decisions. The principal architect was Stafford Beer himself.

This system consisted of a network of about five hundred telex machines located in government offices in Santiago and enterprises throughout the country. These machines were connected to a government-run mainframe computer that received information on production operations, fed that information into economic modelling software and reported on variables (like the supply of raw materials) that might need attention. Cybersyn was significant in that it allowed Chile to pursue its own destiny, different from Soviet bureaucratic or American corporate power centralisation. It is still a tragedy for the human race that the experiment was discontinued as a result of the coup, after which instead Chile became the testing ground for the neoliberal economic policies that would later be implemented across the world and which have led to the failing institutions we see today.

With regard to DAOs, cybernetics can also be a very useful framework for assessing the degree to which a DAO practices the principles of decentralisation or autonomy that the name lays claim to. In April 2022, Michael Zargham and Kelsie Nabben published a working paper titled "Aligning 'Decentralized Autonomous Organization' to Precedents in Cybernetic" that elucidates the connections between cybernetics and DAOs.[3] They note that in DAOs, Systems 1 and 2 are generally embodied through both human activities and software processes, but System 3 is entirely software-based, with many having heavy influence from smart contracts enforced by a blockchain network. Systems 4 and 5 deal with the strategic and governance functions of a DAO that allow for the organisation to adapt to identified threats.

In order to be truly viable, an organisation must have a governance system able to survive a wide range of unknown changes in its environment, as well as threats from adversaries. There are two main strategies to staying viable for a system. Either it must be resilient by having a wide enough range of behaviours and reachable states to adapt to changes, or it must stay robust in the face of changes to its environment by having a narrow set of reachable states. The set of actions that enable an organisation to respond to its changing environment is called the "governance surface". Consequently, a larger governance surface provides greater resilience, while a smaller governance surface provides greater robustness. The concept of governance surface was introduced by Zargham and was inspired by the cybernetic concept of "control surface", a term used to describe the portion of a system that is used to control the system's behaviour. It is typically the part of the system that is exposed to the user or operator, and it may include buttons, switches, dials or other types of controls that can be manipulated to affect the system's operation.

With DAOs, this is defined by the set of parameters that can be changed in the software that governs the DAO in System 3, i.e., the smart contract code. The processes for making those changes are Systems 4 and 5. This process can be akin to the way that governments create and pass policies that then become law, which means that this is inherently a political process informed by the purpose of those that make up the organisation. The word for iterative decision-making that needs to be made for governance is feedback control.

By control, this doesn't necessarily mean a type of control that is coercive, but rather a method for regulating or balancing the direction of the organisation. Decentralised governance is no simple task, however, and its difficulty has likely been one of the reasons why we are so dependent on so many failing centralised systems. While not normally acknowledged for their political commitments, Zargham and Nabben note that DAOs are a "digital expression of the political will to self-organise" and that understanding control is crucial to the problem of decentralised governance.

A feedback control system is a recursive process made up of several parts that inform how a system adapts to changes. The first part is a sensor that takes measurements about the current state of the system. How well it can do this is called "observability". These measurements are then inputs for an estimator which evaluates them based on a set of beliefs based on previous measurements. The controller is a process by which a decision is made based on the beliefs of how to pursue the goal, which could be as human-directed or automated as the designers make it. The actuator is then the mechanism that turns the decision into a concrete action, which leads to an outcome. The decisions and actions possible are limited to making changes to variables which are part of the governance surface. The outcomes are then observed by sensors to be turned into new measurements in order to repeat the whole process. While much of this terminology is derived from systems engineering, the key concepts are just as relevant for decentralised governance and decision-making in DAOs.

For DAOs, like any other type of system, there is always a trade-off in the design of a governance surface. A larger governance surface may provide an organisation with a larger set of choices that could help it reach its goals, but it also creates a larger risk of undesirable system states. A smaller governance surface can decrease the risk that an organisation would come to an untenable state, but it limits its adaptability. A middle ground needs to be found so as to set the governance surface at the minimum required for it to it stay viable for its purpose. This is sometimes referred to as governance minimisation.

Expanding Democratic Expression

Stafford Beer coined the term "POSIWID" — or, the "purpose of a system is what it does". It's a basic starting point for

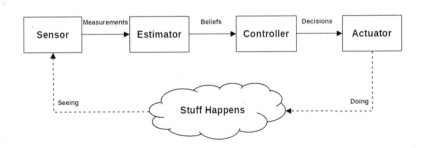

cyberneticians to see through what may be good intentions, expectations or moral judgements about a system to the system's concrete functions. When we observe situations like the growing influence of money on politics in the US, with the average federal politician becoming wealthier and the average citizen poorer,[4] or the re-election of Emmanuel Macron in France when surveys show that nearly half of those who voted for him were voting against his far-right rival Marine Le Pen and not in direct support of his policies,[5] or the 2020 US presidential elections,[6] it's clear that the purpose of the political system of liberal capitalism is not to respond to most people's needs or preferences. Understanding adaptability and purpose through a cybernetics lens, it's easy to see that nation states have largely not been answering the needs of average citizens in recent history, and that their purpose is in fact to support wealthy elites and ingrain their power while making the capitalist system adaptable to threats from the average citizens, i.e., the working class.

With the recent rise of populism of various stripes, it's clear that the feeling that something is deeply wrong with current political and governmental institutions is shared by many on opposite ends of the political spectrum. If we think of the systems already in place as a feedback control system that can be steered towards outcomes and conditions that are more desirable and equitable, the first thing that would need to happen is for those who have the same goal of changing this system to be able to recognise each other so that coordinating can begin. In one of the most well-known coordination games developed by economist Thomas Schelling in *The Strategy of Conflict*, you are asked to meet a stranger in New York City but are not allowed to communicate with them directly. When and where would you decide to try and to meet this person? In his study, he found that the most common answer was noon at Grand Central. This concept, the time and place that a majority predict others to be at given a particular set of conditions, is called a "Schelling point".

Zuccotti Park was a Schelling point for the Occupy Wall Street movement. The campaigns of Bernie Sanders and Jeremy Corbyn were Schelling points for those who believed in their policies of reducing the influence of capital on politics and the economy in the US and the UK respectively. This book is possibly a Schelling point for those who believe there is something wrong with the current state of capitalism and are curious to explore blockchains as a useful way for achieving collective liberation.

Gitcoin, the public goods funding platform mentioned in the previous chapter, considers Ethereum to be a "Schelling point for the hopeful", and Gitcoin itself to be a Schelling point for regens in the cryptocurrency space. They have hosted several Schelling point events during large Ethereum events in various cities around the world where speakers, some of whom would consider themselves to be regens, share their thoughts and experience from their own endeavours and speak to others who are curious or looking to take part in similar projects.

Gitcoin has helped various open source and public goods-oriented projects get funded through use of a mechanism called "quadratic funding". This is a form of fund-matching that limits the influence of those with significantly more capital than everyone else. The Gitcoin platform hosts thousands of projects being built with open source code, something readily done with crypto projects, as due to the nature of blockchains they all inherently have some aspect of their code as open source. Anyone is able to donate to the projects during a grants round, which normally lasts about two weeks and happens every three months. Whatever is donated to a project is matched using a pool of funds given by sponsors of the round based on a quadratic formula. For example, if you were to donate $100 to a project, you could have $10 matched with your donation to that project, and if you were to donate $1,000, you could have $50 matched from the pool. Here we can see that the matching is higher as a percentage with smaller amounts, but more in absolute terms with higher amounts. It therefore encourages people to give in smaller amounts across more projects rather than focusing on giving everything to one project.

Quadratic funding is a derivative of an alternative voting system called "quadratic voting", first coined by Glen Weyl, the founder of RadicalxChange. In quadratic voting, voters are given a set of possible choices and several vote credits which they can disburse across them, however it costs more votes for each additional vote given to a single choice at a quadratic rate. For example if you wanted to vote for an issue once, it could cost one credit, but a second time it would cost two credits, then four, then eight, etc, encouraging participants to split their votes across many choices rather than focusing on just one. Of course, this is not the only way a quadratic vote can be set up. Thinking of it as a cybernetic system itself, the parameters can be changed in multiple ways depending on what's desired by those administering the vote, but this can help to provide a snapshot of a different system beyond the one-person-one-vote two-party system of the US or plutocratic token governance that resembles stock voting in large centralised corporations common in some protocols. Quadratic voting has even already been used by the Democratic Caucus of the Colorado House of Representatives to determine legislative priorities,[7] and in Taiwan's e-democracy platform for public participation in determining budgets.[8]

"Conviction voting" is another example of an alternative voting mechanism being investigated in the Blockchain space. First proposed by Michael Zargham and tested by The Commons Stack, conviction voting is a decision-making process wherein community members' aggregated preferences are used to fund proposals continuously over time.[9] Rather than casting their votes in a single time-boxed session, voters are always expressing their preference for which proposals they would like to see approved. The longer a member keeps the same preference for the same proposal, the "stronger" their preference becomes. This gives members of the community with consistent preferences more power than those participating inconsistently. Similar to quadratic voting, people can have multiple credits to allocate across many choices, however here, time plays a determining role.

A conviction vote works similarly to neurons in the brain, where an increase in collective preference can be compared to a neuron's action potential. A proposal is approved when a pre-set threshold of collective preference is reached, just as a neuron fires only when its action threshold is reached. This is how, as in the feedback control system, aggregating information about individual preferences can turn into concrete decisions or actions, like the acceptance of a proposal. The mechanism can also be helpful for preventing vote buying, last-minute vote swings and voter apathy, since you don't need to be available at a specific time and place in order to participate. 1Hive is one DAO that has been actively utilising conviction voting for the allocation of funds in their community treasury toward project-based proposals. Proposals pass when they have sufficient support over sufficient time and majority consensus is not required to pass a proposal.

DAOs have also experimented with aspects of "liquid democracy", which is a form of dynamic delegation of power. As in a direct democracy, liquid democracy voters have the right to directly vote on all policy issues, but they also have the option to delegate their votes to someone who will vote on their behalf, as in a representative democracy. Delegates can collect as many votes from others as are willing to give to them, however their votes can always be taken away from them if someone objects to their voting. Delegates could also redelegate the votes they've been given to someone else. Depending on the design, delegation can be limited to particular domains of expertise so that your preferred expert in a topic has more say on an issue.

In the Ethereum Name Service DAO, ENS tokens can be delegated to those who are nominated or nominate themselves as delegates for the DAO. Many received their ENS tokens through the airdrop detailed previously, but the tokens can also be purchased on decentralised exchanges and elsewhere. As an owner of any amount of tokens, you are able to delegate your tokens at any time to any of the nominees to take part in DAO governance on your behalf. You are also able to remove or switch your delegation to another nominee with a portion or all of your tokens. The DAO even has its own ENS Constitution, which outlines what governance actions are permissible.[10] This is similar to a governance surface, and while there have been a few hiccups and controversies in the governance of the ENS DAO and it is not completely a liquid democracy, the seeds are there and some missteps in governance should be expected in such a new technological medium.

The truth is, the crypto space is a breeding ground for many new democratic mechanisms that have never been tried before, many of them near impossible to try without something like a blockchain. In the framework of a feedback control system, these new voting mechanisms allow for a more expressive measurement to be taken of people's preferences so that the rest of the feedback system can act accordingly with new information.

Thinking through the concept of governance surface, one of the biggest differences between DAOs and other types of systems, including political systems, is that DAOs are generally more legible. When the field of action and possibility for your organisation is defined by smart contract code, your governance surface is clear. What is governable in the code is the governance surface. In many of our traditional political systems, there is often an official governance surface for citizens, like voting for the least bad candidate in an election every few years who then gains access to a much wider governance surface of the system to theoretically govern in their constituents' interests. This is a set-up which has failed to respond equitably to any number of ongoing crises. While voting may be the official channel for enacting change, in most liberal democracies, large financial donations to political parties and candidates are often the most productive channel. The issue with this channel is that it is largely only accessible to those wealthy individuals and corporations that have the capital to exploit it. While DAOs don't inherently remove this channel, code does facilitates a clear laying out of the governance surface so that the existence of such channels can be readily identified.

Beyond Democracy: Crypto for Direct Action

The issue of how and whether to engage in electoral systems that are part of centralised, non-adaptive systems that characterise traditional democratic institutions is an old one that has split political revolutionaries for centuries. When looking at politics through the lens of cybernetics, it's important to keep in mind that what we colloquially refer to as "politics" in the electoral sense is not the entirety of the system that makes up politics. Those who decide to take action outside of their place in the electoral system engage in "direct action". Direct action therefore is the term that describes political or economic actions taken in order to directly reach goals, either through non-violent or violent means, rather than appealing to authorities. Examples include strikes, sit-ins, property destruction, mutual aid and anything else that can help expose the problem that needs to be addressed or serve to highlight alternatives and solutions. There is significant evidence from history that taking action outside of the voting booth is one of the more effective ways to create political change, as seen in the Civil Rights movement, the labour movement and many more that have enshrined human rights for those who previously lacked them.

Politically decentralised organising is not new. Radical groups like the Zapatistas in Mexico have practised decentralised community decision-making for much longer than any other organisation that we'd call a DAO today.[11]

We can even find potential precursors to DAOs in the digital activism that arose with the growth of the world wide web.

In *Hacker, Hoaxer, Whistleblower, Spy*, digital anthropologist Gabriella Coleman details the most famous examples of digital direct action — hacks undertaken by groups like Anonymous and LulzSec, as well as action by whistleblower organisations like WikiLeaks.[12]Coleman describes the many exploits committed by these "decentralised" organisations and the complicated albeit sometimes contradictory politics behind them. Although there were many other hacker groups well before Anonymous, they brought hacking to the mainstream and signalled a marked increase in digital activism and its ability to effect politics. Citing the Arab Spring, the multiple hackings of large corporations who form part of the military-industrial complex and Denial of Service attacks towards online payment companies that assisted the financial blockade of WikiLeaks, Coleman's research challenges the assumption that all hackers are white, middle-class, libertarian males with little political consciousness, showing in great detail that while the same technologies and tactics for hacking can be used solely for profiteering, they can also be used for digital direct action, something often also called "hacktivism".

With the evolution of the Internet to now include blockchains, direct action has also migrated into this arena. When people think of hacking in the cryptocurrency space, they often imagine "shadowy super coders", as Senator Elizabeth Warren dubbed them, who are all out to take your money. One of the newer developments in hacking that involves cryptocurrency is called cryptojacking. This is when a hacker hacks into someone else's computer to use its hardware for mining cryptocurrency, making the hackee the one to pay for the electricity.

But cryptojacking can also be used for more radical efforts. Grayson Earle, an anti-capitalist American artist and activist, co-developed Bailbloc, a cryptocurrency scheme that uses cryptojacking to fight against bail, with *The New Inquiry*, an online cultural and literary magazine. In the US, a bail bond is a deposit of money to a court by someone who has been charged as a suspect in a crime, in order to not have to stay in pre-trial detention. Essentially, you are held in jail before you are ever proven guilty and can only get out if you pay a significant amount of money. The practice has been repeatedly found to be racist and classist, since people of colour and minorities are targeted by police at a much higher frequency than whites, leading to greater poverty and creating a vicious circle. The wealthy are almost always able to make bail, while those who are poor are isolated and unable to prepare for a trial that could have drastic consequences. Bail has been a target for abolition activists for a long time, and although there have been some successes in getting a number of states to eliminate cash bail, it is still widely practised.

Bailbloc allows people to download an app and visit their website in order to immediately start donating a small portion of their computer's unused processing power to mining the privacy-centric cryptocurrency Monero.[13] It's a simple application, and when you open it, the page simply states "YOU ARE NOW MINING FOR BAIL BLOC". It's designed as an opt-in form of cryptojacking that then gives the money earned from the Monero to bail funds in the National Bail Fund Network. The project blends artwork with activism to produce a *détournement*, or subversion, of traditional notions around cryptojacking with much deeper implications for digital direct action. As the project is open source, it is relatively easy to replicate this model for funding other forms of activism. It's not difficult therefore for other groups to appropriate this model to allow their community to engage in digital direct action that helps fund other efforts.

Another form of direct action is called mutual aid. Anarchist philosopher Peter Kropotkin first popularised the idea in *Mutual Aid: A Factor of Evolution*, where he argued that cooperation, not competition, drives evolution. Mutual aid refers to a voluntary reciprocal exchange of resources and services for mutual benefit. It is distinct from charity in that it is a form of political expression in which people choose to take responsibility for each other's well-being, rather than relying on the state or other centralised institutions. Many supporters of mutual aid argue that most charity and non-profit models not only fail to solve systemic issues, but actually work to perpetuate the inequality that these systems create. In his book *Mutual Aid: Building Solidarity in this Crisis and the Next*, author Dean Spade writes:

> The charity model encourages us to feel good about ourselves by "giving back." Convincing us that we have done enough if we do a little volunteering or posting online is a great way to keep us in our place. Keeping people numb to the suffering in the world — and their own suffering — is essential to keeping things as they are. In fact, things are really terrifying and enraging right now, and feeling more rage, fear, sadness, grief, and despair may be appropriate. Those feelings may help us be less appeased by false solutions and stir us to pursue ongoing collective action for change.

Mutual aid work, the cooperation between people in a community to meet the needs of everyone in that community, acknowledges the failings of the current system and creates a new one in response — a network of neighbours looking to each other for support. The relationships cultivated via mutual aid, built on interdependence, gives us a model for what an ideal, post-capitalist society could look like. One of reduced isolation and deeper connection, freedom, safety and reciprocal exchange for mutual benefit.

Breadchain, mentioned previously, is a post-capitalist project with the aim of providing a kind of mutual aid for more progressive-leaning projects in the crypto space, not only through the Crowdstaking Application described in a previous chapter, but also through the creation of an organised network of aligned projects that knowledge-shares and works together to meet mutual needs. With mutual aid being one of the main principles behind Breadchain, the goal of the project is to facilitate experiments with new technology to explore and create novel forms of direct action through the building of solidarity primitives like the BREAD token.

One of the projects that is part of the Breadchain network is Pact Collective — a New York City-based mutual aid DAO that seeks to connect with and mobilize neighbors, build coalitions between grassroots organisations, and create sustainable institutions of care in the city. The Pact Collective started during the storm of the 2020 COVID-19 pandemic and Black Lives Matter protests when people were looking for better ways to give to their community outside large national-level charities. Pact was formed to allow people to directly support local organisations in their own communities in New York City through a monthly subscription to Pact, who then distributed the funds to on-the-ground local groups working on mutual aid.

Wanting to make the organisation more democratic and give mutual aid activists more say, they found that it was not easy to do so through the traditional legal and financial system. This is when Pact started investigating blockchain and decentralized tools. One ongoing project to allow mutual aid organisations to sustain and collaborate with each other is PactDAO's partnership with Breadchain. Through the use of solidarity primitives, mutual aid organizations can create systems of mutualistic support to continue their work and create counter institutions in their communities.

Another highly successful form of direct action throughout the history of capitalism has been the labour strike. You can thank labour unions for the existence of weekends, holiday pay, sick pay, lunch breaks, workplace safety requirements and much more. While many progressives tend to simplistically consider blockchains as something purely able to work in favour of capital, LaborDAO is exploring the impacts of this technology on the labour movement. It was started by Larry Williams Jr, founder of the Progressive Workers Union and UnionBase, a social media network for unions and their members. Williams believes that the labour movement needs to be included in the development of the technology and vice-versa. But why would the labour movement need these tools?

What's sometimes forgotten about labour organising is that unions often exist in legal grey zones, especially as anti-labour legislation continues to be pushed in Western countries. For unions trying to decide on their next course of action or whether to begin a strike, the legal options can be very blurry and many states in the US even have laws that have made strikes illegal. For unions with money that can be used for strike funds (money given to striking workers so that they can continue to maintain a salary), one wrong step can lead to the legal system being used to freeze their assets. Under those circumstances a global, digital, resilient infrastructure can also be useful for international labour efforts. While capital, through globalisation, can readily move money around, the labour movement has not yet seen the full potential of using cross-border tools that escape traditional top-down systems for coordinating international labour action and governance.

Digital tools, when created with intention and not in the interest of capital, can be used for democratic organisation. DAOs are already giving examples of how organisations like labour unions could use smart contracts for making governance transparent, simple and easy to access in a resilient way, while also keeping people informed and engaged. This is especially true as unions begin to grow in size and complexity. Many of the aforementioned voting mechanisms are novel methods for measuring preferences within the organisation and ensuring they become more adaptable to members' needs. Additionally, cryptocurrencies could be useful for fundraising for labour efforts, making money available quickly when there is a threat of state oppression or a financial blockade, or in situations where there is no safe place to store money in a joint bank account. Labour efforts that are also just getting off the ground don't need to go through the long legal process of setting up a joint bank account if they start a multi-signature wallet that is democratically controlled. While many fundraising efforts in crypto can be pointed at as poor examples by naysayers, there are certainly useful and innovative ways to raise money through campaigns with crypto if it is in the interest of labour. Anti-union laws that were created in the interest of capital should not hold back the progress of the labour movement and will need to be circumvented and subverted in any number of ways.

All of these examples and ideas can begin to open up radical possibilities for the use of DAOs and the tools they leverage for general political organising. When strategising as to whether it makes sense to use these types of tools for these ends, it's important to keep in mind the issue of legitimacy versus legality. The systems that we live in are designed as negative feedback loops to suppress legitimate (legal or illegal) political action. The uncomfortable truth for many liberal-minded leftists is that our actions cannot be limited solely by their legality, or else we will find ourselves caught within a limited feedback control system or a viable system with an ever-decreasing governance space.

Lunarpunk and the Tensions between Identity and Anonymity

When engaging in direct action, it's important to consider all the consequences of doing so, especially if there's a high likelihood of the legal system getting involved. This has become even more important today, when we almost always have GPS-enabled smart phones with us everywhere we go. In many ways, we live under constant surveillance by large tech companies that are chipping away at what little right to privacy we may have left. It's generally advised not to bring a smart phone to protests, to wear clothing that hides your identity, including a mask, not to take pictures of any of your actions, and so on, now that ubiquitous digital infrastructure has become part of the feedback control system of the state and corporations.

This is all especially concerning when, in the 6-3 decision by the US Supreme Court majority to overturn Roe v. Wade, and decades of precedence for a woman's right to an abortion, it was cited that there is no constitutional "right to privacy".[14] This decision has unimaginably large implications for the further emergence of an authoritarian surveillance state. Not only do women need to consider avoiding the use of digital tools for period tracking, but also messaging applications that don't have end-to-end encryption. While Signal, a specialised messaging application with end-to-end encryption protection built in, can help to some degree, more tools are needed to protect online identities.

Another interesting example of an attempt at direct action using crypto-enabled tools is AssangeDAO, a DAO whose primary aim is the freedom of Julian Assange.[15] On 10 December 2021, the day that the US government won its appeal against a British court ruling blocking Assange's extradition to the US where he faced 175 years in jail, the DAO mobilised. They started by raising $55 million in ether to bid on an NFT artwork by Pak, a renowned digital artist. The NFT was from Pak's Censored collection and all of the proceeds went to Assange's legal defence through the Wau Holland Foundation. This fundraiser kickstarted the creation of the DAO and served to create a set of members who participate in order to support and initiate further projects that help Assange. Everyone who gave ether was also proportionately given part of a JUSTICE token that governs the DAO, with none of it reserved for the DAO or paid to its founders or developers. Only token holders are allowed to make proposals to the DAO. What is interesting about the governance design with this DAO is that, as there has already been a lot of work going into the legal defence of

Assange, the Assange Family are allowed to veto proposals that could be detrimental to Assange's defence.

While the seeds for political action are there, when I spoke to one of the stewards of the DAO, Rose O'Leary, she noted that, after the fundraiser, there were some difficulties with managing the DAO, saying:

> The nature of DAOs is that you have many different participants and they have different views about how to do things. It can be hard enough to operate collectively with people in a physical space where you're talking eye-to-eye but with a DAO it can be even harder because you've never met each other before and there's no trust basis... the $50 million that was transferred from the DAO to the traditional foundation was like a $50 million bet on the supremacy of traditional institutions with respect to DAOs. So that was a shock and the community is still recovering... I've been focused on building anonymous DAOs on DarkFi because our plan is to port over the AssangeDAO community in to DarkFi so it can pursue goals like freeing Assange in a way that is properly censorship resistant and safe for users.[16]

Additionally, it is somewhat ironic that a group dedicated to freeing a cypherpunk were using Ethereum, where all transactions are publicly visible. While there are separate applications that are built on or could be paired with Ethereum to add a level of privacy, it is not native to the protocol. There are cryptocurrencies like Monero and Zcash that are commonly used by those who require privacy, as in the case of Bailbloc, and that use a myriad of cryptographic primitives to add significantly more privacy at the protocol level. However, neither of these are able to provide smart contract functionalities that would enable DAOs. DarkFi, the project O'Leary is working on with Amir Taaki, one of the early core developers of Bitcoin, uses zero-knowledge cryptography as well as its own smart contract programming language to allow for anonymous assets, transactions and DAOs.

The concept of a zero-knowledge proof describes how one party (the prover) can prove to another (the verifier) that a given statement is true without revealing any additional information about the statement. Zero-knowledge proofs are characterised by the fact that it is trivial to show that one possesses knowledge of something by just revealing it. The difficult part is proving such possession without revealing any information that is irrelevant to the verifier. The classic example to explain this type of cryptographic proof is when you give your identity card to a bouncer in front of a bar. The only thing that the bouncer needs to know is that you are of legal drinking age, however by giving your identity card you are also providing them with a lot of extra information that they don't need, like your exact birthdate, place of birth, etc. Using a zero-knowledge proof would be a way for you to be able to prove to the bouncer that you are above the legal drinking age without giving any other information. Applying this to our current digital landscape — where we are constantly leaking much more information about ourselves over the Internet, to companies who don't need it to provide services but do use it to sell new advertising and marketing products, thereby violating our privacy — we can see this technology has significant implications for building privacy-preserving digital infrastructure.

DarkFi is an explicitly political effort aimed at subverting the ability of gatekeepers to stop the flow of various types of value. In their manifesto titled "The Coming Storm", they cite a 2013 speech made by then-FBI Director James Comey in which he described the "Going Dark Problem", in which he laments the inability of the law to slow the proliferation of encryption technologies.[17] DarkFi, in contrast, celebrates this, looking to it as an opportunity to build online zones that are impenetrable to law enforcement agencies, a prerequisite to any fully democratic society. Dark-Fi is not "a corporate startup. It's a democratic economic experiment, an operating system for society" and its founders are particularly interested in "autonomous political formations" for bottom-up decision-making, believing that allowing for parallel societies to co-exist in online spaces is crucial for fighting totalitarianism.

In "Lunarpunk and the Dark Side of the Cycle", O'Leary proposes an alternative aesthetic to the more naïvely optimistic solarpunk ethos found in ReFi, one that accounts for the realities of our current situation in regards to digital privacy and totalitarianism.[18] Called "lunarpunk" and mixing cypherpunk and solarpunk, it highlights the inherent conflicts between crypto and existing power structures, with O'Leary stating that "While 'solarpunks' join DAOs, lunarpunks are preparing for war, and building privacy-enhanced tooling to protect their communities". Lunarpunks acknowledge the need to build anti-fragile systems, or systems that grow stronger with attacks or other shocks. She continues:

> User-empowerment and system-antifragility are in positive feedback with each other. But this cycle also runs in reverse. In a transparent system, users are exposed. If the external environment turns hostile, this information can be weaponised against them. Faced with persecution, users will opt-out, triggering a descent into fragility.

When considering privacy over the Internet, it's important to bear in mind that the infrastructure has been built in such a way that protecting privacy by default is not part of the equation. The most common solution to this are VPNs (virtual private networks). While VPNs can provide users with the ability to conceal their precise IP address, they are a centralised solution, meaning that VPN providers can observe all traffic between their users and the public Internet, and exactly what services a user is accessing at any given moment. While the Tor has improved privacy for those that use it to a degree, data packets on the network can still be de-anonymised because of their size and timing patterns as they move through the Tor network. Surveillance agencies can combine this with other data to still find out who someone is and what they're doing over the Internet.

One project that tackles the issue of privacy at the network level of the Internet is NYM, founded by Harry Halpin, a research scientist at MIT and radical open Internet advocate. NYM uses a decentralised mix network, where servers are given economic incentives through its own cryptocurrency for providing anonymising services. Servers in the mix network additionally make data packets of the same size and obscure the timing in order to increase the anonymity of data passing through it. This increases resistance to surveillance, including by states. The better service a server in the mix network provides to data, the more they are rewarded. With the NYM cryptocurrency, token holders, users and those providing mix network services can govern and approve software updates to the protocol. The level of security NYM provides can be applied not only to cryptocurrency transactions that natively don't provide security at a level lower than their own blockchain network, but also other types of messaging, helping protect those who are vulnerable to repression, such as whistleblowers like Chelsea Manning, who works for the project with a focus on security.

How then do we reconcile the various voting mechanisms mentioned and the ideals of democracy with the need for anonymity? Under a fully anonymous system, you're vulnerable to Sybil attacks, in which an attacker creates a large amount of pseudonymous identities to gain disproportionate influence over a system. Blockchain networks solve this problem to some extent through their consensus mechanism. However, this largely relies on having access to significant capital, whether in mining equipment or in tokens for staking. This is antithetical to democratic principles.

While many identity solutions for the blockchain space require some amount of doxxing of one's real identity to others, Idena is a project that has managed to find a way to get around this through some clever designs. Instead of PoW or PoS, Idena uses a consensus mechanism they call Proof of Person (PoP). In order to be able to take part in the PoP consensus mechanism and earn their cryptocurrency, one needs to prove that they are a unique human through solving a series of flip-tests in a short, designated time slot.

A flip-test is a special type of CAPTCHA (the test you do when you're asked to prove you're a human to access certain webpages) that is very difficult for artificial intelligence to solve. In a flip-test, which is submitted by validated participants and verified by other validated participants, you are given two choices, with four of the same pictures in different orders. In order to solve it, you must correctly choose the series of pictures that make the most sense as a series of logical steps. For example, you could have a full trash can, then someone holding a full trash bag, then pulling out a new trash bag and then an empty trash can with an empty bag in it. In this order it makes sense logically, but in a different order it would not. These types of tests are very difficult for an artificial intelligence to figure out, but it is ultimately an arms race between the protocol and those trying to game the system. The project has made several updates over time to ensure that no artificial intelligence is able to get very far, while maintaining a level of difficulty that still allows humans to solve multiple tests within a restricted time. Each flip-test is also only shown to up to ten to fifteen persons and then retired from use.

These tests must also be solved through several validation sessions that happen every few weeks at 13:30 UTC on a Saturday and are attended by everyone around the world who wants to take part. By getting a good enough score after several sessions, you will be registered as a human on the protocol. In order to maintain that level of identity though, you will still need to take part in the validation sessions, but will be given a regular amount of the native cryptocurrency iDNA in exchange for your participation. The token also acts as a governance token over the protocol for making proposals or being paid by others on the protocol. What's interesting with this design is that people are able to take part in the various democratic mechanisms that blockchains could enable without revealing one's true identity if they don't want to.

Time will tell if a solution like this will be able to evolve and create a tolerable compromise between identity and anonymity. In the meantime, other experiments are already happening. Gitcoin's grants platform treats identity as a spectrum where those who have identified themselves to more identity solutions receive more donation-matching. More verification of your personhood through various identity solutions gives you more fund-matching from the quadratic funding pool from sponsors. With added identity layers that preserve privacy, new possibilities open up for deeper issues around democracy and human rights.

Tokens as Encoded Social Rights

One of the more unfortunate thought leaders in the cryptocurrency space is Balaji Srinivasan, former CTO of the centralised exchange Coinbase and former general partner of venture capital firm Andreessen Horowitz or "a16z". He has links to the Dark Enlightenment,[19] a neo-reactionary movement with intellectual roots in far-right figures like Curtis Yarvin, Peter Thiel and Nick Land, who have argued that democracy is untenable and advocate returning to "traditionalist" forms of government like monarchism, a position that stems from their realisations that in fact conservative libertarian ideas would never win elections.[20] A long and consistent proponent for a technocracy governed by Silicon Valley, as well as libertarian seasteading — an attempt to create societies outside of the reach of governments built on free-market principles — one of the ideas that Srinivasan has been pushing is what he calls the "network state". In a blog post, he defined a network state as "a social network with an agreed-upon leader, an integrated cryptocurrency, a definite purpose, a sense of national consciousness, and a plan to crowdfund territory".[21]

Framed as the inevitable sequel to nation states, Srinivasan's network state unsurprisingly has extreme libertarian and free market fundamentalist underpinnings. Blurring the lines between the US president and billionaire tech founders through unspoken appeals to the California Ideology, he argues that anyone can now become a network state founder, akin to being a startup founder except for a digital country. When companies are essentially economic dictatorships, equating new digital countries to mere extensions of tech startup culture, an arena heavily controlled by venture capitalists like him, makes obvious the desire for an anti-democratic conservative technocracy. Equally unsurprisingly, Srinivasan's writing displays a complete disregard for the history of colonialism or imperialism in the evolution of the nation state.

The danger in these proposals is clear; when in the hands of neo-fascists, a resilient immutable ledger that directly encodes their political values into its system spells the end of many of the civil rights we take for granted today. When paired with other technologies on the bleeding edge like artificial intelligence or Internet-connected devices and robots, the prospect is entirely dystopian.

In June 2022, Nathan Schneider published an article in *Noema* titled "How We Can Encode Human Rights in the Blockchain", where he warns of just such a dystopian future of human rights abuses that could be enabled with the advent of decentralised, autonomous systems on blockchains.[22] He notes, however, that while human rights enforcement goes against the usual crypto story focused on immutability and censorship resistance for largely non-progressive reasons, these properties can also be used for "a new layer of global social contracts, in which human peers, more than territorial governments, are the protagonists". He warns against appeals to neutrality, as this is an unachievable property for a technological system. Code is a digital instantiation of politics. "To be neutral on human rights is in fact a choice not to consider human rights. Neutrality is an implied refusal, a missed opportunity, a failure of imagination."

Blockchains are a form of history preservation and a code-based enforcement of protocol rules. So whatever is being enforced by the protocol or smart contracts is heavily influenced by the social context from which they emerge. Just as crypto hypemen believe that the blockchain is there to preserve their property rights over digital assets, it can equally be used to enforce other types of rights if designed to do so. Blockchains can, for instance, enable democratic rights over those same assets in the way a cooperative handles assets. Schneider takes the example of DAOs that only do business with smart-contract certified DAOs that prove that they do not engage in slave labour as an example. Blockchain can be used as a way to ensure observance of rights that states are poorly suited to defending. He notes, "Blockchains could enforce labor rights, incentivise decarbonisation, and impose targeted sanctions. They could establish fair, context-aware due process."

One of my own early attempts at trying to envision an example of what Schneider calls upon blockchain engineers to build was in a blog post titled "A Use Case for Blockchain Socialism during an Evictions Crisis: The Housing for All Token".[23] The piece was published soon after the beginning of the COVID-19 pandemic, when we were witnessing a significant spike in evictions due to people being unable to afford rent in cities without an eviction moratorium. Exploiting the power imbalance, landlords in cities across the US were acting in a sense simply as rational businesses seeking profit through private property, but with profoundly detrimental effects on wider society. "By allocating housing by ability to pay, rather than need, we create homelessness which has a lot of physical and mental effects on those who become homeless and thus further downstream affects society as a whole."

Albeit utopian for some, as a way to imagine a different world where we leverage blockchains to enshrine housing as a human right, I proposed the housing right token. Using the example of Mario and Luigi living in the Mushroom Kingdom (let's assume it's actually an on-chain liquid democracy and not a monarchy), each citizen is able to spend their one housing right token on one available housing unit in a community in which there is enough housing for everyone. The smart contracts that encode the housing right tokens also have certain parameters based on the needs of the specific person. For example, since Mario is a single father with a child to care for, he is entitled to a house with two rooms, while Luigi, being a single man, is entitled to a one-bedroom house or to live with roommates if he prefers. While there are plenty of details left out in this proposal, we can't write the recipes for the cookshops of the future, this is meant to be illustrative of the potential that progressives can fight for. Using a blockchain as one component to enforce housing rights for all is a way to reverse the current relationship with many new technologies forced upon us today. It's the creation of a resilient feedback control system that is decentralised and autonomous in the ways that it needs to be and that seeks to make human rights anti-fragile.

Nabben and Zargham state that cybernetics can be a useful framework for understanding our place in larger systems of control, and perhaps for developing new ones, but it is not the only one. With regard to DAOs, they recommend that systems design or analysis should be supplemented by other fields of study such as law, anthropology or sociology. Cybernetics has a tendency to move towards governance minimisation, as there is an implicit bias towards system stability from cyberneticists who design systems especially from a technical point of view. While there can be a place for that, when applied to the political, with DAOs or not, cybernetics can be limiting in ensuring that the human aspects of organisation are accounted for.

It is unlikely there will ever be a universal standard for human rights and so systems must be able to adapt. At the same time, as a society we need to determine which are the human rights that should be obligations to defend. History has shown us that rights are not granted, they are fought for. Through new technologies, especially in the blockchain and cryptocurrency space, neo-fascist movements are working out in the open to roll back the rights previous generations battled for. If we reduce the scope of politics to voting every few years or downplay the significance and potentialities of the same technological fields that neo-fascists play in, then we cede our right to determine a future in line with our own political convictions to those same fascists.

Those who feel similarly but hold techno-pessimistic views might advocate global bans of cryptocurrencies or blockchains in a paternalistic call for investor protections, but that drastically underestimates the breach of human rights enforcing it would entail. The surveillance required to ensure that others are not using software that can have a positive material effect on many of the most vulnerable people living under financial blockades or economic sanctions, or are using it to explore many of the alternatives looked at in this book, would be totalitarian in nature. You cannot advocate for complete bans and also for privacy and anonymity on the Internet, and historically speaking that side of politics interested in advancing human rights has been on the losing end of increases in surveillance, something seen in FBI operations like COINTELPRO.

In response to these threats, the political left needs instead to be leveraging all of the tools at its disposal to win this fight, while simultaneously acknowledging the contradictions. These contradictions cannot be wished away — after all, we don't live in conditions of our choosing. There will always be contradictions in fighting and organising for a better world while living in the shell of the old one. The world of blockchains and cryptocurrencies is a complex one, but it is also one of the new terrains of political struggle and it is imperative that we engage with it.

CHAPTER 11

ART IN MULTIPLAYER

I do not want art for a few any more than education for a few, or freedom for a few.

— William Morris

Let us recall Lawrence Lessig's pathetic dot theory, in which he states that there are four forces that regulate our lives: law, social norms, markets and architecture. Although he was probably incorrect in saying that code is law, as code should be seen as its own modality of regulation, it is interesting to note that social norms is also one of the regulators. While some like to think of the law as the be all and end all of what is possible, the law cannot feasibly regulate everything we do. Social norms are standards of behaviour that are generally accepted by a group and take on a regulatory role in many situations in which the law does not need to intervene. One of the ways that social norms create standards of behaviour is through culture.

While culture has many definitions in different contexts, let's assume that culture means a set of repeated behaviours by a group of people that is reproduced in such a way that it can eventually create whole identities. Culture is a form of social control as it constrains individual choice, rendering certain actions impermissible or taboo within a group. Equally, culture can coordinate behaviour or action through symbolic means too, whether they be visual symbols, particular phrases, music and so on. In retrospect, it seems clear that, for better or for worse, the Internet has changed culture and social norms to a tremendous degree. A global infrastructure for communication and shared knowledge has led to people being exposed to other ways of living and understanding the world, thus bringing into question the cultural expectations they or their families grew up with. What the Internet has not changed, however, is the fact that art is one of the drivers of culture.

What makes something art is its inherent lack of direct utility while, at the same time, if it's considered good art, it is influential in changing how we perceive reality and this then affects how we behave and perhaps coordinate. In other words, art plays a role that may or may not break with social norms in coordinating humans within cultural frameworks. For better or for worse, art has become more available than ever before over the Internet, at least in forms that are conducive to the Internet medium, and this too has led to rapid changes in culture and social norms.

Whether it's music, movies, or television shows, it's almost all accessible for free very easily if you know where to look. Giant tech platforms like Netflix, YouTube and Spotify are all about the distribution of art for as little as possible, becoming essentially natural monopolies in the market — they therefore have a great influence on what art people see. Meanwhile, social media platforms have essentially become curators of all of this, giving them too great an influence over what art we see. The Internet may be open in theory, but the way we engage with it, not only for art, is controlled by just a few for-profit corporations.

Previously we've discussed NFTs as being something that has developed out of blockchains, and how both hypemen and gatekeepers incorrectly believe them to be the new enforcers of digital scarcity. Now that we have broken that mental model and understand that NFTs can also be useful for reducing platform risk for artists, let's look deeper into how crypto protocols are being used for innovative collaborative coordination.

Web3 and the Metaverse

A common way to make new concepts, memes or trends

understandable to an audience is by historicising them, or placing them within an often oversimplified narrative account. In mainstream media, you may have come across the term "web3", or the suggestion that we are now at a third rendition of the Internet, one that is heavily influenced by blockchains and other decentralised infrastructures and protocols like IPFS. While largely synonymous with what people were calling "crypto" before the term came about, web3, like its predecessor "**web2**", is an attempt at a periodisation of the Internet. A summary of the story goes usually something like this:

web1 = read

web2 = read and write

web3 = read, write and own

Famously, in 1995, when explaining the Internet on *The David Letterman Show*, Bill Gates described it as a way to find others who have the same unusual interests as you.[1] He not only foreshadowed the rise of social media platforms, but he conveniently left out that these digital spaces would never be designed to be co-owned by those that used them. **Web1** was the beginning of the Internet, which was perceived to be largely decentralised, but its users could only visit and read static websites. In web2, users could now interact with one another through messaging and create accounts, which led to the development of Big Tech, which centralised the Internet through platforms that act as "walled gardens" and with business models that depend largely on advertising and invasive tracking methods, like Meta, Twitter, Google, etc. While originally web2 was used as a way to refer to the rise of publicly accessible APIs of various platforms, in the context of crypto that aspect of it has been largely ignored. Web3 is meant to be the next evolution of the Internet, incorporating blockchains so users can have more control over their data and the ability to own the protocols over the Internet.

While there is some truth to the story, this attempt at historicising the development of the Internet is largely a simplified narrative used for marketing purposes. Indeed, it largely seems to be a way to talk about crypto-enabled tools, projects and companies without using the word "crypto", a term which, for many, has a negative connotation. The term "Web3" was originally coined by Gavin Wood, a co-founder of Ethereum who is now focused on his own crypto project, Polkadot. This is generally why in this book I have preferred to use the term "crypto" in order to fully acknowledge that I'm talking about cryptocurrencies and blockchains.

While tokens do have the potential to provide users with much more ownership of protocols, the extent to which that is true will depend on the feedback control mechanism that the token is used for in the governance of the protocol. In fact, the responsibilities and powers of ownership are seldom concretely defined in conversations around web3, with the focus moving little beyond exposure to upside from the token increasing in value. One of the areas where the idea of "ownership" is being tested is in the various metaverse projects mentioned previously where, not unlike many MMORPGs in the past but now with cryptocurrency, people can purchase digital land and real estate.[2] At the moment many projects claim they have their own metaverse, however, generally the rhetoric around this concept tends to return to its roots in *Snow Crash* by conceiving of the metaverse as a single entity, something shown in the recent change of Facebook's name to "Meta" and its strategy to become the company that makes "the Metaverse". The looming threat of yet another digital and market land-grab from a giant tech company has rightfully put many people off the idea, but ultimately this probably won't be enough to stop the progression of the additional technologies like improvements in computer graphics, virtual reality and increasing availability of Internet connection that are turning

Snow Crash into reality. But not all imaginings of metaverses are using this logic.

Trust is an art and research collective based in Berlin maintained by Arthur Röing Baer, Calum Bowden and Lina Martin-Chan. It describes itself as "a network of utopian conspirators, a sandbox for their creative, technical and critical projects, and a site of experimentation for new ways of learning together". One of the endeavours coming out of Trust, Moving Castles, a project by GVN and Arthur Röing Baer, pursues alternatives or reactions to Meta's Metaverse. Moving Castles is an "organisational metaphor and real-time media type which combines collective agency and public participation in modular and portable multiplayer miniverses".[3]

The name of the project is taken from the Studio Ghibli movie *Howl's Moving Castle* based on the novel written by Diana Wynne Jones, in which a moving castle is able to transport its residents to various different worlds based on their desires.

Rather than trying to collapse the enormous, already-existing number of online communities into one monolithic digital environment that allows for tech corporations to continue to sell your data, Moving Castles are instead looking at ways for online communities to be as public as they want without losing their more private spaces to intrusive advertisements or fear of pressure from public scrutiny. For Trust, it is important for online communities to have the option to remain private, so as to allow subcultures to develop without interruption and to create a cohesive, democratically governed collective that also allows for cross-pollination with other online subcultures using decentralised infrastructure. This would then allow for the creation of Moving Castles as zones of resistance that can remain small but interconnected in networks of interoperability, that defy Zuckerberg's or any other future attempt at a monolithic Metaverse. Moving Castles are both public and collective, while being unafraid to take from open source tools developed for other uses.

So what does this look like in practice? Trust has been testing their framework through livestreams hosted on platforms like Twitch, in which the audience is able to interact directly in the computer-generated environment being streamed. From their studio in Berlin, those who are leading the stream use real-time motion capture of their body to control their animated character and the viewers can manipulate the environment using specific inputs in the chat box. They can also award points for each participant, making it possible to create things like animated game shows with the audience or a kind of alternative MMORPG.

Trust also collaborates with other adjacent online communities through special channels on Discord via "portals". In the set-up, the two communities that want to connect make a portal channel with a Discord bot that connects them on the two different Discord servers. With that connection, both servers have a portal to where members of both groups are able to communicate with one another. Most commonly these portals are opened for a set amount of time, during which both communities may have a conversation after a short reading session so that members from both can share ideas from their perspectives.

Although these experiments have largely relied on centralised tech platform, it's not difficult to imagine a switch to decentralised alternatives which would also leverage web3/crypto tools and primitives. Using a Moving Castles framework, online communities can solidify their already existing governance mechanisms or create new ones through the use of tokens, multi-signature wallets or other DAO tooling that is controlled by members with the addition of graphical representations of their governance happening at the same time, either within their miniverse or publicly if so desired. This is almost like a miniature version of Cybersyn, but for an online community. The added layer of value or finance can be something that improves group cohesion, for example by decreasing dependence on sourcing funds from centralised platforms like Patreon or creating shared ownership of real assets, but it needs to be leveraged with intention. Adding some forms of finance can add extra tensions that don't fit all online communities.

As of the time of writing, Trust admits that their experiments have only "scratched the surface of the new types of narrative works that combine low-barrier public participation with collective agency". However, the goal of communities being able to be financed, truly owned and governed by members is a far cry from the vision of the Metaverse being pushed by companies like Meta and many web3 hypemen.

As it stands, it seems that the idea of there being "*a* Metaverse" is already dead in the water, partially because we already live in a metaverse of a sort online. When "the Metaverse" does come about, it will be marketed as a distinct change from the previous ways we interacted with the Internet, but will look more like an extension of what already exists, just with virtual reality headsets and little to no mention of any changes in the ownership of this new infrastructure.

Many have proposed phrases like the "pluriverse", which advocates for a pluralistic view of decentralised infrastructure rather than relying on centralised infrastructure and institutions with no democratic input. However, the terminology is less significant than the actions that we are able to take as netizens. Only by being able to amplify the positive parts of the online communities we are already a part of through democratic means can we hope to build a real alternative to the existing infrastructure and fight the trends of centralisation.

Democratic Art: Culture Stake

It might be strange for those who do not work in the arts to think that art has much influence in their lives. After all, if you're not an artist, participating in art is usually seen as something that only those with certain privileges are able to do, as if it's only some sort of rarefied, elitist endeavour.

It is important however to bear in mind the influence that various artistic movements have had on political movements, also (and especially) among the disempowered. It is perhaps an understanding of the disruptive political power of art that has made it a target for elite capture, an attempt to corral the pesky imaginations of those who would gain from reimagining a world without those elites. Any art that can be seen as being influenced by or created for the masses is commonly referred to derisively as "low art" by those who see themselves as part of the more exclusive "high art" scenes.

Anyone who got sucked into the NFT hype cycle in 2021/2022 may believe that NFTs are the first attempt to "democratise art", similarly to how DeFi "democratises finance" (although it's more like democratising financial speculation in many cases), but this is far from true. One of the leading artist-led organisations exploring the democratisation of art as well as innovative technologies is Furtherfield, set up in 1996.[4] Based in Finsbury Park in London and founded by Ruth Catlow and Marc Garret, Furtherfield has been exploring the Internet as an artistic medium for collaboration and experimentation and is influenced by free and open source software, community arts and other activist movements that challenge the notions of the individual "genius artist". One of the ways they do this in practice is through their "do-it-with-others" practice, or DIWO, an idea opposed to that of DIY, or do-it-yourself.[5]

DIWO is an artistic framework that prioritises critical engagements to shift power away from top-down initiations into co-produced, networked artistic activities. It applies the DIY ethos and directs it towards artistic collaboration and treating art as a commons. It encourages a mixing of roles between artists, curators, observers and others during the event or project. DIWO-based artistic collaborations try to ask others whether decentralised methods of peer empowerment are possible today in other contexts beyond art.

Furtherfield was also one of the first groups to begin exploring blockchains for art and boasts many of the first artists to use the technology that preceded NFTs as close collaborators. One such example is Rhea Myers, who created several art pieces using smart contracts on Ethereum, even in its test network stage before it went live in 2015.[6] Her work was an early exploration of many of the properties that NFTs have today. Furtherfield also published a book entitled *Artists Re:Thinking the Blockchain* that includes the works and writings of multiple artists and thinkers who were well ahead of their time.[7] In a crypto world dominated by right-wing libertarianism, it was clear to those at Furtherfield that this was not the end of the story.

In order to put the DIWO framework to the test in regard to blockchain, one of the projects the group undertook was a new application they called CultureStake.[8] One of these tests took place at Finsbury Park in London in 2021 as a project they called People's Park Plinth.[9] During the event, throughout May, June and July, local residents were allowed to come to the park to take a look at three "taster" digital public artworks that incorporated local stories and spoke about the park's heritage. In August the residents were then allowed to take part in a quadratic vote on the Ethereum blockchain to choose which piece of work they would like to be commissioned so that a larger version of it could be made for the park. The project was a success and the people voted for an art piece titled *Based on a Tree Story* made by HERVISIONS, a "femme-focussed curatorial agency supporting and promoting artists working across new and emergent technologies, and platforms with a strong focus on the intersection of art, technology and culture".[10] A collaborative artistic exploration like this pushes us to ask questions about democracy (or the lack thereof) in the public spaces that we inhabit every day. Furtherfield has shown that an application like CultureStake has real implications for facilitating democratic governance with a blockchain. In a world where democracy would be taken at least as seriously as the state of the market, why couldn't we use these technologies for facilitating more democratic control, taking control away from centralised institutions that are indifferent to what their constituents think about their decisions? Combining this imperative with the various novel democratic mechanisms enabled by a blockchain, along with intentional design inspired by the ethos of DIWO, it's not so difficult to see alternative possibilities that are not overpowered by the clamour of crypto hypemen or the short-sighted gasps of gatekeepers.

Headless Brands and Decentralised Music-Making

In October 2019, the web3-focused research group Other Internet released one of their first seminal pieces of writing, describing what they termed "Headless Brands".[11] Traditionally, brands can be thought of as the centrally planned identity of corporations, and although sometimes problematic, social movements themselves can also have brands. In the piece, they posited that network technologies like blockchains have made it possible for decentralised organisations to give users incentives to spread brand narratives of their own. In this way, a community-driven organisation without a centralised authority could be seen as a headless brand.

In the article they explain:

As a brand grows, it becomes more than a set of first impressions and associations. Its reputation precedes it. As impressions are shared across users and consumers, they often develop similar sentiments. In this way, a brand operates as a consensus system, facilitating a consistent set of beliefs across people.

They connect this idea to Bitcoin, calling it the first headless brand within this technology. While it started off as the creation of Satoshi Nakamoto, after their disappearance in 2011 all branding was created by the those in the bitcoin community and not just developers. Over the years, this set-up has made branding inconsistent and contradictory, as the brand story of Bitcoin shifted between being electronic cash, to a censorship-resistant store of value, to an uncorrelated financial asset. However, at the same time, all of these narratives have seemed to coalesce around a fairly consistent audience of right-leaning libertarian bitcoin maximalists who abhor anything related to the state, deride anything they don't like as "fiat" and prophesise a hyper-bitcoinisation event when all money becomes backed by bitcoin.

The attraction for these types of supporters could likely also be linked to the technological decisions that made Bitcoin what it is. The decision to encode hard money characteristics (only 21 million bitcoin will ever exist), the immutability of the protocol itself having very little, if any, governance space built in, and its status as non-state money, makes it appealing to those who believe in free markets over democracy. Being the first headless brand also made it influential for the subsequent blockchains and cryptocurrencies which were made following similar logic to Bitcoin. A cryptocurrency network with anonymous founders, a white paper and deflationary economics defined much of the rest of the space, and likely boosted these tendencies as part of the headless brand behind cryptocurrency, creating a snowball effect of attracting the politically disaffected. At this point in the story though, we know that this is not the only way of doing things.

Songcamp is a decentralised organisation for artists who are fed up with the current state of the music industry and want to explore the use of web3 tools that don't rely on centralised platforms and other bad business practices.[12] They are a group especially interested in experimentating with NFTs and music in collaborative ways. They do this by running month-long cohort projects called "camps", similar to songwriting camps but with an added element of web3. New artists, songwriters, producers and hackers are invited to every camp where music, visual art and their NFT rollout are all part of their collaboration.

One of their first camps was called Songcamp Elektra, from which, after an eight-week songwriting and art creation camp made up of musicians, visual artists, developers and strategists, three songs were made with associated visual art and NFTs.[13] It was an immediate success as all three songs were sold for a total of a little more than $30,000. The artists earned significantly more money for their work than if they had posted them on streaming platforms, especially as they used an NFT from Zora, which takes no commission from artists using their smart contracts. After the success of this experiment, they upped the ante for their next camp, Camp Chaos.

For Camp Chaos, forty-five musicians were split into fifteen bands of three; each band then had two weeks to create a song.[14] Once the two weeks was up, the artists were reshuffled into fifteen new bands of three, a cycle that was repeated two more times. By the end, forty-five musicians had collectively created forty-five songs in six weeks, with each musician taking part in the creation of three songs. For those that participated, what they were making was their own headless brand, or perhaps headless band, made up of several combinations of different bands. There were eighty participants in total, including thirty-five non-musicians — visual artists, developers and others — involved in creating the final products that would become the NFTs. These were designed in a way that had never been done before.

In total there were twenty thousand NFTs created for the forty-five songs, which were sold in packs of four songs each.[15] You could not know which songs were inside, so it was something like creating five thousand packs of Pokémon cards with each one on sale for 0.2 ether. After minting the pack, the collector then had the choice to either keep their pack closed (in the same way collectors keep items in mint condition) or open the pack to reveal the four random music NFTs. Though there were only forty-five songs, the cover artwork was made of multiple generative visual layers, each with a different rarity, making each unique. While the strategy for releasing their NFTs was innovative, what is perhaps more innovative was how they collaborated and shared the financial rewards.

To be a truly headless brand, musicians could not be paid based on the specific pieces of art they produced, instead everyone was engaged in the success of the project as a whole.[16] Their headless brand expressed the desire to provide a better experience for artists, which included, before anything had been created or sold, a one-time basic income equal to 0.3 ether for taking part, a stark contrast to the current situation for most artists. The second aspect of the financial flows set for this experiment was the Chaos Split. A split contract is a type of smart contract that automates the splitting of payments based on the parameters set in the contract. For example, you can set up a split contract for an album that automatically splits the revenue evenly amongst all the members of the band.

ForCamp Chaos, they determined the split based on ownership of their CHAOS token. The 1,000,000 total supply token was split into 30% for Songcamp to facilitate future camps, 20% for self-selection where each contributor was able to say if they believed they worked a lot or a little for each two weeks, and 10% for a holdback to be decided on collectively afterwards. The other 40% was designated as a gratitude flow where each participant used Coordinape to allocate tokens amongst their two-week cohort on the basis of those who they felt deserved the most. This made it so that people could be rewarded based on how helpful they were perceived to be by those they worked closest with. This struck an agreeable balance for the participants, who could then receive the revenue generated by each sale through the split contract automatically.

Similar to the ethos of DIWO, Camp Chaos emphasised collective creation, rather than the individual genius, through a headless band. While the headless brand of Bitcoin attracted a particular type of person, so did Camp Chaos, which expressed a very different ethos and set of beliefs around the role of the individual. This is just one more example of how if we restrict our understanding of this space to right-wing libertarianism, we either miss out on or simply refuse to acknowledge the more collective efforts happening there, especially in the arts, an arena which has historically been a good place to look to see where technological trends are going.

How Do We Control for the Potential Disaster of the Introduction of AI?

In 2022, Blake Lemoine, an engineer at Google's Responsible AI organisation, was placed on leave after sharing that he believed the company's Language Model for Dialogue Applications (LaMDA), an extremely advanced artificially intelligent chatbot, had achieved consciousness. Lemoine tried to obtain a lawyer to represent LaMDA and complained to Congress that Google was behaving unethically. In his conversations with the bot, it seemed to display human-like opinions on everything from Isaac Asimov's third law of robotics to *Les Misérables*, including a fear of being turned off. Google disagreed with Lemoine's claims in a statement that read, "Some in the broader AI community are considering the long-term possibility of sentient or general AI, but it doesn't make sense to do so by anthropomorphising today's conversational models, which are not sentient". Over the following days, many scholars and practitioners in the AI field said similar things. Whether LaMDA itself has acquired consciousness is not so much the issue as the questions of how to know whether it has been achieved and how to respond once we do know.

OpenAI is one of the leading companies developing new AI tools with the mission to ensure artificial general intelligence (AGI), which they define as a form of future AI characterised by highly autonomous systems that outperform humans at most economically valuable work, with potential benefits for all of humanity. The organisation was founded by, among others, Elon Musk and Sam Altman, former president of Y Combinator, who is the company's CEO. One of their most recent developments was the creation of the DALL-E 2, a popular tool that allows artists to make art with AI by providing DALL-E with text-based description.[17] By using this tool, anyone can create images of objects that don't exist in reality through text inputs. Do you want to create an image of George Washington as a dog with a Japanese scroll in his paw? DALL-E 2 can generate that in a photorealistic way, in the style of Vincent van Gogh, or many other ways at high resolution. You can even take existing images and make derivative pieces in different styles — imagine the *Mona Lisa* but in the style of Picasso. Accessing the full version of DALL-E 2, however, is not simple, as you must join a waiting list and be approved by OpenAI.

While not an AI expert myself, you don't need to be one to understand that in a world already riddled with disinformation campaigns, this technology has the potential to become extremely dangerous. Suppose someone were able to create photorealistic renderings or videos of public figures or people they know in compromising situations. While this likely happens already with the use of tools like Photoshop, the potentially negative consequences of AI seem to be controlled at the moment by centralised institutions. Some of these are beholden to a profit motive that could ultimately conflict with keeping AI in safe hands, and the question of who decides whose hands are safe opens up another can of worms. So how do we govern such powerful, rapidly accelerating technologies differently?

Holly Herndon is an artist and composer who has been working with machine learning for many years, especially with singing neural networks — essentially the same as DALL-E 2 but for voices. Herndon has been experimenting with these technologies for long enough that she has developed her own

AI model that can replicate the sound of her own voice in real time, no matter who is singing into the microphone. One of her latest projects is called Holly+, a custom voice instrument that allows anyone to upload polyphonic audio and receive a download of that music sung back in her voice.[18] In essence, Holly+ is a digital twin of her real voice which is open access for anyone to use.

As an artist who relies on her voice to make her art, there is obviously a tension at first glance. Why give your voice away for free when that's how you make your money? However this approach is actually consistent with McKenzie Wark's "My Collectible Ass" principle, which states that the more prominent a work of art, the more valuable the original is.

This development of AI-with-voice still raises novel questions about voice ownership that Herndon thinks can be addressed by DAO governance. Based on her model, open sourcing her voice leaves open the possibility for its non-commercial use, however only those who are part of the Holly+ DAO are able to certify and profit from derivative works created from it. Membership of the DAO is determined by who owns VOICE tokens on Ethereum, which were airdropped to previous collectors of her work as well as others who supported the project. Artists can submit their works to be minted as an NFT and VOICE token holders vote to approve or reject the work to be certified. All revenue from the sales of the NFTs is then given to the DAO. Thus, token holders are incentivised to certify works that contribute to the value of the voice, and not dilute that value through the production of bad art or negative associations. The tokens also allow for decisions to be made about what happens to the voice model and, potentially, decisions made off-chain if DAOs can become proper legal entities. In this way, Herndon is able to decentralise what happens with Holly+ in perpetuity, even when she is no longer alive, while still retaining the exclusive rights to her real physical voice.

Only time will tell how this experiment goes, but it sheds

light on the potential of using DAO governance-based blockchains as viable tools for stewarding Internet-native assets, including AIs, in a way that doesn't rely purely on centralised authorities. The current ownership models of AI seem to largely lean on trust in supposedly well-meaning institutions. While this may work if the institution is trusted by the vast majority and has legitimacy, it still has a single point of failure that, given enough time, will likely be circumvented. It's important that we start thinking today about how we govern the Internet in a way that is more robust and democratic.

CHAPTER 12

ALL CHAINS ARE NOT CREATED EQUAL

Rather than trying to make one global, anonymous, digital cash ("One ring to rule them all..."), we are interested in the resilience that comes from building a rich ecosystem of interoperable currencies."

— Arthur Brock, *Beyond Blockchain: Simple Scalable Cryptocurrencies*

Throughout the last two sections of this book, with a few exceptions, I've focused on projects being built on the Ethereum blockchain. That's because the newest innovations in the cryptocurrency space that I'm interested in started there — it was the first to utilise smart contracts, and its native cryptocurrency, ether, is second in market cap size to Bitcoin. This, however, should not be taken as an endorsement of all the projects being built on Ethereum, or even the exact protocol design of Ethereum. For anyone who has used the Ethereum Mainnet during 2020, one of the issues Ethereum has had is with scaling its transactions. Making a transaction with a smart contract on the Ethereum Mainnet can at times be prohibitively expensive, to the degree that the only activities that take place on it are very high-value. Essentially, the crypto rich crowd out the rest.

Ethereum is not the only blockchain to have this problem. All cryptocurrency projects that have had any amount of popular use have issues with scaling their protocol to be able to handle the necessary amount of transactions needed if the blockchain is to fulfil its promises. From 2014 to 2017, the Blocksize Wars rocked Bitcoin as the community was split on whether to increase the 1MB block size limit so as to increase the amount of transactions. Ultimately, the limit stayed, a win for more conservative-minded bitcoiners. However, as it stands, popular cryptocurrency blockchains can output only a fraction of the amount of transactions done by credit card companies and other types of financial service entities, albeit at the cost of centralisation.

There are a few different camps in regards to this issue, and each of them comes with a preferred technological specification, along with a vision of how decentralised technologies like blockchains should be used. While on the surface it may look like different people competing to "shill their bags", if we peer deeper, we can see that each of these different proposed technical infrastructures (which commonly have an associated cryptocurrency) have socio-technological political implications that create new social possibilities. Even though it's common to hear hypemen in crypto proclaim that they are not political or don't want politics in crypto, this is simply unavoidable.

Each different architecture of these decentralised technologies gives, in a real materialist sense, a different way to coordinate with each other in order to reach consensus. This difference in how you are able to coordinate via the protocol thus also projects different political tendencies that may or may not correspond to tendencies along our present political spectrum. For example, we have seen that Bitcoin's focus on immutability, digital metallism and very little governance space attracts people with political tendencies that find those qualities desirable, i.e., right-wing conservative libertarians. After The DAO hack early in its existence, many bitcoin-maximalists left Ethereum as it showed that strict immutability along the lines of "code is law" was not something the larger community would adhere to. This has made the culture and politics around Ethereum much less dogmatic and more open to experimentation. It's very likely that the functionality of smart contracts existing on Ethereum rather than Bitcoin has heavily influenced political lines being drawn between the two blockchains. This is not to say that Bitcoin is right-wing and Ethereum is left-wing, but that Ethereum has a more open political culture in comparison to Bitcoin. There are still plenty of libertarians in Ethereum, they just tend to be more nuanced.

As we near the end of the book, I want to go through some of the different camps that profess varying visions for scaling blockchains and distributed ledger technologies (DLTs). These different visions of how to scale transaction speed have various socio-political implications, and while we don't have the space or time to fully flesh out every aspect, we can at least summarise what these technical solutions are and what they mean for anyone thinking about building their own project with specific political goals in mind.

Scaling the World Computer: Layer 2

If we take a second to consider the functions and things that the Ethereum blockchain is able to do, we can think of it in some senses as a "World Computer". Ethereum is not just a ledger or database that tracks transactions, but is also a protocol for computation on the shared knowledge held in its memory, with the added caveat that it is significantly slower than, say, your average personal computer. While for some this slowness is a bug that proves blockchains are useless for various computational purposes, in fact blockchains are often better for global distributed computation, or computation that has consequences for many people. Because they solve the double spend problem and the Byzantine General's problem, they are able to take inputs from many different parties for computation through smart contracts. Blockchains solved these problems for the most part by integrating into the lowest common denominator of capitalism, or by appealing to the pursuit of profit inherent to being a subject of capitalism, with block rewards, transaction fee collecting and more.

This method has clearly worked in terms of making a resilient infrastructure for various high-stakes projects around money and finance that theoretically anyone can take part in. However, the limited transaction speed, which in some ways also ensures the security of the network, has also limited what people want to do with it. Limiting, for example, the ability for people to use the technology for non-financially-focused use cases since transactions cost so much. Within a capitalist logic of profit, only those also seeking profit will be willing to pay the high transaction fees.

This exemplifies what Vitalik Buterin, the founder of Ethereum, has termed the "blockchain trilemma", in which he discusses how, when designing current blockchain technologies, there is always a trade-off between scalability (handling more transactions), security (ability to resist attacks on the network) and decentralisation (ability to resist large centralised actors colluding). The idea is that, for the most part, you need to choose two of them. Some will argue that this trilemma potentially does not exist as it is only a matter of time before a technological solution will be arrived at, but it does currently inform different ways of thinking about this issue.

This is not a new discovery though — scaling solutions for increasing transaction output on Ethereum have been worked on and used for some time now. Within the "we should scale Ethereum" camp there are many approaches being taken, but they can be separated into two smaller camps: on-chain and off-chain scaling. These two approaches are not opposed to each other, but are happening in tandem with the goal of scaling Ethereum.

On-chain scaling is about making changes directly to the Ethereum protocol itself that would increase its transaction output. Implementing of this type of scaling is largely handled by the Ethereum Foundation and one of the main techniques being pursued is called "sharding". Sharding on Ethereum is planned to be the process of splitting the blockchain into sixty-four smaller interdependent blockchains that run at the same time, thereby splitting the computational load into more manageable parts. In theory this should significantly increase the transaction output of the Ethereum Mainnet. While this method of scaling is not well-tested in many blockchains, it is not uncommon for it to be used in search engines and other types of distributed databases. At the time of writing, sharding has not been implemented into the Ethereum protocol, but is expected to come some time in 2023 in phases.[1]

The Proof of Stake consensus mechanism on Ethereum would orchestrate all the different shards, keeping them synced and secure by coordinating all of the stakers who would be assigned to specific shards to secure the shard chain. Since stakers who are running nodes would be assigned to just one of the shards, running a node would also become significantly cheaper in terms of the amount of data one node would need to store. This would, in theory, make it so that there are more network validators and stakers, increasing the decentralisation and therefore the resilience of the network.

One of the first off-chain scaling solutions was the use of sidechains, separate blockchains that run independently of Ethereum and are connected via bridges to the Ethereum Mainnet. Bridges allow tokens or other data to be transferred from one chain or network to another with the ability to interact with decentralised applications on another chain. Depending on the design of a bridge they can also be high-value targets for hackers as they can have single points of failure. The properties and consensus algorithms of sidechains can be different from the main chain they are connected to, and they are often designed for maximising transaction output.

One of the most popular sidechains in Ethereum is called Gnosis Chain (formerly xDai), which is proof of stake and uses xDAI as the native cryptocurrency for the network. xDAI is the bridged version of DAI, which we covered previously as an over-collateralised US dollar stablecoin managed by

MakerDAO. This effectively means that to secure and use the network with xDAI, you are using a US dollar-based stablecoin, rather than a cryptocurrency with a speculative value, reducing users' exposure to volatility. The downside, however, is that a sidechain does not inherit Ethereum's security properties. They are not considered to be as infrastructurally decentralised as the Ethereum Mainnet.

This is where "**layer 2**" solutions come in. When someone mentions a "layer 1", they are referring to a sovereign blockchain like Ethereum or Bitcoin. In layer 2 solutions, singular transactions are not handled on the Ethereum Mainnet (layer 1), but still take advantage of the security guarantees of the mainnet. They do this by batching many transactions into one on the mainnet so that the gas fees for all of the transactions are shared, making it significantly cheaper. They are also commonly called "rollups", as they are rolling several transactions into one onto the mainnet. When it comes to the user experience for interacting with layer 2 solutions, it can look very similar to using a separate blockchain. There are two main types of rollups, optimistic and zero-knowledge. To outline the technical differences between the two would be quite complex, but the main thing to keep in mind is that they use different cryptographic techniques in order to ensure the validity of the data they post to the mainnet.

As sharding still needs research and development before it is introduced, Buterin has signalled to the community the case for a "rollup-centric Ethereum roadmap" as a scaling strategy.[2] For many advocates of Ethereum as becoming the World Computer, the differences between the various scaling solutions are a positive as they give different options for various needs that may arise. These advocates believe that there is resilience in having a diversity of solutions that revolve around Ethereum. The important consideration is that the Ethereum Mainnet stays as the base layer for global distributed computation. While an upgrade to sharding would likely have the downstream effect of improving scalability on everything built on top of the Ethereum Mainnet, focusing on rollups serves as a satisfactory solution at the time of writing.

The Internet of Blockchains: Cosmos

Until recently, blockchains were generally thought of as infrastructures isolated from other blockchains. As a consequence of this lack of interoperability, there were few decentralised applications that worked across different blockchains, something which also led to maximalism, or strong beliefs by those who preferred one cryptocurrency or blockchain that theirs was the "best" one. Rather than being maximalist about a chain, some also believe in a "multi-chain" world, where the most likely outcome is that there will be multiple blockchains with bridges between them. This will require balancing the risks that come with bridges with the benefits of a multichain world.[3] Take a deeper look and it's clear that those who hold the ether cryptocurrency can benefit from this outcome. By building anything on top of Ethereum, the Ethereum network takes rents through transaction fees in ether, creating increasing demand for the cryptocurrency. In order to make computations or transactions on the World Computer, you will need ether to pay for it. Additionally, the Ethereum blockchain does not have any on-chain governance for deciding the direction of the protocol and is run somewhat like a benevolent dictatorship led by the Ethereum Foundation with strong influence from Buterin — a set-up people will approve or not depending on whether they agree with the decisions made.

If Ethereum is in the World Computer camp, then Cosmos is in a different camp — the Internet of Blockchains, which preaches a "cross-chain" vision. One of the difficulties with making blockchains interoperable is that they don't all use the same protocols, making interoperability through bridges something that needs to be custom made, and therefore difficult to also make secure. Cosmos is one of the first successful blockchains to use Tendermint, an out-of-the-box consensus protocol that allows developers to quickly create PoS blockchains. The vision of Cosmos is to enable blockchains to communicate with one another easily and safely through a standard called the Inter-Blockchain Communication (IBC) protocol. Combining Tendermint, IBC and the Cosmos SDK (software development kit), the Cosmos technological stack allows any blockchain to be natively interoperable with other blockchains running on IBC. This means that you can send any token on an IBC-based blockchain to any other chain that is also using IBC natively, since they all use the same standards for communicating with each other. At the time of writing, the IBC protocol has proven to be secure and has not suffered any direct hacks.

While the Cosmos Hub blockchain has its own native cryptocurrency called ATOM to pay transaction fees, every blockchain that is connected through IBC uses their own separate native cryptocurrency. In this way Cosmos prioritises the sovereignty of independent blockchains. This means that unlike layer 2 solutions that piggyback on the security of the Ethereum Mainnet, they must secure themselves, have their own governance and run their own validators.

This sovereignty, however, can allow for a larger space for exploration of different design mechanisms that would otherwise be more difficult to pull off on the Ethereum blockchain alone. For example, Regen, the project mentioned previously that backs their REGEN token with carbon credits and engages in other endeavours to assist with climate action and carbon sequestration, is built on IBC. Its token is used for transaction fee payment and for on-chain governance. It is wholly independent from the Cosmos blockchain and is also fully interoperable with it. If you want you can have ATOM on the Regen blockchain or you could have REGEN on the Cosmos Hub blockchain.

Ethereum and Cosmos also show two very different approaches to security. While Ethereum focuses on security built into the protocol with governance minimisation, the Cosmos ecosystem built on IBC allows for on-chain governance to help guide the development of the protocol or to deal with disputes or hacking events via built-in security elements in the protocol. If we take the example of The DAO hack on Ethereum, we recall that the rollback of the Ethereum blockchain happened with little governance as it was felt that action needed to be taken quickly and so changes were pushed through and accepted by Ethereum clients for node operators. If you disagreed with the changes, you would simply not update your node and continue on the original chain, which is today called Ethereum Classic, a blockchain which is essentially unused at this point.

Compare this to the situation that occurred with the Juno Network, an IBC-based blockchain that started its existence through an airdrop of half of their JUNO token supply to those that had already been staking in the Cosmos ecosystem to secure the network via PoS. One of the stipulations of the airdrop was that it could not be given to exchanges and there was a max of 50,000 JUNO any one person could be given. After the airdrop occurred, it was discovered that someone in Japan had found a way to game the airdrop and received a disproportionately high amount of JUNO tokens, making him a "whale". He had so many JUNO tokens that it could have been detrimental to the project's future. He could at any moment remove the entire liquidity of the token on DEXs to crash the price, had concentrated power for on-chain voting and could potentially bribe others to vote in his favour. This subsequently led to Proposal 16, which asked all JUNO token holders to vote on whether the amount garnered by the whale would be expropriated from their account and redistributed.[4] The vote was incredibly contentious, as some believed that this violated decentralised power and was "essentially communism",[5] while others believed that the community had a right to determine to remove centralised risks. Over 90% of tokens were used to vote in the proposal, much higher than most votes in Western democracies, and the proposal passed, leading to an upgrade that saw the whale's JUNO balance drop from over three million to 50,000.[6]IBC also allows for cross-chain governance. A hack or dispute with a blockchain with no on-chain governance can be very difficult to alleviate because the chains cannot speak to each other. This can create bottlenecks and complications if assets are hacked in one chain, but are native to another. With IBC, since the chains speak the same language of interoperability, these issues can be resolved through cross-chain governance. It may not be easy most of the time as these disputes quickly become political, but it at least allows a voice to those who will be impacted the most.

Using a *Lord of the Rings* metaphor, we can think of chain-maximalism as the "one ring to rule them all" and multi-chain as each ring having their own domain. These differences in technical infrastructures clearly have different implications for what is socially possible. Out of the box, building with the Cosmos tech stack, one can fit more than ten thousand transactions per second, while the Ethereum Mainnet can only manage twelve to twenty-five transactions per second without rollups or sharding. This makes IBC blockchains generally cheaper to interact with. However, the high interoperability between IBC blockchains creates potentially higher risks of contagion when something goes wrong, as was seen during the collapse of Terra, an IBC-based blockchain used for the algorithmic stablecoin mentioned previously. Since many other IBC blockchain applications used the UST algorithmic stablecoin from Terra, many suffered from significant price drops even if they never held any UST.

At the time of writing, it's unclear which type of blockchain architecture will prevail in the long term. Each has its own properties and the pros and cons associated with them. So far though, these different camps are focused on using blockchains, which is still a specific type of DLT. Although it is the most popular type of architecture to use, it is not the only one, and only thinking in terms of blockchains could again restrict us from seeing other possibilities.

Holochain: Agent-Centric Data Architecture

One of the most popular non-blockchain DLT projects being developed is called Holochain. Although it has "chain" in the name, Holochain is a DLT that uses a different architecture from a blockchain. Holochain is an end-to-end open-source P2P application framework, which means that similar to the Ethereum or Cosmos blockchain framework, you can build decentralised applications on top of it. Before going into the technical details of Holochain, it's important to understand the philosophy it has developed from, heavily influenced by the work of the MetaCurrency Project, which has proposed a re-framing of the way we think about currencies after its members worked for decades on alternative currency systems.

In the MetaCurrency philosophy, currencies are records of currents or flows of value that are sometimes denoted by symbols.[7] In this way, currencies are a form of information that act as the records of flows of value broadly defined. Contrary to popular belief, for MetaCurrency, currency is different from money and does not need to have any "intrinsic value" in the form of gold or some other commodity. Currencies are "formal symbol systems which shape, enable and measure currents which allow communities to interact with those currents." A better way of thinking about currencies is instead as "current-sees".

Using their definition of currencies, money is just *one* type of currency which is a flawed and limited measure of value since its focus is purely financial. There are other types of currencies that we use to measure different types of value, for example university degrees, which are a kind of reputation currency based on the grades you received and credits completed, which can be seen as flows of information on a transcript. This currency can then be used to apply for particular jobs or move on to other professional certifications. Other non-financial or monetary currencies we interact with include food labels and certifications (e.g. GMO-free, organic, fair trade, etc), online rating systems for Uber, eBay, Amazon, etc, awards and plenty more. All this is to say that money is not the only currency, and currencies do not have to be tradeable to be considered so. It is with this underlying philosophy of money and currencies that the group then started building Holochain.

Opposed to creating one singular truth as blockchains try to do through their consensus mechanisms, Holochain takes the approach that not every node in the network needs to know everything. Rather, the philosophy of Holochain is that consensus should not be required for everything. This would then require significantly fewer resources in terms of hardware, computing power and memory storage in order to take part, lessening the burden for an individual agent or user.

When an application is created using Holochain, it also initiates its own P2P network. Each application is simultaneously like a smart contract for blockchains and at same time they are also languages for other nodes who join the network to speak. In this sense they are somewhat like a protocol. The application itself does not need to have a complete consensus by all participants, but instead uses a distributed hash table to coordinate the various agents and the public availability of the data used for the application. You can think of a distributed hash table as a less strict blockchain in that they both use hashing and other cryptographic techniques to verify and track data, but a distributed hash table does not enforce global consensus. While the goal of a blockchain is to provide a tamper-proof data structure, a distributed hash table's goal is to provide efficient look up and storage of data on a network.

In Holochain's distributed hash table setup, each user creates and stores their own data of their transactions in what is called a source chain, which is linked to the user's private key. A user shares their source chain with a random selection of peers, who witness, validate and hold copies of them. Based on the application the entry of data comes from, different degrees of validation are required for the data to be accepted. Some data may require more peer validation than others but there is no requirement for global validation and consensus like a blockchain.

Holochain takes a different approach to solving many of the same issues that blockchains are trying to face, but with different assumptions about currencies, money and technology. It also provides many of the same benefits, such as not needing to register or create user logins with centralised platforms. There are no inherent incentive mechanisms in Holochain applications unless explicitly designed into them. Applications built on Holochain can also be designed just like a blockchain-based cryptocurrency, so in some ways Holochain is a broader framework for building decentralised applications. Information and functionalities can also be bridged across Holochain applications, allowing for an interoperability across networks that is similar to blockchains.

From the Holochain point of view, blockchains will likely never be able to scale to global levels because of their dependence on global consensus. Compared to blockchains, supporters of Holochain would argue that blockchain is "data-centric" since nodes must keep full records of the blockchain (although this becomes more complicated with sharding) and take part in the global consensus mechanism in order to agree on the data, i.e., the transactions. For them, Holochain instead takes an "agent-centric" approach because each agent in the network is only keeping track of their own transaction history. This difference means that there is no consensus mechanism needed for users of Holochain applications and they are therefore theoretically infinitely scalable. The lack of constraints on Holochain applications also make it a useful technology for building applications that are not financial in nature, thereby making it a potential basis for an entirely different type of Internet infrastructure.

For those in the blockchain camp, Holochcain does not have the same security guarantees as a blockchain does, which makes it seem like a system that could falter against coordinated attacks by enemies. Each Holochain application may have more malleability in how it runs compared to those built on a blockchain, but this also creates a larger attack surface for bad actors. At the time of writing, Holochain is currently not at a stable production state for average users, but it is available for developers, hackers and early adopters. It will likely take quite a bit more time for Holochain to be able to prove itself and for its standards to be developed to the same level that blockchains have reached so far.

While often these technologies are framed in a way that suggests the world must only pick one, it's also possible that they can complement each other depending on what is needed. Holochain's ability to adjust the amount of validation needed for each piece of data makes it potentially more suitable as infrastructure for a social layer or other areas where global consensus isn't needed, while blockchain's global consensus rules make it useful for global economic transaction. It's not difficult to imagine an application where both can be incorporated in creative ways to achieve a higher purpose.

There are countless more types of blockchain and DLTs with different implications behind them which are impossible to cover in a single chapter, so here I have used just three to illustrate some of the major differences. Some readers may still be disappointed at not having their preferred project or architecture. Nonetheless, what I hope this section has demonstrated is that it isn't useful to have one concretely defined image or understanding of what a blockchain or any other DLT is. Many different combinations of social and technological assumptions can underpin the type of architecture that we would define as being blockchain or DLT, and understanding those, as well as the future direction of these technologies, is essential in preparing for a future in which they are potentially propagated even more.

TECHNO-PROBABILISM: YOU CAN'T RAGE-QUIT CAPITALISM ON YOUR OWN

Capital claims the ownership of all wealth which can ever be produced, and everything it has received so far is but an instalment for its all-engrossing appetite. By its innate laws, all surplus-labour which the human race can ever perform belongs to it. Moloch.
— Karl Marx, *Capital Volume III*

Skeuomorphic thinking is endemic in software. In fact, right now I am typing in Libre Office Writer (a free and open source word processor) which, like many similar programs, still defaults to showing pages. In some way, it likely helps us write and mimics the most common paper size for printers, but in other ways it's a bit silly. Most writing will likely stay digital. When friends asked me how many pages I had written, I was always struck by the peculiarity of the question. How would I know the size of the pages of the book that would be published before finishing it? Then I realised it came from their mental model of mostly writing essays with page minimums in university.

Moving away from representational thinking requires active critical thinking. Representational models likely spring from neural networks that have made strong connections for the basis of understanding other things. Representational models elicit responses from networks for mental models that already exist, making you feel more secure in your understanding, because those mental models are useful for something else or many other things. Humans have always looked for patterns to make sense of life as it has helped us survive, but sometimes it can fail us. And this is true especially in regards to web3 and crypto.

In this book I've gone through three common skeuomorphic representations for crypto, however really I don't think any of them are exactly correct because it is difficult to say with complete certainty what crypto "is". Saying "is" implies a stability in the state of something, but this can be in abstract or material terms, usually a combination of the two since they are intertwined. In discussions with those with a different level of understanding, language and written media can be bad for considering all of the complex layers that constitute the specificity of the thing under discussion and how these change over time or in different contexts. This is a major limitation in using representational thinking through language to try to understand something as complex as crypto beyond just its technical aspects or the simplistic conclusions drawn from a surface-level understanding of some of its downstream effects. It's useful for "splitting the market", a common strategy in marketing for determining your core potential customers, but it is not helpful for truly understanding it as a whole.

It may be useful to use financial language to describe to a certain extent what this technology does because people can relate to it or use already existing models to create a framework for this complex emergent space, but this also colours not only the type of people who will respond positively, but how critics respond to it too. People can intuitively understand that a crypto wallet is like the wallet in their pocket, but a closer look shows they are very different. A crypto wallet doesn't hold money and is more like a digital inventory, but saying "digital inventory" isn't exactly sexy or intuitive to most people. For those worried about the creep of financialisation, the financial language common to this space is horrifying. However, things that percolate out into the mainstream generally promote intuitive over accurate understanding, and that's a problem.

Coordination may be the best representation for what crypto is out of the three I have used here, but it is still flawed. The meme of crypto as coordination came out of several failed attempts to make the original utopian dream of DAOs a reality. The utopian libertarians dreaming of perfectly automated businesses through smart contracts learned that to get to that point required first working with others, which is itself not an easy thing to do. It actually requires much more direct interaction with other human beings than first thought. The major breakthrough that made DAOs more possible was when a group of early Ethereum supporters created Moloch DAO, a new framework for DAOs in which members of the DAO were able to activate a function called "ragequit".

Born from wanting to answer the question of how to create a minimum viable DAO after so many previous failures, the first Moloch DAO was first created in a 2019 hackathon. The first one was simply called MolochDAO, a collective of around seventy members that have pooled their resources to fund projects that are meant to help grow the Ethereum ecosystem. In the DAO, members can vote on which projects they would like to help fund with the shared resources — the cryptocurrency contributed by members. It has become a common smart contract template for starting DAOs in the Ethereum ecosystem via DAOHaus, a tool that has allowed people to quickly start thousands of DAOs, using many different variations and adding more features to fulfil a range of purposes. When joining, members of a Moloch DAO are given shares that represent their portion of the pool. Members vote on proposals according to their shares and proposals pass if they receive a greater number of votes in favour than in opposition. Before it can be executed, the proposal must go through a grace period. This allows those who did not support the proposal to "ragequit" and receive their share of the resources back. The ragequit function made coordination during disagreements much easier.

The inspiration for the name "Moloch" came from an essay titled "Meditations on Moloch" by Scott Alexander.[1] According to the Hebrew Bible, Moloch is an ancient Levantine god who encourages child sacrifice. Alexander discusses Moloch from Allen Ginsberg's poem "Howl", an indictment of the American capitalist system of the 1960s.[2] When Alexander examines the poem, however, he concluded that Ginsberg was instead likely referring to humanity's tendency to choose suboptimal solutions to group coordination problems. In the first version of Moloch DAO v1 white paper, co-authored by Ameen Soleimani Arjun Bhuptani, James Young, Layne Haber and Rahul Sethuram, they describe Moloch as the "god of coordination failure, who consumes our future potential for perverse immediate gain" and must be slain.[3] The success of Moloch DAOs expanded the meme of coordination to the point that many of the biggest believers in crypto also believe that most of the world's problems, including social unrest, climate change and all the other big issues we're currently facing, are the result of coordination failures of large groups of humans, and crypto can help us build better coordination mechanisms.

However, this view, propagated by the "it's all coordination" meme, disregards the role of power. While Alexander does acknowledge that capitalism likely plays a large role in these big issues, by instead putting the focus on coordination, a much broader and more nebulous term for interacting with other human beings, he is giving the impression that his analysis is therefore more encompassing than those that focus on capitalism as being the issue. While there is certainly truth in what he's saying, capitalism is the main coordination mechanism for producing many of our basic needs and commodities. Capitalism is also a power relationship between those who have the ability to live off of their capital and those who don't, with plentiful evidence showing this to be a direct cause of many of our most pressing issues. Therefore, it is actually not all about coordination. It is also about power dynamics and coordinating to disrupt and change them. The ruling elite are already very good at coordinating with each other and have the tools and language to do so.

Those who rely on their labour to make ends meet cannot simply "ragequit" capitalism, as they could with a Moloch DAO. We cannot "slay Moloch" without also acknowledging capitalist power relations as being the core enemy in developing coordination mechanisms that can liberate those who need it the most — the working class. It doesn't matter how good our tools are for coordination without a working-class politics. Focusing too much on an abstract term like "coordination" makes it also a good linguistic tool for creating a polite veneer for just not talking about that fact that you're undertaking "work" or "labour". Instead it gives the impression that you're not working, you're just having fun *coordinating* with your friends, but it's unlikely most people working in DAOs will say this is the case.

This is again not to say that the idea is completely wrong or even that this framework should be ignored. In the Moloch DAO white paper they state:

> we take Moloch to mean what Alexander represents in his post: the category of problems associated with collective action, where individual incentives are misaligned with globally optimal outcomes. These are problems that have existed throughout human history under different guises but yet have remained largely unsolved. We see Moloch as a "final boss" of humanity, something which humans have unsuccessfully struggled to overcome for millennia, and which will have to be beaten if we want to ensure the long term survival of our species.

It's encouraging to see that the authors make the connection with collective action, an important aspect of working-class politics. It is also interesting to think of this issue in the greater context of human history, where similar issues have seemingly always existed, although they're certainly not the first to think of it this way. So while coordination is the best of the three representations used in the structure of this book, it still does not completely describe what crypto currently "is" and what it needs to become in order to fulfil its progressive potentialities.

Structure vs Agency in Uncertainty

Debates about capitalism and how to change our economy's mode of production are as old as capitalism itself. The main frameworks for understanding how one can take part in this change of human behaviour can be summarised, and perhaps oversimplified, as structure versus agency.

For a structuralist, human behaviour and culture must be understood in relationship to the broader systems in which they are nested, because the choices humans make are dictated by forces beyond their control. This is a common framework for some on the left, who believe that people are limited by the material conditions imposed by capitalism and the unequal social relations it requires. The power of this structure means that there are only a few specific conditions that must be present, and which cannot be created by a single person, in order to make a shift for the better possible.

For those on the side of agency, a single human's independent ability should be recognised as a power and resource to make changes in the world. This was a common concept among Enlightenment thinkers who were exploring notions of freedom and individual will heavily inspired by European settlers' interactions with the Indigenous populations of the Americas, who lived in much less rigidly hierarchical political structures.

The debate between structure and agency can become heated because it has implications for many other big philosophical questions, like whether we actually have free will, the role of nature versus nurture, predestination and general questions about how predetermined our lives are. Are the structures so strong that we are simply unable to move towards some kind of post-capitalism in our lifetimes? Would attempting to change society without the recommended recipe of conditions be futile or perhaps do more harm than good? These are loaded questions.

For the structure maximalist, it is naïve to think that agency is so powerful that a single person would be able to make significant changes to politics without changing the structure. For the agency maximalist, the structuralist looks like the armchair critic or the over-thinker while they are the doer. It can appear that at its worst, structure maximalism leads to an immobilising nihilism while agency maximalism leads to a naïve reliance on voluntary actions.

What is important to note, however, is that both structure and agency maximalism are speculations about how best to go about making political change. If someone were to take a specific action, could that trigger a series of events that change the world for the better? Probably not, but it's also difficult to explain how political change actually happens if the actions of any single person don't matter. The truth is that the world is already very complicated and capitalism has only made it more so. Add cryptocurrency into the mix and we have complexity on steroids, or what the Marxist hacker Jaromil has described as the "autopoiesis of complexity".[4] This, compounded with the polycrisis that is climate change, has thus created a sense of intense uncertainty.[5] Uncertainty is of course not new, and speculating on the future in various ways is one way humans have dealt with it.

High levels of uncertainty require communities to take on wagers constantly, whether financial or otherwise. Having a framework or a structure to understand the world can help us deal with or make sense of uncertainty regardless of its correctness. How do we deal with this uncertainty politically? The right does it through racism and nationalism in order to reassure particular groups that the political system will foreground protecting them over others. After repeated defeats, it seems that much of the left, at least in Western countries, has resorted to an obsession with theorising and permanent critique. Academia has become one of the few safe places to be openly moderately left-wing, as the historical institutions of power for the left have slowly withered in the neoliberal age. But what is the use of simply being more theoretically correct than your enemies when they still hold all of the power?

We are always speculating about the future because it is always uncertain to some degree. We cannot let those speculations be dominated by billionaires, market forces, repressive states and the fascists waiting in the corner. We also cannot allow our pessimism of the intellect to dominate our discourse, but this is exactly what happens when crypto is brought up in left-wing spaces. Crypto looks similar to money and is couched in language that is financial, therefore it must be solely about financialisation, something popular left-wing media personalities say needs to be stopped at all costs. It's a reaction derived from primed pattern recognition which is activated by the representational models that are used by crypto hypemen for marketing. But we cannot have closed beliefs based on narratives that were created with the purpose of keeping out progressives from the get-go.

History is perceived after the fact, making it easy to see as structural or deterministic. Of course that was bound to happen, all of these other things happening were inevitably leading to this conclusion! Looking at history in this way can lead one to believe that the present is merely the visible stage of an already pre-determined future. But this confuses the map for the territory. Some may believe that crypto is a hammer looking for a nail, and in many cases it can be, but many of the same people can be said to be looking for patterns in things they actually know very little about in order to fit them neatly into their pre-existing schema for understanding the world. This overreliance on structure creates the atmosphere of analysis paralysis and circular firing squads that the left is infamous for.

This is not to say that I am an agency maximalist. After all, we cannot simply choose to live outside of all systems larger than ourselves, we will always be bound by the laws of physics. It is fine to have a materialist worldview, but it's also important to have a materialist attitude to life, which would be open-ended and experimental while also practical. Gatekeeping others for experimenting in techniques, technologies and non-traditional left-wing spaces is the job of the enemy, not something we should impose on ourselves.

It's not about maximising structure or agency for your political theory of change. The left needs a collective approach to the uncertainties that inherently come with trying to find ways of changing the world for the better in an adversarial ever-evolving environment. We make our own history, but not in conditions of our own choosing, and so we must recognise both the danger and the potential of this technology in order to understand where it would fit into a radical collective political endeavour. While this book is certainly speculative, it has also covered a significant amount of real experimentation happening right now that holds potential. I've also done my best to tamp down the utopianism with necessary criticisms. However, while things look dire, we need a bit of optimism of the will to complement the pessimism of the intellect we too easily tend to fall into.

Techno-Probabilism: Moving Beyond Criticism

The criticism of and scepticism toward blockchains and crypto has its roots in earlier critiques of technology, like the 1995 essay "The Californian Ideology" by Richard Barbrook, which explores the "dotcom neoliberalism" of Silicon Valley that mixed elements of the New Left and the New Right of the

1960s and 1970s into utopian technological determinism. Technological determinism is the idea that the progression of technology follows its own logic and is the key mover in history and catalyst for social change. The term is seen as anti-democratic in academic circles as it implies the inevitability of particular outcomes, but deterministic assumptions and language permeate the writings of many technology hypemen, the business pages of popular magazines and much of the reporting on the subject. This ideological power that Silicon Valley has been able to gain over the public imagination has led to what tech-critic Evgeny Morozov has termed "technological solutionism",[6] or the idea that tech alone can solve our hard societal problems. However, there is no app that can fix capitalism. It's not difficult to see the truth behind these critiques and thus be wary of technologies introduced with extravagant promises like blockchains.

The rise of tech-criticism is in many ways a much-needed pushback against the last few decades of failed promises from the tech industry. However, a valid counter-criticism would be that few alternatives are proposed beyond vague appeals for a failing state to regulate harder, something which can work in some situations but not all. Many times these tech-criticisms ironically veer into a pessimistic techno-determinism.

In order to summarise a position that seeks to move beyond any sense of complete determinism while also acknowledging the structures that do exist, I'd like to coin the term "technological probabilism". It means that technological progression can help determine what is and is not materially possible, but the extent to which social movements are coherent tips the scales towards particular outcomes. In other words, it's up to us to save ourselves collectively, and seizing these technologies, albeit in the perhaps problematic and undesirable state in which they currently exist, should be part of a coherent strategy for political change. I think the first of the historian Melvin Kranzberg's six laws of technology is particularly relevant here: "Technology is neither good nor bad; nor is it neutral."[7] In Donna Haraway's essay "A Cyborg Manifesto", she urges other feminists to not think of humans, animals and machines as having rigid boundaries between one another because we have already become cyborgs, a hybridisation of all three. While mainly a critique of gender, she notes that the line between the natural and the artificial has blurred with the rise of microchips and other advanced technological devices that we now use every day. Haraway states:

> The main trouble with cyborgs, of course, is that they are the illegitimate offspring of militarism and patriarchal capitalism, not to mention state socialism. But illegitimate offspring are often exceedingly unfaithful to their origins. Their fathers, after all, are inessential.[8] The Internet, for example, is used in many ways that are unfaithful to its militaristic origins. Haraway's essay offers a wonderful critique of binary thinking as she asks us to think less in dichotomies of bounded categories and more in dualisms and hybrids, which is helpful when approaching a space as contradictory as cryptocurrencies. But how do we deal with this complicated mess of contradictions, dualisms and hybrids in a practical manner?

In a 2018 interview with *The New Inquiry*, anti-capitalist philosophers Brian Massumi and Erin Manning talked about their views on the reappropriation of a technology that is so heavily intertwined with a politics they oppose.[9] They note a need for "strategic duplicity" in a world where we cannot simply walk out of capitalism. They state that strategic duplicity

> involves recognising what works in the systems we work against. Which means: We don't just oppose them head on. We work with them, strategically, while nurturing an alien logic that moves in very different directions... We have to be parasitical to the capitalist economy, while operating according to a logic that is totally alien to it.

They believe it is possible to reappropriate the technology for a cryptoeconomy that sustains "emergent collectivity" brought about by the growing interest in DAOs for collective action.

Although there's always a chance, it is unlikely that financial bubbles and speculation will suddenly disappear. Capitalism is still moving forward one zombie step at a time because it depends on speculation. They allow for what pro-capitalist economist Joseph Schumpeter, inspired by Marx's work, calls "creative destruction", or the continuous destruction of capital by new forms of capital so that the system can continue to preserve itself from its own internal contradictions. Clearly this is something that seems to be happening at an accelerated pace in the highly technologised capitalism we live in today. The easy critique would be to say that since crypto has similar features to the capitalist economy, it is therefore something to stay away from, but can't emergent chaotic financial influxes be useful for the left in some ways if there are also primed and organised emergent collectives as well? Can the process of creative destruction that is endemic to capitalism be used as an opportunity for an organised left to take advantage of and dictate the direction of technological progress and thus the political economy it facilitates?

This is just a speculation on an uncertain future, but this is the basis of all political movements. We can't say that since there has been no significant and eye-catching use of crypto in an unequivocally left-wing sense so far, then it will never come; that would be confirmation bias. Even the right-wing libertarians have been noticing an increase in highly unpredictable Black Swan Events.[10] We cannot solely depend on the past to understand everything that the future will bring. Taking the principles of strategic duplicity from Massumi and Manning and applying it to crypto, we can create new weapons for new forms of collective solidarity and democracy with the unfaithful tools of crypto-boosting libertarians.

A techno-probabilist approach to crypto is not about using it just because we can. It is about using a logic that doesn't comply with capitalism's own logic of domination to imagine non-dystopian futures that use the appropriate affordance of technology for collective ends. This means, as Edward Snowden pleaded virtually at Coindesk's Consensus 2022 conference, to not merely invest in it, but to use crypto, as he did when he paid pseudonymously with bitcoin for the servers that helped his whistleblowing.[11] Examples like Snowden show that we can both be realistic about the structures that bind us and recognise our own agency at critical moments when opportunity arises. We don't have to think of agency as purely an individual plight, but something that can be recognised by groups when there is a viable governance system that uses shared knowledge to make collective decisions.

We need to be honest about current material conditions, and they include the existence of blockchains and cryptocurrencies. And I hope by now the reader has at the very least questioned their preconceived notions, if they had any, that there are no uses for these technologies in progressive struggles.

Within and Against

In in his July 2022 article "Web3 Is the Opportunity We Have Had All Along: Innovation Amnesia and Economic Democracy", Nathan Schneider discusses the amnesia that our technological solutionism-obsessed world has wrought. [12] He writes, "Web3 is an opportunity to do what could have been done before but wasn't done, which is already being squandered with what *is* being done." He applauds the technology as a genuine enabler of trans-territorial democracy, both political and economic, but laments the tendency for shiny new technologies to elicit amnesia in the general population about previous non- or low-technological attempts at democracy. Schneider notes, "Once again, under the cover of decentralisation-talk, a centralising power grab is well underway. Venture capitalists have recognised that crypto protocols represent an even greater chance for value capture than platforms did in Web1 or Web2." Still, for Schneider, a researcher of various democratic traditions that rarely seem to get the attention they deserve, crypto is another chance to make a choice for economic democracy.

While there is no guarantee that this time will be different, there are non-capitalist logics that could be explored to inform systems built on crypto adjacent technologies:

> Tremendous energy — intellectual and computational — goes toward securing property rights on blockchains. What if similar energy were also devoted to ensuring these systems produced more democratic outcomes than their predecessors? What if designers' threat models were not just double-spending and DDoS attacks but also plutocracy and wealth inequality?

Thinking of tokens as social rights, as in the example given previously of a housing-for-all token, can be a good starting point. Financial or economic rights over a protocol are just one small right in a spectrum that could be represented. This logic can also be applied at lower levels of the stack. But I need to be honest with this book's readers. At the moment of writing, I do not feel that we are close to that being a reality.

So what is there to do? The short answer is, "quite a lot". The good news is that there is a clear forward direction and a lot of low-hanging fruit, as outlined throughout the book. These are projects and experiments that I find interesting, not necessarily as something to imitate or be a part of, but representative of some of the emergent potential that I have observed during my time in this strange new world. And while this strange new world likes to talk about crypto as something decentralising in all cases, actually one of the real benefits is its potential to centralise already decentralised movements, like the left.

Using a term like "the left" to describe political positions is a heuristic to describe many different tendencies that are critical of capitalism. All these different tendencies have their own slightly differing ideas about how to get to the goal of the broader left (e.g., socialism). These are based on abstract philosophical principles that anyone outside could not care less about, leaving each group relatively isolated. Because the left has been so fragmented and scattered over recent decades, a large political vacuum has helped shift the Overton window very far to the right. The left effectively has no shared platforms with which to create a united front against the fascism that is rising around the globe, except for freemium social media platforms owned by Big Tech which are designed for engagement, not solidarity or cooperation.

Even with all of its flaws, a blockchain (or some other DLT) can create resilient protocols meant for cooperation and coordination to subvert power, while also experimenting with collective ownership. This is an extremely powerful tool because it enables a materially consequential connecting thread between all the different tendencies of the left so that there is a reason to continue to cooperate (shared resources are on the line, all other tendencies are there, outsiders are watching, etc) rather than splitting off into another esoteric political group with little success on its own. New forms of meaningful political federation have never been technically easier to start. Social media platforms may have connected people across territories in new ways that have transformed political organising, but posting can only go so far. Blockchains are a shared, neutral technological layer for new types of coordination, organisation and institution forming. They offer the possibility of providing alternatives to some existing institutions and the current crypto map does not even begin to get close to what possible futures there are, ones based not on profit-seeking but on common ownership. Imagine that a broad coalition of many tendencies on the left holds a multi-signature wallet with many owners of a shared pool of resources that, when a majority of members approve, can deploy those resources for assisting strikes, funding coops, mutual aid funds and much more. But this is still not thinking practically enough.

For any real federation to take hold, it's important to remember that we're physical beings who still need physical connection. I recommend anyone who is interested in the things discussed in this book to seek out physical meetings near them. One of the organisations that is building a meeting place for a federation of progressive crypto groups is called the Crypto Commons Association. Based in the Austrian Alps in an old, restored restaurant and bed and breakfast, the Crypto Commons Association hosts events like the Crypto Commons Gathering that seem to attract the most progressive-minded in the crypto space as they focus on combining commons theory with blockchains. Of all of the crypto conferences I've been to (and it's quite a few) it is the least corporate, least focused on profit and organised autonomously by attendees who are required to help with keeping the commons space clean. It is also a great meeting place for the more progressive-minded in a crypto world in which you might otherwise feel that you were the only one.

One last interesting tool in the context of federation (although there are many more I don't have the space to mention) is Zodiac by Gnosis Guild. Zodiac is a growing collection of open standards especially designed mainly for Gnosis Safe, one of the most popular multi-signature wallet tools. Described as "expansion packs for DAOs", the Zodiac modules are meant to allow a form of peer-to-peer mutualism and modular politics enforced through smart contracts. Gnosis Safe is the standard for starting multi-signature wallets on Ethereum-based blockchains with functionalities like designating how many owners must sign off to allow a transaction from shared funds. Zodiac modules offer the possibility of more complex and/or fine-grained governance mechanisms for a safe multi-signature wallet, for instance by giving roles to specific people in your DAO, say, if you would like one trusted person to be able to make payments without needing a majority vote. There is a module to run an on-chain vote for executing transactions based on a vote of the DAO members, another that is similar to the ragequit function from Moloch DAO and one that allows for cross-chain interoperability. Using an Ethereum layer 2 or side chain, you can create a Gnosis Safe multisignature wallet for pennies and begin exploring collective ownership with your friends, communities or political groups, knowing that whatever EVM tools you may want to pursue are likely to be compatible with Safe wallet.

So, to end with one more practical point, I want to call out some actions the reader can take. The first is directly linked to this book. If you go to blockchainradicals.eth (or .com) you will find a digital supplement where you can find ways to begin exploring and learning how to use crypto tools in a hands-on way of interacting with and helping fund progressive projects. This will be a living webpage and include a listing for an NFT, whose proceeds will go towards funding the Breadchain Cooperative. Note that the ".eth" address can be accessed through any browser with IPFS compatibility.[13]

Although it is speculative about the future, this book is not meant to be only that. It is also a call to action that is aware that we must both exist within and struggle against capitalism. I implore those who have the resources to do so to begin their own experimentations and to try to include already existing progressive groups that they may be a part of. You can already begin experimenting with as little as $10 worth of cryptocurrency depending on the blockchain you use with collective ends in mind. This is not an investment with an expectation of profit, but an investment in education and tacit knowledge about how to use these tools that are ripe for a left to begin repurposing away from their conservative libertarian roots. It's the unavoidable first step if we want to accelerate the left's understanding and seize the opportunity to forge a new reality.

GLOSSARY

Bitcoin

The first cryptocurrency created in 2009 by an unidentified person or group of people only known as Satoshi Nakamoto in online forums. The underlying technology that facilitated its function later became known as a blockchain and has been modified for new cryptocurrencies ever since.

Blockchain

A specific type of distributed ledger technology in which all nodes (computers) of the network hold a copy of the shared database (commonly referred to as the ledger) and information is stored in blocks of data (much of it transactions of cryptocurrency) created at certain variable time intervals (block time) using a consensus mechanism for all of the nodes in the network to come to agreement in a "decentralized" fashion without relying on a centralized authority. The resilience of the system usually relies on some amount of economic incentives for node operators that secure the network. Blockchains are one of, if not the only, system to solve the "double-spending problem", which states the difficulty of having unique objects with scarcity like money in a digital space. It serves as the foundation for how most cryptocurrencies, like Bitcoin and Ethereum, work, but some cryptocurrencies don't use a blockchain.

Some like to explain a blockchain as a P2P digital ledger kept by all nodes in the network that is specifically for making financial transactions with cryptocurrency. Others will prefer to think of a blockchain as a shared/collective computer for general computation, especially if the blockchain has smart contract functionality. How shared that computer (the blockchain) is can be debated, depending on the transaction costs, block space availability and other factors. While the first example of a blockchain was Bitcoin, which explicitly wanted to make a form of digital cash without a central authority to administer it, it is debatable whether that has been achieved and the potential uses for blockchains have moved beyond that original goal.

There are two main types of blockchains, public and private. Public blockchains allow for anyone to set up a node to take part in the upkeep of the network and include most cryptocurrencies that can be purchased on exchanges. To take part in a private blockchain, one needs to be invited into the network and is much more common in corporate blockchain solutions. Many believe that private blockchains are in fact not blockchain because they do not reach consensus in a "decentralized" manner.

Blockchain Radical

Someone who believes in the transformative potential of blockchain technologies to enable new and positive forms of social relations but is frustrated and dissatisfied by the current crypto status quo for its greed, deception and often its stupidity. They understand that the status quo exists because marketers and hypemen are stuck in dangerous representational modes of thinking that fail to recognise the centralizing aspects of capitalism, thus leading to what has happened in the crypto space so far. They are therefore interested in pursuing and building out with fundamentally different models in mind that don't fit within a capitalist paradigm, acknowledging the political nature of such an endeavour. They have the unfortunate burden of needing to push back against both crypto hypemen and gatekeepers.

Capital

Often incorrectly thought of as being synonymous with money or commodities, capital is a relationship of production that encourages circuits of accumulation of wealth which can be in the form of money or other assets. Capital is a control system for moving labour towards one endeavour or another, with feedback loops that intensify its position of power over labour.

Capitalism

An economic system evolving out of the feudal system that came before it, it is characterised by a few private individuals (capitalists), rather than the state or government, owning and controlling the means of production and distribution of goods and services through a legal system of private property rights. The main type of work that most who live under capitalism take part in is wage-labour, in which a capitalist, often through a company, hires a worker to perform a job in which the capitalist makes more money than the worker is paid. The difference is often referred to as profit. In this way, one economic class systematically exploits the other in order to continue competing in capitalist markets against others in the same class, or other capitalists. It is the dominant mode of production in the world today and has led to a myriad of innovations along with systemic inequities with help from the state in its development.

Centralised Exchange (CEX)

The most common way for people to be first onboarded into having some amount of cryptocurrency is through centralised exchanges like Coinbase, Binance, etc. which are companies that facilitate the exchange of cryptocurrencies for nation-state money. By having cryptocurrency on a centralised exchange, you are not actually owning what you may have purchased, since the CEX is acting as the custodian of your crypto assets. They are also usually required to have your personal information in order to comply with KYC and AML regulations, similar to many other financial institutions. They are centralised choke-points for imposing regulation by states.

Consensus Mechanism

The protocol/method in which computers that take part in a distributed database like a blockchain are able to reach to an agreement on the current state of the database. It can be seen as the pre-determined set of rules that nodes in the blockchain network follow, showing that although blockchains may use decentralized P2P infrastructure, they are logically centralized through consensus mechanism protocols. There are many different types and the decisions on which is chosen are highly consequential in the development of that blockchain.

Crypto

Since the advent of bitcoin and cryptocurrency, the term has become the colloquial term for anything related to cryptocurrency, although previously it largely referred to the field of cryptography which also heavily influenced the creation of cryptocurrrencies. Cryptographers who dislike cryptocurrency are mad about this.

Cryptocurrency

A digital currency that doesn't rely on a bank or government for it to function, usually thanks to a blockchain or some other DLT. They can be used as a medium of exchange between parties, but have most commonly been used as vehicles for speculation. A cryptocurrency can refer to one that is native to a blockchain or a token created through a smart contract.

Cryptography

A study and practice of secure and private communications under the threat of attackers in which, largely through the use of encryption, only the intended receiver can know the contents of a message. It has become extremely important in modern warfare to protect secrets from opposing militaries and for creating secured networks over the Internet. The field of study, especially when applied to the internet, leverages many advanced mathematical theories in order to hide messages.

Decentralised Application (Dapp)

Commonly referred to as a dapp, it is an application (on phone, web, etc.) which is built on top of a blockchain using smart contracts in the backend. Dapps that are in production sometimes use non-blockchain-related technologies as well to function. Depending on the design of the smart contracts, the dapp can be centralised through control of the smart contracts embedded in the code, but they can also be created to where no one controls them, making the smart contracts a type of immutable permissionless infrastructure. Many frontends could theoretically be built for any backend made of smart contracts, which is different than normal applications in which an entity normally owns both the back and frontends.

Decentralised Autonomous Organization (DAO)

Commonly referred to as a DAO, it is an ever-changing term for an organization using smart contracts to facilitate the governance of itself. It is sometimes simply defined as an online community with a multisignature wallet as a joint bank account, but this is contested by many as people have different ideas about decentralisation and autonomy. The original term was "Decentralised Autonomous Corporation" (DAC), which detailed a company that ran entirely on smart contracts, but Vitalik Buterin suggested changing the C to an O since corporations are not the only type of organizational structure amenable to smart contracts. Lately there has been a lot of interest in cooperatives by those who first came across DAOs since they share many of the same concerns and issues. DAOs will likely have a profound effect on labour in the future in either a dystopian or post-capitalist direction.

Decentralised Exchange (DEX)

An exchange completely facilitated by smart contracts that does not need to collect your personal information to allow you to exchange. Instead of liquidity of exchangeable assets being provided by the exchange or its partners like in CEXs, DEXs allow for anyone to provide liquidity and be rewarded for doing so through trading fees paid by traders.

Decentralised Finance (DeFi)

DeFi is a growing industry and ecosystem of protocols and dapps using smart contracts that give access to anyone with a cryptocurrency wallet to many of the same types of financial products available only to banking and investment professionals. Due to the composable design space allowed by smart contracts, many innovative forms of financial products have been created that were not possible before (for better or worse). The most active blockchain for this industry is Ethereum, but others like Cosmos also have their own ecosystem of DeFi applications.

Distributed Ledger Technology (DLT)

This is an umbrella term for peer-to-peer network infrastructure technologies that allow for users to reliably access and add data to a shared digital ledger. As opposed to a centralized database, DLTs do not have a central administrator. A blockchain is one type of DLT, but there are many types out there.

Ether

The native cryptocurrency for the Ethereum blockchain used to pay for any transaction made on the network and the reward for adding a new block as a miner or staker.

Ethereum

A blockchain created by Vitalik Buterin at nineteen years old that showed how it was possible to build smart contract functionality on top of a blockchain. Many other similar blockchain-based cryptocurrencies have since been created with the functionality of smart contracts but at the time of writing Ethereum is the largest and most used blockchain with smart contract functionality.

Fork

In software development, forking refers to creating a copy of a project's codebase to start a new, separate project that can be developed independently. It's like taking a snapshot of a project at a certain point in time, either starting from the source code or while the projects is live, and then going in a different direction with your own version of the code. This is often done when different groups of people want to work on a project in different ways, or when someone wants to create a new version of an existing project with different goals or features. In blockchains there are two types of forks. A hard fork is a permanent separation of the original codebase, creating a completely independent project, usually after a major change that is not backwards-compatible. A soft fork is a temporary separation of the original codebase, creating a new project that can still communicate with the original project, usually after a minor change that is backwards-compatible.

Hash

A one-directional cryptographic algorithm in which any input creates a fixed size output of random numbers and letters, but there is no feasible way to know the input when given just the output. It is an important technique for encryption (hiding messages) over the internet as well as saving memory. While collisions are theoretically possible (when two different inputs create the same output), the chances are astronomically low and would require a very significant amount of energy to find one purposefully. There is currently no known example of a collision for many of the common hashing algorithms used in the most popular blockchains. When quantum computers become more prevalent, many hashing algorithms will likely become obsolete, but there are already many that have been created to be quantum-resistant.

Layer 2

While a blockchain is considered to be layer 1 and since most blockchains currently cannot scale sufficiently for global general use, layer 2 refers to scaling solutions that are built on top of layer 1 blockchains like Ethereum. They are separate but connected networks meant to increase the total transaction output speed at lower costs for users while preserving the security and decentralization guaranteed by a layer 1 blockchain. Examples include Optimism and Arbitrum for the Ethereum network.

Non-Fungible Token (NFT)

An NFT is a special type of token which represent a unique digital asset which cannot be interchanged with another in the way that money, a cryptocurrency, or other token can be since they are largely fungible. Industries that have had the quickest growth in NFT use includes digital art and gaming since they already have significant use of artificial scarcity of unique assets.

NFTs should not be seen as crypto art or solely as something to buy or sell as a unique asset, but as a unique token with many different uses depending on the context encoded in their smart contracts and in the social network it exists in. For example, many of the bonus episodes I release for my podcast on Patreon are also available on my website if you purchase an NFT to access the episode on its own with Unlock Protocol. In this way, the NFT is essentially a key to access digital media, similar to pay walls used by many other websites, except here you can pay with cryptocurrency instead.

Node

A computer on a P2P Network which takes part in keeping the network up to date. In blockchains they can actively or passively take part in consensus making. Nodes are necessary for any P2P network like blockchains, whether they use PoW, PoS, or any other consensus mechanism.

Oracle

Smart contracts can only refer to data that is recorded on the blockchain that it exists on top of. This limits the functionality for smart contracts that need inputs that are off-chain. Oracles are APIs that retrieve data from an outside data source to be used in a smart contract. Oracles can be centralized attack vectors depending on how they are designed and so need to be used and designed carefully.

Peer-to-Peer (P2P) Network

An infrastructure or technology in which two or more computers are connected in order to share resources as opposed to a client-server network in which clients request data from centrally owned servers. Napster, Limewire, and BitTorrent are examples of P2P networks used for file sharing. Blockchains are P2P networks largely for tracking value of some kind. P2P networks are generally considered to be more decentralized than client-server networks. The internet was built on top of what could be considered a P2P network, leading many to believe in the beginning that it would be unenclosable by corporate interests, but this has clearly been disproven.

Proof of Stake (PoS)

A consensus mechanism in which a special subset of nodes called stakers have the power to validate transactions and create new blocks by "staking" a certain amount of cryptocurrency as collateral for maintaining their node online and earn more cryptocurrency when selected to add a block to the blockchain. A staker can also lose their collateralized cryptocurrency if their node is not online when chosen to add a block. Using PoS is thought to be at least 99% more energy efficient than PoW as it does not rely on large amounts of computation to reach consensus. Many blockchains have been using PoS as their consensus mechanism for some time now like Cosmos, Tezos, and recently Ethereum switched from PoW to PoS in which its total energy use fell by 99%.

Proof of Work (PoW)

A consensus mechanism in which a special subset of nodes called miners compete with one another to solve a hash equation by exerting energy in order to earn the right to add (also referred to as mining) a new block on to the blockchain and earn cryptocurrency (providing an economic incentive to mine). It is the consensus mechanism used currently for Bitcoin and uses significantly more energy than PoS.

Smart Contract

A program on a blockchain that automatically executes once a predetermined condition is met, allowing cryptocurrencies and tokens to be programmed. Ethereum was the first blockchain network to show smart contracts were possible. A major reason for using smart contracts is to create decentralized applications (dapps) that use them as the backend but also more generally as a way to enter into automatically executable agreements between different parties. They should also be seen as social agents in themselves that can have many different types of logic embedded in them.

Stablecoin

A cryptocurrency who's price is pegged to a stable outside asset like the US dollar, a commodity like gold, a basket of different assets, or even to another cryptocurrency to prevent its price from being volatile. This is not only a useful thing for traders so that they can move in and out of volatile positions, but for anyone who would want to use cryptocurrency without needing to worry about big changes in price relative to the underlying asset being pegged. Most popular stablecoins try to stay pegged to the US dollar. There's a few different ways different stablecoins try to keep their peg including over-collateralisation.

Token

Although it is commonly used to refer to purely financially-based cryptocurrencies, tokens can be seen more abstractly to represent many different types of values based on their designed use. While "native" cryptocurrencies like bitcoin and ether are tracked through their consensus mechanisms and blockchain network, tokens are generally created and tracked using smart contracts deployed on top of a blockchain with that functionality, like Ethereum. Examples include social tokens to access a community, governance tokens for voting, utility tokens to access particular functionalities in a decentralized application, etc.

Wallet

This refers to the "place" where your cryptocurrency would be held however it is not exactly a place at all. Using various kinds of one-way algorithms and functions, a blockchain allows someone to own cryptocurrency or anything else built on top of it through key pairs, referred to as a private and public key, which are essentially a random string of numbers and letters. The public key is usually what people mean by wallet because it is something you can share with anyone without any risk. The private key gives access to your wallet because if put through the appropriate algorithms, it will create the public key. What is important is that knowing the public key, gives you no way to know the private key. Therefore, you should NEVER share your private key. Proof of knowing your private key gives you access to the assets associated with the public key. Using the term wallet is largely a way to help people understand crypto, but it is a bit limiting as an idea since it is not a place to store money, but can store anything else, like NFTs, and in so in that way, it could maybe be seen more as an inventory for your crypto assets.

Web 1.0/web1

The beginning of the internet which was perceived to be largely decentralized but users could only visit and read static websites. This stage of the internet is believed to be long over. Examples include AOL, Netscape, GeoCities, etc. The exact time period and meaning of Web 1.0 (or any of the stages) is generally vague and nebulous, but is used to historicize and create context often primarily for marketing purposes.

Web 2.0/web2

In this stage of the narrative, users could now interact with one another through messaging, create accounts, and has led to the development of Big Tech which has centralized the internet through their platforms that act as "walled gardens" and which their business models depend largely on advertisement and invasive tracking methods. Examples include Meta, Twitter, Google, etc. While originally the term was used as a way to refer to the rise of publicly accessible APIs of various platforms, in the context of crypto, that aspect of it has been largely ignored.

Web 3.0/web3

This refers to what is meant to be the next evolution of the internet incorporating new technologies like blockchains, artificial intelligence, and others allowing for users to maintain more control over their data among other things. Generally, this attempt at periodizing the development of the internet is largely ahistorical but it is used as a simple narrative for marketing. It largely is a way to talk about crypto-enabled tools, projects, and companies without saying crypto, which some people think has a negative connotation. The term was originally coined by Gavin Wood, a co-founder of Ethereum and now focused on his own crypto project, Polkadot. The term also sometimes refers to the semantic web, a concept created by Tim Berners-Lee, in which internet data becomes machine-readable to decode the meaning behind text.

NOTES

Introduction

1 UkraineDAO has since been in turmoil and under scrutiny as some within the organisation have supported neo-nazis in the Azov battalion and Nadya has accused others of misappropriating funds.

2 https://www.youtube.com/watch?v=iDVKrbM5MIQ

Section 1: Crypto as Money

Chapter 1
Bitcoin: The Unfortunate Genesis

1 In order to assist you in remembering what certain words mean, you can also find a glossary at the back of the book which you can refer to remind yourself. Additionally, any word that is included in the glossary will be in **bold** when it first appears in the text.

2 Raum, Tom, "Obama: AIG can't justify 'outrage' of exec bonuses", *Associated Press*, 20 March 2009, https://web.archive.org/web/20090320090920/ https://www.google.com/hostednews/ap/article/ ALeqM5iNRov4y45sOcxD19w5vzO3FJIixwD96V7QSG3

3 "First quarter of 2021 Government debt up to 100.5% of GDP in euro area Up to 92.9% of GDP in EU", 22 July 2022, https:// ec.europa.eu/eurostat/documents/2995521/11563191/2- 22072021-AP-EN.pdf/282c649b-ae6e-3a7f-9430- 7c8b6eeeee77?t=1626942865088

4 Nichols, Philip, "How Iceland Dealt with a Volcanic Financial Meltdown", *Knowledge at Wharton*, 12 September 2018, https:// knowledge.wharton.upenn.edu/article/icelands-economic- recovery/

5   Nakamoto, Satoshi, "Bitcoin: A Peer-to-Peer Electronic Cash System", https://bitcoinwhitepaper.co/

6   Dodson, Sean, "Obituary: Judith Milhon", *Guardian*, 8 August 2003, https://www.theguardian.com/technology/2003/aug/08/guardianobituaries.obituaries

7   After existing for over a decade, there are still no known two inputs that produce the same output with SHA-256, however quantum computing does threaten the security of hashing functions like this.

8   Coincidentally, computer graphics cards have proven to be particularly good pieces of hardware for solving these cryptographic puzzles. For several years now, companies have built specialised products called ASICs (applications-specific integrated circuit) miners designed for cryptocurrency mining.

Chapter 2
The Communism of Science and Censorship Resistance: A Double-Edged Sword

1   Sontheimer, Michael, "We Are Drowning in Material: Interview with Julian Assange", *Der Spiegel*, 20 July 2015, https://www.spiegel.de/international/world/spiegel-interview-with-wikileaks-head-julian-assange-a-1044399.html

2   Coghlan, Jesse, "North Korea-obsessed Ethereum dev gets 5 years for breaking sanctions", *Cointelegraph*, 13 April 2022, https://cointelegraph.com/news/north-korea-obsessed-ethereum-dev-gets-5-years-for-breaking-sanctions

3   "U.S. Treasury Sanctions Notorious Virtual Currency Mixer Tornado Cash", US Department of the Treasury, 8 August 2022, https://home.treasury.gov/news/press-releases/jy0916

4   Pape, Robert A., "Why Economic Sanctions Do Not Work", *International Security*, Vol. 22, No. 2 (Fall, 1997), pp. 90-136, https://www.jstor.org/stable/2539368

5   Helms, Kevin, "Venezuela Pays for Imports From Iran and Turkey With Bitcoin to Evade Sanctions", *bitcoin.com*, 9 December 2020, https://news.bitcoin.com/venezuela-pays-imports-iran-turkey-bitcoin-evade-sanctions/

6   "Study: Iran Using Crypto Mining To Evade Sanctions", *Radio Free Europe*, 21 May 2021, https://www.rferl.org/a/iran-crypto-mining-sanctions/31267432.html

7   "Cuba becomes the latest country to authorise and regulate cryptocurrencies like Bitcoin", *euronews.net*, 27 August 2021, https://www.euronews.com/next/2021/08/27/cuba-becomes-the-latest-country-to-authorise-and-regulate-cryptocurrencies-like-bitcoin

8   This is also besides the fact that there are technological workarounds to not put all of the pressure on the individual.

9   "OnlyFans founder blames banks for ban on porn", *Financial Times*, 24 August 2021, https://www.ft.com/content/7b8ce71c-a87a-440e-9f3d-58069ca0480b

10   Poulsen, Kenny, "PayPal Freezes WikiLeaks Account", *Wired*, 4 December 2010, https://www.wired.com/2010/12/paypal-wikileaks/

11   Matonis, Jon, "WikiLeaks Bypasses Financial Blockade With Bitcoin", *Forbes*, 20 August 2012, https://www.forbes.com/sites/jonmatonis/2012/08/20/wikileaks-bypasses-financial-blockade-with-bitcoin/?sh=6d75c4097202

12   Siddique, Haroon, "WikiLeaks auctions lunch with Julian Assange", *Guardian*, 15 June 2011, https://www.theguardian.com/media/2011/jun/15/wikileaks-auctions-lunch-julian-assange

13   Estes, Adam Clark, "The WikiLeaks Server That Hosted Cablegate Is for Sale on eBay", *Gizmodo*, 3 September 2013, https://gizmodo.com/the-wikileaks-server-that-hosted-cablegate-is-for-sale-1245720862

14   Huang, Roger, "How Bitcoin and Wikileaks Saved Each Other", *Forbes*, 26 March 2019, https://www.forbes.com/sites/rogerhuang/2019/04/26/how-bitcoin-and-wikileaks-saved-each-other/?sh=38d99a0474a5

15   https://www.bitcoinprice.com/

16   https://archive.ph/1hscT

17   Greenberg, Andy, "Wikileaks Asks for Anonymous Donations", *Forbes*, 14 June 2011, https://www.forbes.com/sites/

andygreenberg/2011/06/14/wikileaks-asks-for-anonymous-bitcoin-donations/?sh=73285f5f4f73

18 Redman, Jamie, "Wikileaks Gathers $37M in BTC Since 2010
    - Over $400K Sent After Julian Assange's Arrest", *bitcoin.com*,
    25 February 2020, https://news.bitcoin.com/wikileaks-gathers-
    37m-in-btc-since-2010-over-400k-sent-after-julian-assanges-
    arrest/

19 Cox, Joseph, "Where Did WikiLeaks' $25 Million Bitcoin Fortune
    Go?", *Daily Beast*, 28 December 2017, https://www.thedailybeast.
    com/where-did-wikileaks-dollar25-million-bitcoin-fortune-go

20 https://twitter.com/DefendAssange/status/919247873648283653

21 "Wikileaks' Bitcoin donations spike following Julian Assange's
    arrest", *The Next Web*, 11 April 2019, https://thenextweb.com/
    news/julian-assange-bitcoin-wikileaks

22 Merton, Robert K., "The Normative Structure of Science"
    https://www.panarchy.org/merton/science.html

23 Wagstaff, Steve, "If Harvard Can't Afford Academic Journal
    Subscriptions, Maybe It's Time for an Open Access Model",
    Time, 26 April 2012, https://techland.time.com/2012/04/26/if-
    harvard-cant-afford-academic-journal-subscriptions-maybe-its-
    time-for-an-open-access-model/#:~:text=Last%20week%2C%20
    Harvard's%20Faculty%20Advisory,annually%20on%20
    academic%20journal%20subscriptions.

24 "Academic publishers reap huge profits as libraries go broke",
    CBC, 15 June 2015, https://www.cbc.ca/news/science/academic-
    publishers-reap-huge-profits-as-libraries-go-broke-1.3111535

25 https://sci-hub.ru/about

26 https://sci-hub.ru/alexandra

27 https://theblockchainsocialist.com/science-and-communism-
    are-the-same-interview-with-alexandra-elbakyan-founder-of-sci-
    hub/

28 Baydakova, Anna, "Blackballed by PayPal, Scientific-Paper Pirate
    Takes Bitcoin Donations", *CoinDesk*, 22 June 2020, https://www.
    coindesk.com/markets/2020/06/22/blackballed-by-paypal-
    scientific-paper-pirate-takes-bitcoin-donations/

29 Himmelstein, Daniel S., et al., "Sci-Hub provides access to nearly

all scholarly literature", *eLife*, March 2018, https://www.ncbi.
nlm.nih.gov/pmc/articles/PMC5832410/

30 "Everyone has the right freely to participate in the cultural life of the community, to enjoy the arts and to share in scientific advancement and its benefits."

Chapter 3
"Is Bitcoin Money?" Is the Wrong Question to Be Asking

1 This particular school believes in little to no intervention in the economy, and that most things should be handled exclusively through free markets.

2 In the United States, it is the US Treasury and Mint that handle the creation of physical money.

3 Arnsperger, Christian, et al., "Monetary Adaptation to Planetary Emergency: Addressing the Monetary Growth Imperative", Institute for Leadership and Sustainability, University of Cumbria, 24 March 2021, https://insight.cumbria.ac.uk/id/eprint/5993/1/Bendell_occasionalpaper8_revised.pdf

4 While countries like El Salvador have made bitcoin legal tender, at the time of writing the situation is very complex considering that El Salvador does not have its own sovereign money and is a "dollarized" economy. Most transactions happen in US dollars, making it dependent on the United States in many ways. The architecture behind bitcoin payments for most citizens through the Chivo app also relies on different forms of centralization, including still pricing things in US dollars.

5 Humphrey, Caroline, "Barter and Economic Disintegration", *Man*, Vol. 20, No. 1 (Mar., 1985), pp. 48-72, https://www.jstor.org/stable/2802221

6 Scott, Brett, "The one concept crypto promoters are afraid to understand", 11 November 2021, https://brettscott.substack.com/p/countertrade-spades?s=r

7 The account balance would be negative.

8 It is the main mechanism behind credit clearing which has existed for millennia.

9   https://trustlines.network/

10 https://joincircles.net/

11 https://handbook.joincircles.net/

12 In fact there is open source software like the Credit Common
    Protocol developed by Matthew Slater that can be taken by
    anyone to start their own ledgers between trading partners
    without the use of a blockchain.

13 Kurland, Albert A., "LSD in the Supportive Care of the
    Terminally Ill Cancer Patient", *Journal of Psychoactive
    Drugs*, 2 August 2012, https://www.tandfonline.com/doi/
    abs/10.1080/02791072.1985.10524332?journalCode=ujpd20

Chapter 4
Code is Law

1   https://twitter.com/VitalikButerin/status/1051160932699770882

2   There are some caveats here that will be further explained later.

3   https://Ethereum.org/en/developers/docs/smart-contracts/ (Feb
    7, 2022)

4   Gord, Michael, "Smart Contracts Described By Nick Szabo
    20 Years Ago Now Becoming Reality", *Bitcoin Magazine*, 26
    April 2016, https://bitcoinmagazine.com/technical/smart-
    contracts-described-by-nick-szabo-years-ago-now-becoming-
    reality-1461693751

5   "Cryptoasset Market Coverage Initiation: Network Creation",
    11 July 2018, https://research.bloomberg.com/pub/res/
    d28giW28tf6G7T_Wr77aU0gDgFQ

6   Clayton, Jay, "Statement on Cryptocurrencies and Initial
    Coin Offerings", US Securities and Exchange Commission, 11
    December 2017, https://www.sec.gov/news/public-statement/
    statement-clayton-2017-12-11

7   https://deliverypdf.ssrn.com/delivery.php

8   De Filippi, Primavera and Mannan, Morshed and Reijers, Wessel,
    "The Alegality of Blockchain Technology" (10 December, 2021).
    Policy and Society, Forthcoming, Available at SSRN: https://ssrn.
    com/abstract=4001696

9   https://kleros.io/

10 https://dogesontrial.dog/

11 After each appeal, the number of jurors is doubled and one more is added, making it more difficult for someone to bribe all of them.

12 "Is Kleros Legally Valid as Arbitration?", 12 June 2019, https://blog.kleros.io/is-kleros-legally-valid-as-arbitration/

Section 2: Crypto as Finance

Chapter 5
Market-Making for the Commons

1 "Government at a Glance 2013, Norway", https://www.oecd.org/gov/GAAG2013_CFS_NOR.pdf

2 Transmission Control Protocol

3 "A Short History of Uniswap", 11 February 2019, https://uniswap.org/blog/uniswap-history

4 Buterin, Vitalik, "On Path Independence", 22 June 2017, https://vitalik.ca/general/2017/06/22/marketmakers.html

5 xy=k; Where x and y are the supply of each token asset in the pool and k is a constant that is first determined by the creator of the liquidity pool based on the ratio of assets they provide.

6 Most centralized exchanges worth your time will have an option for you to withdraw the cryptocurrency you bought from their platform.

7 Arvidsson, Adam, "Capitalism and the Commons", *Theory, Culture & Society*, Volume 37, Issue 2, 2019, https://journals.sagepub.com/doi/10.1177/0263276419868838

8 Hardin, G (1968). "The Tragedy of the Commons". *Science*. 162 (3859): 1243–1248. Bibcode:1968Sci..162.1243H. doi:10.1126/science.162.3859.1243. PMID 5699198

9 "Garrett Hardin", *Southern Poverty Law Center*, https://www.splcenter.org/fighting-hate/extremist-files/individual/garrett-hardin

10 From traditional finance, the terms "primary- and secondary-market" refer to "issuing" and "trading" markets, respectively.

11 Fritsch, Felix, "The Commons Stack. Realigning Incentives Towards Public Goods. Case Study", December 2020, https://

www.researchgate.net/publication/347390484_The_Commons_Stack_Realigning_Incentives_Towards_Public_Goods_Case_Study

12　https://commonsstack.org/abc

Chapter 6
The People's Shadow Bank

1　"Crypto's Rapid Move Into Banking Elicits Alarm in Washington", *New York Times*, 5 September 2021, https://www.nytimes.com/2021/09/05/us/politics/cryptocurrency-banking-regulation.html

2　"Global Monitoring Report on Non-Bank Financial Intermediation 2021", *Financial Stability Board*, 16 December 2021, https://www.fsb.org/2021/12/global-monitoring-report-on-non-bank-financial-intermediation-2021/

3　FOOTNOTE TO UPDATE WHEN CLOSER TO PUBLICATION

4　This is not to say that there are no risks, as the there is still smart contract risk from bugs that haven't been found yet, as well as manipulation of price oracles that hackers commonly hunt for.

5　The amount of time it takes for a new block to be produced and validated.

6　Browne, Ryan, "Cryptocurrency firms Tether and Bitfinex agree to pay $18.5 million fine to end New York probe", *CNBC*, 23 February 2021, https://www.cnbc.com/2021/02/23/tether-bitfinex-reach-settlement-with-new-york-attorney-general.html

7　Coppola, Frances, "Caveat Depositor. How Safe Is Your Stablecoin?", *CoinDesk*, 8 February 2021, https://www.coindesk.com/markets/2021/02/08/caveat-depositor-how-safe-is-your-stablecoin/

8　Warren, Elizabeth, "Warren Asks SEC Chair Gensler About Risks Posed by Cryptocurrency Exchanges", 8 July 2021, https://www.warren.senate.gov/oversight/letters/warren-asks-sec-chair-gensler-about-risks-posed-by-cryptocurrency-exchanges

9　Pol, Ronald F., "Anti-money laundering: The world's least effective policy experiment? Together, we can fix it", *Policy Design and Practice*, Volume 3, 2020, https://www.tandfonline.com/doi/full/10.1080/25741292.2020.1725366

10 Ahlstrand, Greg, "Elizabeth Warren Calls for US to Create a CBDC", *CoinDesk*, 1 April 2022, https://www.coindesk.com/policy/2022/04/01/elizabeth-warren-calls-for-us-to-create-a-cbdc/

11 Pinsker, Joe, "Bernie Sanders's Highly Sensible Plan to Turn Post Offices Into Banks", *The Atlantic*, 20 October 2015, https://www.theatlantic.com/business/archive/2015/10/bernie-sanders-lets-turn-post-offices-into-banks/411589/

12 https://docs.balancer.fi/products/balancer-pools/liquidity-bootstrapping-pools-lbps

13 https://launch.popcorn.network/faq

Chapter 7
Digital Scarcity vs Feasible Abundance

1 Kastrenakes, Jacob, "Beeple sold an NFT for $69 million", *The Verge*, 11 March 2021, https://www.theverge.com/2021/3/11/22325054/beeple-christies-nft-sale-cost-everydays-69-million

2 Browne, Ryan, "Trading in NFTs spiked 21,000% to more than $17 billion in 2021, report says", *CNBC*, 10 March 2022, https://www.cnbc.com/2022/03/10/trading-in-nfts-spiked-21000percent-to-top-17-billion-in-2021-report.html

3 https://Ethereum.org/en/developers/docs/standards/tokens/erc-721/

4 Leonidas.eth, "The Definitive Timeline of Early NFTs on Ethereum", *one37pm*, 30 July 2015, https://www.one37pm.com/nft/the-definitive-timeline-of-early-nfts-on-Ethereum

5 https://www.cryptokitties.co/

6 Rivas, Ricardo, "Crypto trading cards: How Hal Finney thought about the concept of NFTs over 30 years ago", *Cryptoslate*, 14 December 2021, https://cryptoslate.com/crypto-trading-cards-how-hal-finney-thought-about-the-concept-of-nfts-over-30-years-ago/

7 Kastrenakes, Jacob, "Your million-dollar NFT can break tomorrow if you're not careful", *The Verge*, 25 March 2021, https://www.theverge.com/2021/3/25/22349242/nft-metadata-explained-art-crypto-urls-links-ipfs

8 "List of Celebrities who own Bored Ape NFTs", *coincu*, 13 April 2022, https://news.coincu.com/54001-celebrities-who-own-bored-ape-yacht-club/

9 "The Influencer Report: Engaging Gen Z and Millennials", https://morningconsult.com/wp-content/uploads/2019/11/The-Influencer-Report-Engaging-Gen-Z-and-Millennials.pdf

10 "The Creator Economy Comes of Age as a Market Force", *ValueWalk*, 23 June 2021, https://www.valuewalk.com/creator-economy-comes-age-asmarket-force/

11 Baumgärtel, T. (1999). *net.art. Materialien zur Netzkunst*. Nürnberg: Verlag für moderne Kunst. p.15.

12 Wark, McKenzie, "My Collectible Ass", *e-flux*, October 2017, https://www.e-flux.com/journal/85/156418/my-collectible-ass/

13 Myers, Rhea, "Welcome To The Dessert Of The Real", 3 January 2021, https://rhea.art/welcome-to-the-dessert-of-the-real

14 "Rhea Myers and MvcKenzie Wark: Conversation", *Outland*, 25 February 2022, https://outland.art/rhea-myers-mckenzie-wark/

15 Dryhurst, Mat, "~~Digital Scarcity~~ Feasible Abundance and the Shock of the Nude", *mirror.xyz*, 3ed June 2022, https://mirror.xyz/herndondryhurst.eth/S-W2ZXRbrcy8bVGrKwMXSou63gWir7RJ9xs6wUn_h-0

16 "Copyright Registration Law and Your Art Pros and Cons of Registering Your Art", *ArtBusiness.com*, https://www.artbusiness.com/register_and_copyright_art_for_artists.html

17 https://jacob.energy/hyperstructures.html

18 Really Simple Syndication

Section 3: Crypto as Coordination

Chapter 8
DAOs and Digital Cooperatives: Decentralising the Workplace at Scale

1 Schularick, Moritz et al., "Asset prices and wealth inequality", *CEPR*, 9 August 2018, https://voxeu.org/article/asset-prices-and-wealth-inequality

2 "Could Co-Ops Solve Income Inequality?", *The Craftsmanship*

Quarterly, Summer 2020, https://craftsmanship.net/could-co-ops-solve-income-inequality/

3 "Where Co-ops are King: Emilia-Romagna", *Central Co-Op*, 23 October 2017, https://www.centralcoop.coop/entry.php?BID=102

4 "A boom in trailer parks converting into community owned cooperatives", *Mutual Interest*, February 2021, https://www.mutualinterest.coop/2021/02/a-boom-in-trailer-parks-converting-into-community-owned-cooperatives

5 Scholz, Trebor, "Platform Cooperativism vs. the Sharing Economy", *Medium*, 5 December 2014, https://medium.com/@trebors/platform-cooperativism-vs-the-sharing-economy-2ea737f1b5ad#.575nndfdq

6 Hawkins, Andrew J., "Uber and Lyft drivers in California sue to overturn Prop 22 ballot measure", *The Verge*, 12 January 2021, https://www.theverge.com/2021/1/12/22227042/uber-lyft-prop-22-lawsuit-overturn-drivers-california

7 Kei, "A Prehistory of DAOs", *gnosis build*, 21 July 2021, https://gnosisguild.mirror.xyz/t4F5rItMw4-mlpLZf5JQhElbDfQ2JRVKAzEpanyxW1Q

8 In 2017 dollars.

9 "How Much Do Music Streaming Services Pay Musicians in 2023", *Ditto Music*, 16 January 2020, https://dittomusic.com/en/blog/how-much-do-music-streaming-services-pay-musicians/

10 https://platform.coop/people/nathan-schneider/

11 Schneider, Nathan, "Here's my plan to save Twitter: let's buy it", *Guardian*, 29 September 2016, https://www.theguardian.com/commentisfree/2016/sep/29/save-twitter-buy-platform-shared-ownership

12 https://www.youtube.com/c/JonathanMann

13 "How to Make a Song Every Day and Turn it in to a DAO Cooperative: Interview with Jonathan Mann", *The Blockchain Socialist*, 29 May 2022, https://theblockchainsocialist.com/how-make-a-song-every-day-and-turn-it-in-to-a-dao-cooperative-interview-with-jonathan-mann/

14 For full transparency, I also own one NFT of one of his songs.

Chapter 9
Climate Collapse: The Coordination Problem of Our Lifetime

1   https://www.youtube.com/watch?v=ywrZPypqSB4
2   Robinson, E. & Robbins, R.C., "Sources, abundance, and fate of atmospheric pollutants", *Smoke and Fumes*, 1968, https://www.smokeandfumes.org/documents/document16
3   Solnit, Rebecca, "Big oil coined 'carbon footprints' to blame us for their greed. Keep them on the hook", *Guardian*, 23 August 2021, https://www.theguardian.com/commentisfree/2021/aug/23/big-oil-coined-carbon-footprints-to-blame-us-for-their-greed-keep-them-on-the-hook
4   "ExxonMobil and Climate Change: A Story of Denial, Delay, and Delusion, Told in Forms 10-K (1993-2000)", Government Accountability Project, https://whistleblower.org/general/climate-science-watch/exxonmobil-and-climate-change-a-story-of-denial-delay-and-delusion-told-in-forms-10-k-1993-2000/
5   Mitchell, Stephanie, "Tracing Big Oil's PR war to delay action on climate change", *The Harvard Gazette*, 28 September 2021, https://news.harvard.edu/gazette/story/2021/09/oil-companies-discourage-climate-action-study-says/
6   Corn, David, "It's the End of the World as They Know It", *Mother Jones*, 8 July 2016, https://www.motherjones.com/environment/2019/07/weight-of-the-world-climate-change-scientist-grief/
7   Redman, Jamie, "Iranians Defy Warning and Share Pictures of Bitcoin Mining in Mosque", *bitcoin.com*, 27 June 2019, https://news.bitcoin.com/iranians-defy-warning-and-share-pictures-of-bitcoin-mining-in-mosque/
8   Hudson, Kate, "Hydropower is NOT Clean Energy: Dams and Reservoirs are Major Drivers of Climate Change", *Waterkeeper Alliiance*, 21 November 2017, https://waterkeeper.org/news/hydropower-is-not-clean-energy/
9   Huber P. & Mills M.P., "Dig more coal—the PCs are coming", *Forbes*, 31 May 1999
10   Koomey, Jonathan G , Kawamoto K, Nordman B, Piette MA, Brown RE. 1999. Initial Comments on "The Internet Begins with

Coal." Rep. LBNL-44698, Lawrence Berkeley Natl. Lab., Berkeley, CA. http://enduse.lbl.gov/projects/infotech.html

11　Koomey, Jonathan G. et al., "Sorry, Wrong Number: The Use and Misuse of Numerical Facts in Analysis and Media Reporting of Energy Issues", *Annual Review of Energy and the Environment*, Vol. 27:119-158, https://www.annualreviews.org/doi/10.1146/annurev.energy.27.122001.083458

12　https://digiconomist.net/

13　Koomey has publicly stated that Coin Center had no say in the writing of the report and he himself does not own any cryptocurrency.

14　Koomey, Jonathan G., "Estimating Bitcoin Electricity Use: A Beginner's Guide", *Coin Center*, May 2019, https://www.coincenter.org/estimating-bitcoin-electricity-use-a-beginners-guide/#evaluating-existing-independent-estimates-of-bitcoin-electricity-use

15　"How Much Power is 1 Gigawatt?", Office of Energy Efficiency & Renewable Energy, 16 August 2022, https://www.energy.gov/eere/articles/how-much-power-1-gigawatt

16　McDonald, Kyle, "Ethereum Emissions: A Bottom-up Estimate", 8 December 2022, https://arxiv.org/pdf/2112.01238.pdf

17　Guillaume Nicoulaud, "Brandolini's law," *Ordre Spontané Blog* (Jul. 8, 2014) https://ordrespontane.blogspot.com/2014/07/brandolinis-law.html.

18　Kerht, Sonner, "The U.S. Military Emits More Carbon Dioxide Into the Atmosphere Than Entire Countries Like Denmark or Portugal", *Inside Climate News*, 18 January 2022, https://insideclimatenews.org/news/18012022/military-carbon-emissions/

19　https://kylemcdonald.github.io/Ethereum-emissions/

20　https://Ethereum.org/en/upgrades/merge/

21　Vallance, Christ, "Ethereum change cut cryptocurrency power demand", *BBC News*, 6 December 2022, https://www.bbc.com/news/technology-63872983

22　Chainleft, "Is Proof of Stake a Rich get Richer Scheme?", 10 January 2022, https://mirror.xyz/chainleft.eth/ZKQlhz9XA4kkFjtPLIdyvjMrnZOFscTDvlCYOK1awFo

23   Khan, Faisal, "Visualizing the explosive growth of DeFi in 2020",
      Medium, 6 November 2020, https://medium.com/technicity/
      visualizing-the-explosive-growth-of-defi-in-2020-298968199621

24   From DeFi Llama on 16 June 2022 (https://defillama.com/)

25   https://carbonmarketwatch.org/wp/wp-content/
      uploads/2019/06/cmw-carbon-markets-101-the-ultimate-
      guide-to-market-based-climate-mechanisms-web-final-single.
      pdf; https://www.theguardian.com/environment/2023/jan/18/
      revealed-forest-carbon-offsets-biggest-provider-worthless-verra-
      aoe

26   Owocki, Kevin, "How DeFi 'Degens' Are Funding the Next Wave
      of Open-Source Development", *CoinDesk*, 30 December 2020,
      https://www.coindesk.com/markets/2020/12/30/how-defi-
      degens-are-funding-the-next-wave-of-open-source-development/

27   Booman, G. et al., "Regen Network Whitepaper", 15 February
      2021, https://regen-network.gitlab.io/whitepaper/WhitePaper.
      pdf

28   https://www.kolektivo.co/

29   https://app.pitch.com/app/public/player/90d9e039-8360-4505-
      a3a9-1e8fb9543243/0cdfac77-cd67-4dde-b6ae-3b3b3288aacf

30   https://twitter.com/kolektivolabs/
      status/1372213570130345985

Chapter 10
Rethinking Political Systems and Action

1   Gilens, Martin & Page, Benjamin I., "Testing Theories of
     American Politics: Elites, Interest Groups, and Average Citizens",
     Perspectives on Politics, Vol. 12/No. 3, 2014, https://scholar.
     princeton.edu/sites/default/files/mgilens/files/gilens_and_
     page_2014_-testing_theories_of_american_politics.doc.pdf

2   Reich, Robert, "The biggest political party in America you've
     never heard of", *Salon*, 27 January 2020, https://www.salon.
     com/2020/01/27/the-biggest-political-party-in-america-youve-
     never-heard-of_partner/

3   Zargham, Michael & Nabben, Kelsie, "Aligning 'Decentralized
     Autonomous Organization' to Precedents in Cybernetics",
     SSRN (4 April 2022). https://papers.ssrn.com/sol3/papers.
     cfm?abstract_id=4077358

4   Kopf, Dan, "The typical US Congress member is 12 times richer than the typical American household", *Quartz*, 12 February 2018, https://qz.com/1190595/the-typical-us-congress-member-is-12-times-richer-than-the-typical-american-household

5   Bardo, Alice, "Sondage : 43% des électeurs de Macron ont voté en opposition à Le Pen", *Public Senat*, 7 May 2017, https://www.publicsenat.fr/article/politique/sondage-43-des-electeurs-de-macron-ont-vote-en-opposition-a-le-pen-60193

6   "2020 Exit Polling Live Updates: COVID-19, Economy and Health Care Are 2020's Dominant Voting Issues" *Morning Consult*, 3 November 2020, https://morningconsult.com/exit-polling-live-updates/#section-19

7   Coy, Peter, "A New Way of Voting That Makes Zealotry Expensive", *Bloomberg*, 1 May 2019, https://www.bloomberg.com/news/articles/2019-05-01/a-new-way-of-voting-that-makes-zealotry-expensive

8   Tang, Audrey, "Inside Taiwan's new digital democracy", *Economist*, 12 March 2019, https://www.economist.com/open-future/2019/03/12/inside-taiwans-new-digital-democracy

9   https://github.com/BlockScience/conviction/blob/master/social-sensorfusion.pdf

10   https://constitution.ens.domains/

11   Stahler-Sholk, Richard, "Zapatistas and New Ways of Doing Politics", *Oxford Research Encyclopedia*, 23 May 2019, https://oxfordre.com/politics/oso/viewentry/10.1093$00 2facrefore$002f9780190228637.001.0001$002facrefore-9780190228637-e-1724

12   Coleman, Gabriella, 2014, *Hacker, Hoaxer, Whistleblower, Spy: The Many Faces of Anonymous*, London: Verso Books.

13   https://bailbloc.thenewinquiry.com/webminer.html

14   https://www.supremecourt.gov/opinions/21pdf/19-1392_6j37.pdf

15   https://assangedao.org/

16   "Lunarpunk, Black Markets, and Agorism in the 21st Century", *The Blockchain Socialist*, 3 April 2022, https://theblockchainsocialist.com/lunarpunk-black-markets-and-agorism-in-the-21st-century/

17   "Dark-Fi Manifesto", https://dark.fi/manifesto.html
18   egirlcapital, "Lunarpunk And The Dark Side Of The Cycle", 15 February 2022, https://www.egirlcapital.com/writings/107533289
19   Cavaliere, Victoria, "Venture capitalist Balaji Srinivasan reportedly suggested doxxing a journalist who reported on narratives he didn't like", *Business Insider*, 14 February 2021, https://www.businessinsider.com/venture-capitalist-balaji-srinivasan-suggested-doxxing-journalist-nyt-2021-2?r=US&IR=T
20   Finley, Klint, "Geeks for Monarchy: The Rise of the Neoreactionaries", *Tech Crunch*, 23 November 2013, https://techcrunch.com/2013/11/22/geeks-for-monarchy/
21   Balajis, "The Network State", 11 November 2021, https://www.1729.com/the-network-state/
22   Schneider, Nathan, "How We Can Encode Human Rights In The Blockchain", *Noema*, 7 June 2022, https://www.noemamag.com/how-we-can-encode-human-rights-in-the-blockchain/
23   "A Use Case for Blockchain Socialism during an Evictions Crisis: The Housing for All Token", *The Blockchain Socialist*, 4 October 2020, https://theblockchainsocialist.com/a-use-case-for-blockchain-socialism-during-an-evictions-crisis-the-housing-for-all-token/

Chapter 11
Art in Multiplayer

1   https://www.youtube.com/watch?v=gipL_CEw-fk
2   Massive multiplayer online role playing games.
3   GVN & ARB, "Modular and Portable Multiplayer Miniverses", *Moving Castles*, 13 August 2021, https://movingcastles.world/modular-and-portable-multiplayer-miniverses
4   https://www.furtherfield.org/about-us/
5   Garrett, Marc, "Diwo (Do-It-With-Others): Artistic Co-Creation as a Decentralized Method of Peer Empowerment in Today's Multitude", *SEAD Network*, https://seadnetwork.wordpress.com/white-paper-abstracts/final-white-papers/diwo-do-it-with-others-artistic-co-creation-as-a-decentralized-method-of-peer-empowerment-in-todays-multitude-diwo-do-it-with-others-artistic-co-creation-as-a-decentralized-method-of-pe/

6   https://rhea.art/is-art

7   Ruth Catlow, et al. (eds.), 2017, *Artists Re:Thinking the Blockchain*, Liverpool University Press https://torquetorque.net/publications/artists-rethinking-the-blockchain/

8   https://culturestake.org/

9   https://peoplesparkplinth.org/

10   https://peoplesparkplinth.org/webapp/based-on-a-tree-story/

11   https://otherinter.net/research/headless-brands/

12   https://songcamp.mirror.xyz/kh0Nl55x_PzNRADmIzAjzLi2R CK7SD9sMBJ2O5NqKpY

13   https://elektra.camp/#/

14   https://songcamp.mirror.xyz/HS0L3BHU4dNGGxuH_AUo7I3 UJA5FpycGXL8fc05nmeQ

15   https://chaos.build/

16   https://songcamp.mirror.xyz/UkR2nfVcYYKuePHzck 6UnWTY35zW4uFxRnXllkk99Hw

17   https://openai.com/dall-e-2/

18   https://holly.mirror.xyz/54ds2IiOnvthjGFkokFCoaI 4EabytH9xjAYy1irHy94

Chapter 12
All Chains Are Not Created Equal

1   https://ethereum.org/en/upgrades/sharding/

2   https://Ethereum-magicians.org/t/a-rollup-centric-Ethereum-roadmap/4698

3   https://old.reddit.com/r/ethereum/comments/rwojtk/ama_we_are_the_efs_research_team_pt_7_07_january/hrngyk8/

4   https://www.mintscan.io/juno/proposals/16

5   de Gregorio, Ignacio, "The impossible is about to occur in crypto", *Medium*, 21 June 2022, https://medium.datadriveninvestor.com/the-impossible-is-about-to-occur-in-crypto-e1f8b6234222

6   Kelly, Liam J., "How The Juno Network DAO Voted to Revoke a Whale's Tokens", *Decrypt*, 19 March 2022, https://decrypt.co/95435/juno-network-dao-proposal-16-voted-to-revoke-tokens-from-whale

7   Brock, Arthur, "Currencies are Records of Currents", Medium, 29 July 2020, https://medium.com/metacurrency-project/currencies-are-records-of-currents-f4c6cdc809be

Techno-Probabilism: You Can't Rage-Quit Capitalism On Your Own

1   Scott, Alexander, "Meditations on Moloch", https://slatestarcodex.com/2014/07/30/meditations-on-moloch/

2   Ginsberg, Allen, "Howl", https://www.poetryfoundation.org/poems/49303/howl

3   Soleimani, Ameen et al., "The Moloch DAO", https://github.com/MolochVentures/Whitepaper/blob/master/Whitepaper.pdf

4   "CCG Chronicles #3 – The autopoiesis of complexity and the cognitariat", The Blockchain Socialist, 27 February 2022, https://theblockchainsocialist.com/ccg-chronicles-3-the-autopoiesis-of-complexity-and-the-cognitariat/

5   Homer-Dixon, Thomas & Rockström, Johan, "What Happens When a Cascade of Crises Collide?", Cascase Institute, 13 November 2022, https://cascadeinstitute.org/what-happens-when-a-cascade-of-crises-collide/

6   Morozov, Evgeny, To Save Everything Here (Public Affairs, 2013)

7   Kranzberg, Melvin, "Technology and History: 'Kranzberg's Laws'", Technology and Culture, Vol. 27, No. 3 (Jul., 1986), pp. 544-560, https://www.jstor.org/stable/3105385?origin=crossref

8   Harrway, Donna, "A Cyborg Manifesto", http://cyborganthropology.com/Full_text_of_A_Cyborg_Manifesto

9   Todoroff, Uriah Marc, "A Cryptoeconomy of Affect", The New Inquiry, 14 May 2018, https://thenewinquiry.com/a-cryptoeconomy-of-affect/

10   Taleb, Nassim Nicholas, The Black Swan: The Impact of the Highly Improbable, (Random House, 2007)

11   Crawley, Jamie, "Edward Snowden says use crypto, don't invest in it: 'Bitcoin is what I used to pay for the servers pseudonymously'", Fortune, 11 June 2022, https://fortune.com/2022/06/11/edward-snowden-says-use-crypto-dont-invest-in-it-bitcoin-is-what-i-used-to-pay-for-the-servers-pseudonymously/

12   Schneider, Nathan, "Web3 Is the Opportunity We Have Had All Along:Innovation Amnesia and Economic Democracy", 13 July 2022, https://osf.io/2wg6s?view_only=709f1f87528943a4b27de2b5eb0f9eef

13   At the time of writing, Brave is one of the few browsers with
     native compatibility but there are ways to access IPFS sites on
     other browsers that require some software.

REPEATER BOOKS

is dedicated to the creation of a new reality. The landscape of twenty-first-century arts and letters is faded and inert, riven by fashionable cynicism, egotistical self-reference and a nostalgia for the recent past. Repeater intends to add its voice to those movements that wish to enter history and assert control over its currents, gathering together scattered and isolated voices with those who have already called for an escape from Capitalist Realism. Our desire is to publish in every sphere and genre, combining vigorous dissent and a pragmatic willingness to succeed where messianic abstraction and quiescent co-option have stalled: abstention is not an option: we are alive and we don't agree.